Philosophy of Law

Praise for *Philosophy of Law: Introducing Jurisprudence*:

'*Philosophy of Law: Introducing Jurisprudence* is an exceptionally clear, comprehensive, and engaging introduction to philosophy of law. Brand succeeds at doing justice to the complexity of the subject matter while making it accessible. It will be an excellent resource for undergraduate and law school courses in legal philosophy.'

John Oberdiek, Professor of Law,
Rutgers University School of Law, USA

'*Philosophy of Law* is a well-written guide to the important ideas and figures providing students with a clear guide to complex material in a useful companion to any legal philosophy course or module.'

Thom Brooks, Reader in Law,
University of Durham, UK

'Jeffrey Brand's *Philosophy of Law: Introducing Jurisprudence* is a highly accessible, highly engaging, and at the same time fundamentally fair-minded, introduction to a wide-range of legal issues that are at the core of contemporary legal education and practice. It would be an excellent resource for an undergraduate survey course in law, whether as a primary text or secondary text to accompany other primary materials.'

Alec Walen, Associate Professor of Law,
Rutgers University School of Law, USA

'Jeffrey Brand has managed to write the best introduction to legal philosophy yet available. The book is sophisticated yet accessible, and the range of issues covered is impressive. Those who read the book will not only learn about legal philosophy's main questions and the position of some of its major figures, but will actually learn how to do legal philosophy by observing the manner in which Brand meticulously crafts arguments and counter-arguments for the competing views. If you are looking for one book to adopt in class, then this is the one, and I certainly plan to use it with my students in Brazil.'

Noel Struchiner, Professor of Law and Philosophy at the
Pontifical Catholic University of Rio de Janeiro, Brazil

'Pitched at just the right level to be both accessible and illuminating, master teacher Jeffrey Brand takes the reader on a sure-footed tour of contemporary legal philosophy. Written with the student in mind, it is packed with examples and applications that make clear the importance of the issues it studies. An additional strength is the attention Brand gives to topics that other textbooks tend to shortchange, such as private law, international law, and the ideal of rule of law itself. Highly recommended.'

Craig Duncan, Associate Professor and Chair of the
Department of Philosophy and Religion, Ithaca College, USA

'Brand offers an exceptionally clear presentation of an almost encyclopedic list of topics addressed by analytic legal philosophers. These include not only questions concerning law per se – e.g. its nature, the source of its normativity, and its interpretation - but also questions specific to particular areas of law such as criminal law, property and torts, and international law. The organization of the book allows instructors a great deal of flexibility in what they wish to cover, in what order, and in what depth, and enables them to select among the many different connections they might wish to draw between various concepts and arguments. Brand presents students with just the right amount of material on a given topic to spur productive classroom discussion and essays. Reading this book will surely awaken in many students the same passion for doing legal philosophy Brand clearly enjoys.'

David Lefkowitz, Associate Professor of Philosophy,
University of Richmond, USA

'Jeffrey Brand is a highly original and astute legal philosopher. Teachers seeking a clear and comprehensive introduction to the subject, aimed at undergraduate students, will not easily find a better book than this.'

Jeffrey Goldsworthy, President of the Australian Society of
Legal Philosophy and Professor of Law, Monash University, Australia

Also available from Bloomsbury

Anatomy of Failure, Oliver Feltham
Introduction to Political Philosophy, Alexander Moseley
Law: Key Concepts in Philosophy, David Ingram

Philosophy of Law

Introducing Jurisprudence

Jeffrey Brand

Online resources to accompany this book are available at: www.bloomsbury.com/philosophy-of-law-9781441141897.

Please type the URL into your web browser and follow the instructions to access the Companion Website.

If you experience any problems, please contact Bloomsbury at:

companionwebsites@bloomsbury.com

B L O O M S B U R Y

LONDON • NEW DELHI • NEW YORK • SYDNEY

Bloomsbury Academic
An imprint of Bloomsbury Publishing Plc

50 Bedford Square   1385 Broadway
London   New York
WC1B 3DP   NY 10018
UK   USA

www.bloomsbury.com

Bloomsbury is a registered trade mark of Bloomsbury Publishing Plc

First published 2013

British Library Cataloguing-in-Publication Data
A catalogue record for this book is available from the British Library.

ISBN: HB: 978-1-4411-0484-7
        PB: 978-1-4411-4189-7
     ePDF: 978-1-4725-1507-0
     ePub: 978-1-6235-6889-4

Library of Congress Cataloging-in-Publication Data
Brand, Jeffrey.
  Philosophy of law : an introduction to jurisprudence / Jeffrey Brand.
     pages cm
  Includes bibliographical references and index.
ISBN 978-1-4411-4189-7 (pbk.)—ISBN 978-1-4411-0484-7 (hardcover)—
ISBN 978-1-62356-889-4 (epub) 1. Law–Philosophy. I. Title.
K231.B73 2013
340'.1—dc23
2013018687

Typeset by Newgen Knowledge Works (P) Ltd., Chennai, India
Printed and bound in India

Contents

Preface

This book provides a general introduction to the philosophy of law, aiming for breadth rather than depth. The subject as I conceive it goes by many names, including "jurisprudence," "legal theory," and "legal philosophy" (which I prefer).[1] We can divide legal philosophy into three main divisions: *analytical jurisprudence, descriptive jurisprudence*, and *normative jurisprudence*.

Analytical jurisprudence studies the nature of law (what makes something law and not something else?) and the implications of law (what necessarily follows from the fact that something is law?). Philosophers call these *conceptual* and *metaphysical* questions.

Descriptive jurisprudence examines actual laws and legal systems and offers general accounts of them. For example, a scholar might examine the Japanese law of inheritance and try to determine what general values, ideas, and principles it reflects.

Normative jurisprudence concerns what the content of the law ought to be, from the perspective of a conscientious lawmaker. What makes a law good and just? Normative jurisprudence evaluates existing laws and prescribes revisions.

Legal philosophy is somewhat peripheral to the field of philosophy as a whole, but it is extraordinarily broad, nevertheless. I have had to make difficult decisions about what to include in this short book. I have chosen to concentrate on topics that occupy two, interrelated groups of scholars: (1) professional analytical philosophers who write about law; and (2) legal scholars who study these philosophers and are studied by them. Giving the book this focus aligns it with what is widely considered the mainstream of legal philosophy in the English-speaking world.

Within this set of topics, I emphasize those that are accessible to undergraduates and least likely to be covered in other philosophy courses (e.g. applied ethics, political philosophy, feminist philosophy) or elsewhere in undergraduate curricula, in the other humanities or social sciences. I also give preference to topics encountered by law students and topics that interest law professors, as opposed to historians, social scientists, or philosophers whose primary specialization is not legal philosophy. For example, I include sections on the philosophy of private law (tort, contract, property), which is foundational for law students and which undergraduates rarely encounter in other courses.

Philosophers will quickly recognize this book as emerging from the "analytical" tradition rather than the continental European tradition of Hegel, Marx, Heidegger, Merleau-Ponty, Sartre, Foucault, and Derrida. Some legal philosophers writing in English draw from the continental tradition. They ask some of the same questions posed in this book, although most of their questions are quite different. There has been little interaction, unfortunately, between continental legal philosophers and the core group of scholars defined above. Someone should write a good, English-language introduction to continental legal philosophy.

This book contains little discussion of feminist jurisprudence, Critical Race Theory, and Queer Theory, although these are major schools of thought which I readily classify as legal philosophy in the broader sense. Each deserves its own introduction. Many of the questions posed by these "critical" scholars are questions of normative jurisprudence. Critical scholars examine ways in which actual laws, and ideas about law, work to perpetuate the subordination of women, people of color, lesbians, gay men, and others. Critical scholars develop new ways of thinking about law. They challenge the status quo and advocate for law reform. Unfortunately, there has been little dialog between critical scholars and my "core" group. Bridges should be built between these groups and they are being built, but critical scholarship still represents a separate intellectual tradition from the one introduced in this book.

I believe that legal philosophy has improved substantially in the past 50 years and is more sophisticated today than it has ever been. I also believe that undergraduates benefit from exposure to the most recent work, even without a foundation in the history of philosophy. This book gives more emphasis to the past five decades than to the history of the subject. This is not to understate the importance of Plato, Aquinas, Hobbes, Blackstone, Kant, or Bentham. Fortunately, there are abundant resources on these giants.

In my sections on analytical jurisprudence, I break from the convention of having separate chapters on "schools of thought," such as positivism, natural law, realism, and economic analysis. I discuss all of these theories, but I do not organize my chapters in the conventional way because I believe that the classics of jurisprudence address many different questions. Of course, any jurisprudential question receives competing answers, but in many cases two writers are actually asking and answering different questions, not disagreeing with one another. Therefore, the book is not organized by "competing" schools of thought, but rather by philosophical questions that can be posed from the standpoints of different actors within the legal system (judges, lawmakers, private citizens). How can I learn what the law says? How should I decide cases, given what the law says? What laws should I make? What obligations do I have under the law? I think analytical jurisprudence is less confusing when approached in this way.

American undergraduates sometimes ask me if studying legal philosophy will help them in law school. This is an empirical question that no empirical study has addressed, so I do not know the answer. My suspicion, which has no scientific basis, is that studying legal philosophy probably has some value as preparation for law school. Students of mine who have gone on to study law sometimes report that my courses helped them as law students. Perhaps, they are just being kind. They have no basis for comparison, having never attended law school without first having taken my courses.

A better question would be: is there another liberal-arts course that would be *more* helpful to a law student than legal philosophy? Perhaps not, as yet, although I suspect that such a course could be designed. In the meantime, legal philosophy may be as good as it gets for prelaw students.

Whatever the preparatory value of legal philosophy, the best reason to study the subject is that one finds it intrinsically interesting. Learning legal philosophy makes studying the law more interesting, as well. I hope this thought will excite current and future law students as they read the book.

I am grateful to many students and teachers who have helped me learn legal philosophy. I also thank my wonderful colleagues at George Washington University for their continuing support. I am grateful to my parents, Donald and Gabriella, my brother, Thomas, and my precious children, Maresca, Quentin, and Felix. I dedicate this book to Kelly in love and gratitude.

Website

www.bloomsbury.com/philosophy-of-law-9781441141897

Online resources for lecturers and students:
Sample Syllabus
Sample Essay Questions
Sample Exam Questions
Glossary

1

Aspects of Law and Legal Systems

If you ask a chemistry teacher "what is glycerol?" then she might tell you that it is a colorless, odorless, syrupy, sweet liquid. That is a good, preliminary answer, but hardly a complete one. Other liquids are also colorless, odorless, syrupy, and sweet (e.g. dextrose), so the teacher's answer does not even distinguish glycerol from everything else. She could do better by referencing its chemical formula: $C_3H_8O_3$. Nothing but glycerol has this formula and nothing with a different formula is glycerol. And there is more to know about glycerol than even its chemical formula conveys to you. Why is it liquid at room temperature? Is it toxic to humans? How does it react with other substances? What are its industrial uses?

Now imagine that you are questioned by a young child who does not know what law is, or by a visitor from a strange land without a legal system. If the child or visitor asks you "what is law?" then you could answer that law is "the principles and regulations established in a community by some authority and applicable to its people." This is part of a dictionary definition. It is an acceptable preliminary answer, but again far from complete. It contains words such as "established," "community," "authority," and "applicable" that must themselves be understood.

Glycerol has a unique chemical formula: a set of characteristics possessed by all glycerol and only glycerol. Law, by contrast, has no chemical formula. Might there be, nevertheless, a set of characteristics that all law and only law possesses? This chapter begins by introducing a branch of legal philosophy—*analytical jurisprudence*—that tries to answer this question and to identify the defining characteristics of law (see Preface). There are other ways of phrasing the question, such as "What is law?" and "What is the nature of law?" It comes down to the same thing. Analogous questions can be asked about other institutions: religion, sports, families, war, higher education, social etiquette, and so on. What are the distinctive features of sports? What makes etiquette different from other things? These are philosophical questions, too, but our subject in this book is law.

Analytical jurisprudence is difficult, partly because law is not tangible or visible. It is not a physical substance or self-contained physical object. Even if we succeed in identifying the defining characteristics of law, they will be less concrete than the chemical formula of glycerol. Perhaps the search for these characteristics is hopeless, but we cannot know until we try.

The fundamental purpose of analytical jurisprudence is simply to understand what makes law different from everything else and what all legal systems have in common. You might wonder why anyone should care about these inquiries. Most of us can manage perfectly well in life without asking these questions, much less answering them. Of course, each of us should know what the laws of his own legal system require of him, but analytical jurisprudence does not tell us about any particular legal system. The answers to questions of analytical jurisprudence may or may not have practical implications. It is worth noting, however, that statements made about the law by prominent people often presuppose that law has a certain nature. Analytical jurisprudence may bear on the truth of such statements. Consider, for example, a famous 1977 statement by President Richard M. Nixon: "If the President does it, that means it is not illegal." Whether Nixon's statement is true or false depends on what makes an act illegal which depends, in turn, on the nature of law, among other things.

Since the time of St Thomas Aquinas (1225–74), a great philosopher and theologian, legal philosophers have distinguished between *positive law*, *divine law*, and *natural law*. Positive law, our main subject, is law made by human beings. Divine law is made by a deity (e.g. the God of the *Bible*, if He exists). Natural law is a set of conduct rules that are, supposedly, knowable to every rational person. All of these are distinct from scientific "laws" (e.g. the four laws of thermodynamics). All legal philosophers today are interested in positive law, although some also discuss natural and/or divine law.

Has law existed wherever human beings have lived? Only if we define "law" so broadly that it is no longer a useful term. Legal philosophers assume that some societies, such as ours, have law while others do not. If a society has law, then it has a *legal system*. The concepts of law and legal system are logically related—understanding one requires understanding the other. One way of studying the nature of law is examining a familiar legal system and trying to identify its distinctive features. That is what I shall do in this chapter.

1. The command theory

Law is a *concept* of which different thinkers have different *conceptions* (Hart 1994/1961: 155–9). Philosophers offer different models or "theories" of law, each of which identifies different features as the distinctive features of a legal system. One influential theory is the *command theory*, which defines a legal system in terms of a human lawmaker or "sovereign." The command theory is closely associated with a great English legal philosopher, John Austin (1790–1859), although Austin borrowed from a fellow Englishman, Jeremy Bentham (1748–1832). The theory has earlier roots in Thomas Hobbes (1588–1679), also English.

According to the command theory, every legal system has a human *sovereign* who is himself above the law (Austin 1995/1832). Austin defines the sovereign as someone[1] who is usually obeyed by most people, and who does not usually obey any other human being (Austin, who lived in Christian England, allowed his sovereign to obey God). If no one in a society fits that description, then the society has no sovereign and hence no legal system. The sovereign issues commands to his subjects: he orders them to act, or to refrain from acting, and he threatens them with *sanctions*—unpleasant consequences—if they disobey. Laws are simply the sovereign's commands.

2. Critique of the command theory

The command theory dominated legal philosophy in the English-speaking world for many decades. In 1961, the theory was dealt a devastating blow, from which it has never recovered, at the hands of H. L. A. Hart (1907–92), another English positivist and one of the most important legal philosophers of his century. Hart challenges three aspects of the command theory. First, he notes that legal rules often remain in force even after the sovereign dies or resigns, so their validity cannot depend on the sovereign's commands (1994/1961).

Secondly, Hart rejects one of Austin's basic assumptions about how laws function. Austin assumes that all laws require subjects to act or to refrain from acting. Many laws are like this, of course. Consider, for example, laws requiring parents to feed their children and laws forbidding rape. But what about other laws, for example, the estate laws that specify how I must draft my last will and testament if I wish to leave my wristwatch to my brother upon my death? In Australia, as in many jurisdictions, a will is not legally valid unless signed before two adult witnesses. Australian law does not require anyone to draft a will in the first place, but it grants everyone the *legal power* to do so and it specifies how one must draft and execute a will if it is to be legally valid. Similarly, the law of contracts does not require anyone to make contracts, but it empowers some people (normally adults) to enter into contracts and it specifies the conditions that contracts must satisfy if they are to be enforceable in court (see Chapter 5, sec. 5).

These are examples of laws that "enable" or "confer powers," rather than requiring action or inaction. These examples are not mere anomalies. In fact, some of the foundational laws of modern legal systems are also *power-conferring*. Consider any law that establishes a public office (e.g. police officer, magistrate, Member of Parliament, etc.) and specifies who may hold it. Modern legal systems could not function without such laws, yet they are not easily characterized as commands. Some legal philosophers since Austin have characterized all laws as orders directed at public officials (Kelsen 1967), but even these efforts have not been widely embraced.

This brings us to the third aspect of the command theory that Hart criticizes: its account of our obligation to obey the law (see Chapter 4). When Austin claims that you are obligated to obey the law, he simply means that the sovereign threatens to sanction you if you disobey. Hart thinks this account of obligation is incomplete. Someone can feel obligated to obey the law even if she faces no threat of sanctions. This might be because the authorities are not paying attention, or because the law in question has no sanctions associated with it. Hart takes these feelings of obligation as evidence that one really *is* obligated. Yet, this obligation cannot be explained in terms of sanctions if no sanctions are threatened.

Having identified these flaws in the command theory, Hart proceeds to improve upon it. He rejects the idea that all laws are commands of a sovereign, or of anyone, for that matter. In fact, he rejects the basic premise that a legal system must have a sovereign. Some legal systems do, but most modern systems do not. In modern legal systems (including, ironically, the England of Austin's day), there is no legally unlimited lawmaker. Even the monarch and the House of Lords must obey the law. (In rejecting the idea that every legal system has a domestic sovereign, Hart does not mean to reject the idea that the modern nation-state is itself "sovereign" relative to other nation-states.)

If laws are not the sovereign's commands, then what are they? According to Hart, laws are *rules* of a certain sort. This suggestion, on its own, is unsurprising. We can understand the sovereign's commands as rules, too. Hart and Austin also agree that the mere fact that a certain rule is a rule of law can obligate one to obey it. But Hart diverges from Austin by holding that one can be obligated to obey a rule of law without threatened sanctions. According to Hart, rational persons have the ability to see rules as reasons for action, even if no sanction is threatened. To accept a rule as a reason for action is to adopt what Hart calls the *internal point of view* with respect to that rule. If one adopts the internal point of view with respect to a rule, then one justifies and criticizes behavior—one's own and that of others—by reference to the rule.

Despite Hart's criticism of Austin, the two agree on two basic theses. The first is the *social fact thesis*: what constitutes the law in a certain society is ultimately a matter of social facts—facts about the mental states and behavior of certain individuals. Put more simply, the social fact thesis states that the laws of a society exist and have meaning if and only if human beings create them and give them meaning. The second thesis shared by Hart and Austin is the *separability thesis*: there is no necessary connection between law and morality (see sec. 8). For many years, the social fact and separability theses jointly defined the position known as *legal positivism*, but in the late twentieth century, positivists began to abandon separability, leaving the social fact thesis as their sole defining thesis.

3. Primary and secondary rules

So laws are rules of a sort, in Hart's view, with which sanctions may or may not be associated. But not all rules are laws. The rules of grammar, etiquette, or rugby, for example, are not rules of law. What makes some rules, but not others, rules of law without a sovereign? Hart's answer is "other rules." The most familiar legal rules are those that require or forbid action and those that confer powers, as described earlier. Hart calls these *primary rules*. But modern legal systems also employ *secondary rules*: rules concerned with other rules. A small, primitive society can function with primary rules alone, if most people accept certain essential primary rules that forbid violence, require parents to care for their children, and so forth. But a system using only primary rules will encounter difficulties, especially as the society becomes larger and more complex. In a system consisting only of primary rules, there is no centralized way to change the primary rules when circumstances require. There is no reliable means of resolving disputes and enforcing the rules when they are disobeyed—people must rely on their own muscles and sympathetic members of the community. Finally, there is no authoritative way to establish what the primary rules actually are when people disagree about them.

Secondary rules can solve these problems. *Rules of change* specify ways of modifying outdated rules. *Rules of adjudication* specify procedures for establishing that violations have occurred and for enforcing the rules. *Rules of recognition* specify conditions that a rule must meet in order to be legally valid in the system. Rules of recognition are the rules that make some rules, but not others, rules of law. Legal systems contain more than one rule of recognition. A rule of recognition can validate a subsidiary rule of recognition, which can validate a more subsidiary rule of recognition, and so on. But Hart believes that all the rules in a legal system are ultimately validated by a single master rule, the *ultimate rule of recognition*. This master rule is often simply called "the rule of recognition," as I will call it from now on. Hart borrows here from the great Austrian legal philosopher, Hans Kelsen (1881–1973), who suggested that every legal system has a "basic norm" (*Grundnorm*) at its core (1967). The basic norm of the Canadian legal system might be "The original Constitution of Canada is to be obeyed." Hart takes from Kelsen the idea that a legal system must have a single master norm, although Hart's understanding of the norm is otherwise very different from Kelsen's. Kelsen's basic norm is a standard that (according to Kelsen) one must simply assume to be true before one can

see any other rule as legally valid. The basic norm exists if and only if someone accepts it. Whereas Hart's rule of recognition is a social rule that exists if
and only if most public officials accept it.

4. H. L. A. Hart's theory of law

I have now introduced the basic elements of Hart's theory of a legal system,
but they must be combined. Hart holds that a legal system exists if and only
if two conditions are met: (1) the rules that are valid according to the system's
ultimate rule of recognition are generally obeyed by the public; and (2) the
rule of recognition is effectively accepted as a common public standard of
official behavior (i.e. from the internal point of view) by the officials of the
system. A law, accordingly, is a rule that has been validated by a legal system's
rule of recognition.

In order to understand Hart's position, consider the following rule of recognition: "All rules enacted by the Canadian Parliament are valid rules of law."
This rule of recognition is unrealistically simple, but it will serve our purposes.
Let us suppose that Canadian public officials accept this rule of recognition
from the internal point of view. At a minimum, this means that they treat the
rule as a reason to enforce rules enacted by the Canadian Parliament and to
criticize officials who fail to do so. If Canadian officials accept the rule of recognition in this way, then the rules enacted by Parliament are legally valid.

We can now return to a major point of divergence between Hart and
Austin. Hart agrees with Austin that a sovereign's threatened sanction gives
one a reason to obey, but Hart believes that the mere fact that a rule is a valid
rule of the legal system gives one a reason to obey it, even without a threat.
Hart's position is easily misunderstood. Hart does not claim that most people
obey the law for moral or "altruistic" reasons. He knows that sanctions are
important, as a practical matter, for enforcing an acceptable level of obedience. He does not propose that we stop punishing criminals. Hart's point is
that a rational individual has the ability to obey the law just because it is the
law. This can happen after one adopts the internal point of view. Hart also
believes that the fact that a rule is the law is what gives one a reason to obey it,
whether or not one appreciates this fact.

In the English-speaking world in the past five decades, legal philosophers
have often defined their theories in relation to Hart. Many important contributions to legal theory have been challenges to Hart's theory or efforts to fill in
missing details (Finnis 1980; Raz 1980; MacCormick 1978; Dworkin 1977c).

5. Predictive theories

Hart and Austin are typical of legal positivism insofar as they agree that law consists of rules. One important alternative view is the *predictive theory* of law. This theory is often associated with a famous justice of the US Supreme Court, Oliver Wendell Holmes, Jr (1841–1935) and various *legal realists* (see Chapter 2), although this association is debatable (Leiter 2001).

According to the predictive theory, a legal statement is true if and only if it accurately predicts how courts would rule. For example, the statement "Luis is the legal owner of the apple orchard on highway A24" is true if and only if a court actually would rule in Luis' favor if his claim to the orchard were challenged. To make the statement about Luis is not to describe a preexisting legal state of affairs, according to the predictive theory, but to predict the future.

The predictive theory, however, suffers from some serious limitations. If legal statements are merely predictions of judicial behavior, then there can be no such thing as a judicial mistake: whatever a court decides is legally correct. At least this is true of the highest court. A decision from a lower court can be overturned on appeal, and thus deemed mistaken, but when a high court rules, we cannot criticize the ruling as legally incorrect. We can always object on moral grounds, but legally speaking the high court is always correct, according to the predictive theory.

But how could this be? Judges on high courts make mistakes, as everyone does. They can misread statutes, ignore precedents, reason fallaciously, and so forth. The predictive theory seems unable to account for these facts.

6. Rules and principles

The centrality of rules to law probably comes as no surprise to you. Legal philosophers agree that understanding law requires thinking about rules, but they disagree about the nature of rules and the precise role that they play in the law. What is a rule, exactly? Does law consist entirely of rules or is there more to it?

On a simple theory of law, law consists entirely of rules. Specifically, law consists of all and only the rules made by the lawmakers identified in the rule of recognition. Courts hear disputes, identify the applicable rules from within the set of legally valid ones, and apply those rules to the facts. Consider a town ordinance stating, "Animals shall not be brought into the Public Library." Someone who brings a Great Dane into the library has definitely violated the ordinance. A child who brings his plush bear into the library has definitely not violated the ordinance. These are both cases in which the rules apply unequivocally, dictating definite results. But what if someone brings a goldfish in a plastic bag of water? In that case it is unclear how the rules apply. Is a goldfish an "animal" or not for the purpose of the ordinance?

Hart contends that cases such as these are inevitable in any realistic legal system. Natural languages are, he observes, *open-textured*. Every word has "fuzzy edges": a *core* of settled meaning and a *penumbra* of unsettled meaning. Great Danes fall in the core of "animals" (at least in the context of this ordinance). Goldfish fall in the penumbra. Plush bears fall outside the penumbra: they are definitely not what the ordinance means by "animals."

Hart claims that there are no legally correct answers to questions involving the penumbra. We can say neither that the law allows goldfish in the library, nor that it forbids them. Accordingly, before the court decides the case, we can say neither that you are legally permitted to bring your goldfish into the library, nor that you are legally forbidden to do so. In such cases, Hart concludes, courts must exercise *discretion*, deciding on the basis of extralegal considerations.

In a famous paper of twentieth-century legal philosophy, "The Model of Rules" (1977b), the American philosopher, Ronald Dworkin (1931–2013), challenges the model just described. Dworkin's key observation is that lawyers do not limit themselves to rules in crafting legal arguments. Rules are important, but lawyers use other kinds of standards, too. Sometimes they appeal to what Dworkin calls *policies*: standards that set goals for improvement of the economic, political, or social life of the community. Keeping the public roads safe is a common policy (the policy of "public safety," for short). Lawyers also appeal to what Dworkin calls *principles*: standards required by justice, fairness, or some other dimension of morality. "Innocent until proven guilty" is one familiar legal principle.

In interesting cases, lawyers commonly appeal to principles in their arguments. Dworkin illustrates this by recounting the facts of two court cases.

The first of these, *Riggs v. Palmer*[2] is an appeal from probate court decided in 1889. In this case, Elmer Palmer murdered his grandfather and then sought to collect his inheritance under the terms of his grandfather's will. Interestingly, as of 1889 the rules of estate law in New York made no exception for cases of murder. If the court had followed the rules, then it would have awarded Elmer his inheritance. But the high court of New York ruled against Elmer, holding that all law must be interpreted in light of fundamental maxims of the common law such as "no man shall profit from his own wrongdoing." Dworkin sees this maxim as a legal principle upon which the court relied, disregarding the rules.

The second case that Dworkin uses is *Henningsen v. Bloomfield Motors*,[3] a New Jersey case from 1960:

> The plaintiff in *Henningsen* purchased a car from the defendant, signing a contract that limited the defendant's liability in case of accident. According to the contract, if the car crashed because of a manufacturing defect, the defendant was liable only to repair the defect, not to pay for other damage to persons or property. Again, the rules on the enforcement of contracts would require the court to find in favor of the defendant (see Chapter 5, sec. 5). But the Supreme Court of New Jersey found for the plaintiff. The court decided that purchase agreements must be examined closely for fairness. The court stated that it would not allow itself to be used as an "instrument of inequity" and would not enforce a bargain where one party took "unfair advantage" of the economic necessities of another. As in *Riggs*, the court disregarded legal rules in favor of certain stated principles.

Dworkin references these cases not because he believes that the courts made mistakes, but because they gave legal weight to principles at the expense of rules. Although this is not always appropriate, sometimes it is. Dworkin has three basic points. First, rules and principles are different kinds of standards. Secondly, lawyers appeal to both kinds of standards. Third, both are part of the law.

Dworkin's work encouraged legal philosophers to recognize that legal reasoning often appeals to standards other than rules. They have debated what makes a rule a rule and what makes rules different from other standards. However, Dworkin's original discussion of these matters is confusing. He describes rules as applying in an "all-or-nothing fashion." If a case falls under a rule, then the rule applies. Any exceptions to the rule could, in theory, be stated explicitly. Principles, by contrast, do not apply in an all-or-nothing fashion. Consider, for example, the principle used by the *Riggs* court: "no man shall profit from his own wrongdoing." This principle looks absolute. It seems to require courts to prevent any party from profiting from his own wrongdoing, but courts are not actually so strict. As Dworkin notes, there are many cases in which courts allow people to profit from wrongdoing: illegal squatters can eventually acquire title to land under the doctrine of adverse possession; employees who breach job contracts in order to take higher-paying jobs are permitted to retain their higher salaries, and so on. The "no man shall profit" principle does not always control the outcome, even when it applies. Rather, it operates as a *pro tanto* reason (Kagan 1989) to prevent wrongdoers from profiting.

A pro tanto reason (originally known as a *prima facie* reason; Ross 1930) is a reason that has some weight, but that can be overridden by stronger reasons. When a principle applies to a case, other principles usually apply, as well. In any given case, the correct outcome depends on the balance of applicable principles.

Writers since Dworkin's 1967 paper have generally agreed that rules differ from principles, although they have not always agreed with Dworkin's way of drawing the distinction. There is a growing literature on what makes rules special (Goldman 2002; Alexander and Sherwin 2001; Schauer 1991).

Dworkin also claimed boldly that his observations about the role of principles in legal reasoning undermined some central positivist theses, including the idea that laws are primary rules enacted in accordance with procedures specified in a rule of recognition. Cases such as *Riggs* and *Henningsen* were decided on the basis of principles that were not passed by legislatures. Such principles are not formally enacted or formally repealed in accordance with procedures specified by a rule of recognition. Rather, such principles emerge gradually as courts begin to cite them in their reasoning. When principles erode, they do so gradually as well—courts make decreasing use of them over time. No formal test, such as a rule of recognition, exists for whether a given standard is a "valid" legal principle, or how much weight to give it at any given time. To determine how much weight to give a principle in the case at hand, we examine precedent and see where the principle has or has not prevailed in the past.

Dworkin's theory of law continued to develop over the years, culminating in his monumental book, *Law's Empire* (1986). There Dworkin presents the theory he calls *law as integrity*, which has been influential. Dworkin understands the content of law from a judicial, rather than a legislative, perspective. Consider the proposition that swimming in the River Thames is against the law. According to Dworkin, this proposition means that judges have a reason to uphold convictions of people who swim in the Thames. Dworkin equates "what the law requires" with "how judges ought to rule." In this respect he differs from positivists, who see a gap between the laws of a jurisdiction and how judges there should rule (see Chapter 2, sec. 7). Positivists can maintain that judges should sometimes decide on the basis of considerations other than the laws of their own jurisdiction. On Dworkin's definition of "law," this suggestion is nonsensical—the standards that judges should use are all there is to the law.

Because Dworkin equates "the law" with "how judges ought to rule," I shall discuss his theory at greater length in Chapter 2 on courts and legal reasoning.

7. Legal validity and the sources thesis

In section 4, I distinguished between Austin's and Hart's respective *criteria of legality*—criteria that determine which rules are legally valid. For Austin, a rule is legally valid if and only if the sovereign commands us to obey it. For Hart, a rule is legally valid if and only if it satisfies criteria specified in the rule of recognition. Legal philosophers agree that Hart is closer to the truth than Austin, but they continue to argue about the rule of recognition. This debate becomes complicated. This section will simply introduce it.

Recall the simple rule from section 6: animals shall not be brought into the Public Library. How might this rule become legally valid in the City of Hartford, Connecticut? Let us suppose that the rule of recognition in Hartford states that all norms enacted in accordance with the City Charter are legally valid (a *norm* is a rule or other standard of conduct). The Charter, in turn, specifies that any proposed ordinance that receives a majority of votes in the cabinet shall be published in the official register of ordinances and become law in Hartford. Here we have several elements: the cabinet, composed of human beings; the vote, an event that takes place in accordance with an established procedure; and the text of the ordinance published in the official register. Each of these elements is, in its own way, a *source* of law. The cabinet creates the law. The vote is the means by which they do so. The text of the ordinance tells us what the law is. Although each of these is a source of law, when writers refer to "sources of law" they often mean to refer to self-contained texts, such as the register of ordinances or specific sections thereof. But it is understood that those texts constitute sources of law only because they have been so designated by certain officials who are themselves designated as "sources" of law.

For the purpose of our discussion in this section, a source of law could be a text (e.g. the ordinance), an event (e.g. the vote), specified actors (e.g. cabinet members), or something else entirely. The important point is that these sources of law are identified by the rule of recognition, which is itself a social phenomenon, according to Hart.

Keep in mind the idea of conventionally specified, social sources of law. Now we can examine the *sources thesis* (also known as the "pedigree thesis") which states that all law is based on social sources (Raz 1979a). The sources thesis is important in contemporary legal philosophy, but it is difficult to understand. Let us begin by comparing two possible rules of recognition:

> (RR1) Any norm enacted in accordance with the Hartford City Charter is legally valid.
>
> (RR2) Any norm enacted in accordance with the Hartford City Charter is legally valid, unless it is unfair to the poor.

RR1 specifies only social sources of law. RR2 specifies both social and non-social sources. According to RR2, whether a certain norm is legally valid in Hartford depends in part on the *content* of the norm, not just on whether it was enacted using specified procedures. RR2 entails that a norm that is unfair to the poor cannot be legally valid in Hartford, even if the City Council votes for it. In order to apply RR2, one would have to decide whether the proposed norm is or is not unfair to the poor. This is a moral judgment, what might be called a judgment of "value" rather than "fact."

The sources thesis entails that, whereas RR1 can actually function as a rule of recognition for a legal system, RR2 cannot. Philosophers who accept the sources thesis are *exclusive positivists*. Those who reject it are *inclusive positivists*. There are many arguments for and against the sources thesis (Shapiro 2011; Coleman 2001; Himma 2000; Kramer 2000; Waluchow 1994; Raz 1979b).

The debate between exclusive and inclusive positivists over the sources thesis is about whether a rule of recognition could, in principle, make the validity of a norm depend on its morality. But even inclusive positivists accept that the validity of a norm only depends on its morality if the rule of recognition says so. If the rule of recognition in a particular legal system specifies no moral criteria of legality, then even inclusive positivists will agree that morality is irrelevant to validity in that system.

Dworkin agrees with the inclusive positivists in their rejection of the sources thesis. Most inclusive positivists also believe that morality is relevant to legality in modern Anglophone legal systems. Dworkin agrees with them on this point, as well. But his reasoning differs from theirs. Inclusive positivists believe that such systems have moral criteria of legality only because their rules of recognition so dictate. Whereas Dworkin denies that these systems have rules of recognition in the first place. He has his own account of what gives these systems moral criteria of legality (see Chapter 2, sec. 7).

In another respect, however, Dworkin's position converges with positivism. For Dworkin, as for inclusive positivists, the fact that modern Anglophone legal systems have moral criteria of legality is merely a contingent fact about these systems. There could be legal systems with strictly social criteria of legality.

8. The separability of law and morality

Legal philosophers have long argued about the relationship between law and morality. They disagree about whether law and morality are separable, as the separability thesis holds (see sec. 2), or whether there is some necessary connection between them.

Before examining the separability thesis, however, we must examine the concept of morality itself. Many topics in legal philosophy cannot be understood without some background in moral philosophy or "ethics." Unfortunately, the words "moral" and "morality" confuse readers, so it is worth pausing to make sure we are all speaking the same language. Nonphilosophers sometimes think of morality as a mysterious domain, the stuff of superstition, tradition, taboo, and religious dogma. One dictionary defines "morals" as "Rules or habits of conduct, especially sexual conduct, with reference to standards of right and wrong" (*American Heritage Dictionary* 2000). In philosophy, however, morality concerns matters of right and wrong in the broadest sense, with no special emphasis on sexuality. Here are examples of simple statements that express *moral judgments* (it is another question whether any of these judgments is *true*):

(1) She was wrong to shoplift that magazine.
(2) South African apartheid was unjust.
(3) You have no right to spank your children.
(4) It would be unethical for him to use a pseudonym on his résumé.
(5) It's OK to have sex with an unconscious person.
(6) Genocide violates inalienable human rights.

Ethics is "the study of the general nature of morals and of the specific moral choices to be made by the individual in his relationship with others" (*American Heritage Dictionary* 2000). Some moral questions are, of course, difficult to answer, leading reasonable people to disagree. But there is broad agreement that actions of the following types are, at least in some circumstances, wrong:

 (1) Killing
 (2) Maiming/injuring
 (3) Causing physical pain
 (4) Inflicting emotional distress
 (5) Physical detention or confinement
 (6) Deception/misrepresentation/fraud/lying
 (7) Breaking promises
 (8) Theft/misappropriation/destruction of property
 (9) Exploitation
(10) Partiality/unfairness/bias
(11) Damaging the natural environment

There is broad agreement in the modern world that actions in these categories are, at least in some conditions, wrong. There are also easy cases that command broad agreement: all reasonable people agree that maiming an innocent child for one's own amusement is wrong. The more interesting cases are ones about which reasonable people disagree. We disagree about the conditions under which doing these things is wrong.

With this overview of what philosophers mean by "morality," we can return to our main question: are law and morality connected? The answer is surely affirmative if "morality" means "moral beliefs" and "connected" mean "causally connected." Throughout history, positive law has partly reflected the moral beliefs of lawmakers. Lawmakers use law in order to encourage moral behavior, to punish immorality, and to serve moral purposes in other ways. Most lawmakers believe that it is immoral to maim innocent people for no good reason. They create the crime of *mayhem*. Lawmakers in Iran believe that it is immoral for a married woman to speak to men other than her husband. That is a crime in Iran. Lawmakers who believe that blackmail is immoral often outlaw blackmail. Law and morality overlap considerably in modern legal systems, but the overlap is only partial. Laws do not perfectly reflect anyone's moral beliefs. I believe, for example, that publicly mocking someone for his mental disability is immoral, but it is entirely legal in the United States.

Positive law may also influence our moral beliefs (although individual ignorance of the law is often remarkable; Darley 2001). In the United States, for example, the development of a civil cause of action (a legal basis for a lawsuit) for victims of workplace sexual harassment may have influenced opinions about the wrongness of harassment (Tinkler 2008).

So law can influence our moral beliefs and our moral beliefs can influence law. Law and morality are "connected" in these ways. But these are merely *contingent* connections—they vary from one legal system to another. The existence of contingent connections does not contradict the separability thesis, which denies that law and morality are *necessarily* connected. This is a controversial claim.

In contrast to Dworkin and the positivists, some theorists contend that morality is relevant to validity in *all* legal systems, regardless of what their rules of recognition say. This claim asserts a necessary connection between law and morality, thus contradicting the separability thesis. The claim is popular with *natural lawyers*, for whom moral standards derive from natural or "higher" law. Consider the traditional slogan, *lex iniusta non est lex*—translated as "an unjust law is no law at all." This slogan is associated with Aquinas, although his writings do not contain the exact phrase. Aquinas states that a positive law that contradicts natural law is "no longer law but a perversion of law." Such laws are "acts of violence rather than laws" (Aquinas 1969/1274). The idea goes back at least to Cicero, a roman orator of the first century BCE. The *lex iniusta* slogan is suggested also in the works of St Augustine (354–430 CE) and the great English jurist, Sir William Blackstone (1723–80). It has caused much confusion. Austin (see sec. 1) misunderstood it as the empirical statement that unjust laws are never enforced. This is false, as Austin sarcastically observed.

To other readers, *lex iniusta* has seemed logically incoherent, both affirming and denying that an "unjust law" is a "law." But there are less literal, more charitable ways of interpreting it. We can avoid the logical incoherence if we allow that the first occurrence of "law" has a different meaning from the second (Kretzmann 1988). Interpretations such as the following then become available:

(1) Every unjust norm is legally invalid (at least in a certain sense).
(2) Every unjust law is defective as a law.
(3) One has weaker moral reasons to obey an unjust law than a just law.
(4) No one is morally obligated to obey unjust laws.
(5) Public officials are not morally obligated to enforce unjust laws.
(6) Public officials are morally forbidden to enforce unjust laws.

I shall examine the third and fourth theses in Chapter 4. For now, I shall merely note that Aquinas himself accepted at least the third. In this section, I shall consider the first two.

First, we should try to clarify what an "unjust" norm is. Mark Murphy (2003) suggests that, for traditional natural lawyers, a norm is unjust if and only if it cannot guide the conduct of rational agents. There may, however, be reasonable disagreement about which norms can guide the conduct of rational agents. Natural lawyers offer elaborate substantive theories of justice, the good, and practical reason (reasoning about what to do). For the purposes of this section, we need something generic to use as an example of a norm that cannot guide:

(N) Everyone must keep his or her eyes shut for the hour between noon and 1 p.m. daily.

Can (N) guide the conduct of rational agents? In one sense it can: if you have eyes, then you can simply keep them closed at the noon hour every day. So (N) can guide conduct, unlike a norm that requires you to freeze time or swallow the moon. But in another sense, (N) cannot guide *rational* agents because it serves no good purpose, while interfering with many good purposes. Rational agents do not perform actions that serve no good purpose. (Even idly bouncing a ball off the wall of one's bedroom can serve the slight purpose of amusing oneself.) Because (N) serves no good purpose, it cannot guide rational agents in the sense intended by the first thesis above. (In unusual circumstances, (N) might serve a good purpose: if a nuclear device is detonated at noon, then shutting your eyes could protect them from injury.) On Murphy's reading, the first thesis means that every norm that cannot guide rational agents is legally invalid. It entails, therefore, that (N) is legally invalid, even if (N) is enacted in accordance with procedures specified in the rule of recognition. The first thesis thus contradicts the social fact thesis, according to which legal validity is exclusively a matter of social fact (sec. 2).

Unlike the first thesis, the second thesis allows that irrational norms can be legally valid, but it claims that they are still defective as laws. This claim presupposes that laws, as such, have an *essential proper function*. The claim that some things have essential proper functions dates back to the great Greek philosopher, Aristotle (384–322 BCE) and continues to receive attention from philosophers (Foot 2001; Finnis 1980). It is a controversial claim, but easy enough to grasp intuitively. Flying, for example, is an essential function of bluebirds. Even a bluebird that cannot fly has this essential function, so it is a defective bluebird. By contrast, a turtle that cannot fly is not defective because flying is not among its essential functions. The analogous idea in legal philosophy is that guiding rational agents is an essential function of laws. A norm that cannot guide the conduct of rational agents is therefore a defective law. Its defect is relative to its essential proper function.

Suppose, again, that (N) is enacted in accordance with procedures specified in the rule of recognition. The second thesis is consistent with the claim that (N) is, in that case, legally valid—it is a law. However, if it cannot guide rational agents, then it is a defective law. Some natural lawyers would say that it is not a law "in the fullest sense of the term."

Some philosophical questions must be answered before we can evaluate the second thesis. Do norms actually have essential proper functions? Is guiding rational agents one of them? Which norms can, in fact, guide rational agents? I shall not attempt to answer these questions. I shall turn, instead, to the implications that the first two theses would have if one of them were true. First, there is a methodological implication concerning how we do legal theory. If one of the theses is true, then legal theory cannot be done in a purely descriptive way, which entails that the separability thesis is false. The separability thesis—that there is no necessary connection between law and morality—has important implications for the very enterprise of legal theory. Some of the basic tasks of legal theory are *descriptive*. Legal theorists attempt to describe law in general (distinguishing it from other things), to describe particular legal systems, and to describe particular norms as legally valid or invalid. The separability thesis implies that a theorist can engage in these descriptive tasks while remaining *value-neutral*. Consider, for example, questions about whether a particular norm is legally valid. Separability implies that you can arrive at correct judgments about legal validity without presupposing any moral premises. If, however, unjust laws are invalid or at least defective by nature, then we cannot describe any of these things without moral evaluation. We cannot know whether a particular norm is a law in the fullest sense before we know whether it is just. We cannot know whether a system is a legal system before we know whether its laws are just. And we cannot completely and accurately describe law in general without noting that laws, in the fullest sense, are just norms.

A similar position is taken by John Finnis (1940–), a leading natural lawyer in the tradition of Aquinas. Finnis agrees with Hart that an adequate theory of law must take into account the "internal" perspective of participants (see sec. 2), but Finnis defines the relevant perspective more narrowly than does Hart. Hart describes the distinctively legal standpoint as that of a participant who obeys the law for whatever reason. She might obey the law because she feels morally obligated to do so, or she might obey for entirely self-interested reasons. Finnis's participant, by contrast, obeys the law because she sees it as imposing moral obligations. This participant, whose perspective is necessary for the correct description of a legal system, is a morally engaged participant. Therefore, Finnis (2000) concludes, even descriptive legal theory cannot be done in a morally neutral way—the separability thesis is false.

Do the first two theses also have practical implications? That is best answered after considering the basic question whether one has reasons to obey the law as such, on which see Chapter 4. But here is a preview. Suppose (N) is enacted in accordance with procedures specified in the rule of recognition. What does it mean to say that (N) is, nevertheless, legally invalid or defective, as theses 1 and 2 entail? One plausible answer is that individuals have a weaker reason to obey (N) than to obey legally valid norms. If unjust laws are invalid or defective, then we may have reason to accept one or more of theses 3–6, above. However, someone who accepts the social fact thesis, thereby rejecting the first two theses, could nevertheless accept 3–6. Suppose you believe that (N) is legally valid and not defective. You might nevertheless believe that (N) is unjust, and therefore you might conclude that you have a weaker reason to obey (N) than to obey just laws. So the injustice of a norm could have practical implications in at least three different ways: by rendering the norm invalid, defective, or otherwise simply unworthy of obedience.

9. The authority of law

Legal philosophers often refer to law as having *authority*. Here we can distinguish several issues:

(1) What does it mean to say that law has authority over someone?
(2) Under what conditions, if any, does law claim to have authority over us?
(3) Under what conditions, if any, does law actually have authority over us?
(4) Does the authority of law entail that anyone is obligated to obey it?

What do philosophers mean by the authority of law? People refer to authority in various contexts. The physicist Stephen Hawking, for example, is an authority on the origins of the cosmos. This is *theoretical authority*: expertise in a subject matter. If Hawking tells you that the universe is roughly 13 billion years old, then you have a reason to believe this. The law may also be a theoretical authority on some matters, but we are mainly interested in its *practical authority*—law as a source of practical reasons (i.e. reasons for action).

If law gives us practical reasons, then it does so by giving us instructions. But there must be more to authority than that. Anyone can give you instructions, but most of these lack authority: a bossy neighbor can tell you to plant tulips in your yard, but he has no authority over you. So giving instructions is necessary, but not sufficient, for authority. What is missing? One might imagine that sanctions are the missing element, but this is not so. Your neighbor cannot acquire authority over you by threatening to vandalize your home unless you obey him. Perhaps, you will obey him if you fear his threat, but he still lacks authority over you. The state, similarly, cannot acquire authority over you simply by employing sanctions.

The state might, however, succeed in securing general obedience by means of sanctions. The subjects of such a state might come to believe, correctly or not, that the state had authority. Such a state enjoys at least de facto authority. Someone has de facto authority if and only if most people usually obey him and believe him to have authority. De facto authority, however, is not necessarily *legitimate* authority. When philosophers discuss the authority of law they are mainly interested in the question of its legitimate authority. In the rest of this book "authority" means legitimate authority.

To say that a state, or the law of a state, has authority over you is to say that it is *justified* in instructing you. But when is the state so justified? What reasons does the state give you? Are you obligated to obey the law?

I shall discuss the last of these questions in Chapter 4. In this section, I shall focus on the special role that law plays in practical reasoning. First, consider an ordinary case of practical reasoning, not involving law. You are trying to decide whether to quit smoking. You have a *first-order* reason to smoke: you enjoy it. But a friend presents you with first-order reasons to quit. She reminds you that you value your health and recounts the latest research on the health hazards of smoking. She emphasizes that you are trying to save money and computes for you the cost of a smoking habit. She notes that your friends are nonsmokers who hate the smell. First-order reasons compete with one another in your deliberation. You weigh them against each other and follow whichever reason ultimately seems to you to have more weight.

Now imagine that your state outlaws the purchase of cigarettes. It is trying to discourage you from smoking, as does your friend, but in a different way. Your friend draws attention to the reasons you already have to quit, whereas the state creates a new reason for you to quit. This reason is special in that there is "no direct connection between the reason and the action for which it is a reason" (Raz 1986: 35). It is what Hart calls a *content-independent* reason (1982: 254). Threats create content-independent reasons for the threatened party. Promises create content-independent reasons for the promisor. Laws create content-independent reasons for legal subjects. Or so many writers claim. When buying cigarettes becomes illegal, you acquire a reason not to buy them—a reason that has nothing to do with the nature of cigarettes. If, by contrast, the law *required* you to purchase cigarettes, then you would acquire a reason to do so. In other words, laws provide content-independent reasons.

Many writers, following the important Israeli philosopher, Joseph Raz (1939–), claim that laws provide reasons that are distinctive in another respect as well. According to Raz, laws provide *exclusionary reasons*, which are a type of second-order reasons, not just ordinary, first-order reasons. Imagine, again, that purchasing cigarettes is illegal. Someone offers to sell you cigarettes illegally. You want to buy them. Let us suppose, however, that you are a certain sort of person, whom I shall call *law respecting*. As a law-respecting person, you treat the fact that cigarettes are illegal as an exclusionary reason—a reason simply to ignore your desire for them in deciding what to do. Thus, the illegality of cigarettes is more than a competing first-order reason for you. Exclusionary reasons always trump first-order reasons.

Raz holds that the law claims authority over us and that it thereby claims that we ought to be law respecting: to treat laws as exclusionary reasons. Several questions arise. Some writers have questioned whether laws actually provide exclusionary reasons (Alexander 1990; Perry 1989; Regan 1989). Others have questioned whether law actually claims authority over us, as Raz believes (Soper 2002).

Another question is whether law actually has the authority that, according to Raz, it claims. Hart believes that law both claims and has authority. Hart also maintains that law has authority even without a threat of sanctions. Where, then, does this authority come from? Hart claims that it comes from the rule of recognition. The rule of recognition has authority, Hart writes, because it is accepted from the internal point of view. Hart's reasoning, however, is invalid. The fact that officials believe that a rule of recognition has authority for them does not entail that it actually has such authority. So Hart's way of defending the authority of the rule of recognition fails. But that flaw does not doom his theory of law. He must simply defend the authority of the rule of recognition in some other way. Some philosophers have suggested, for example, that the rule of recognition has authority for public officials because it is a social rule for them—a generally accepted convention within their group. Social conventions often create reasons for participants who desire to coordinate their behavior with others (Marmor 2009; for another view see Shapiro 2011).

Let us suppose that, one way or another, the rule of recognition has authority for public officials. Does this entail that legal rules have authority for ordinary legal subjects? Hart thinks so, but he does little to convince his reader. It is not obvious that legal rules can inherit authority from the rule of recognition that validates them. We are assuming that the rule of recognition has authority for public officials, so perhaps the rules validated by the rule of recognition also have authority for public officials. But why would such rules also have authority for other legal subjects? Hart gives us no reason to think that they do.

Many other writers deny that law has authority in the first place. Some argue that the individual's autonomy (see Chapter 3, sec. 2.7) and rationality preclude accepting practical authority in any form (Wolff 1970). One such argument runs as follows. Whatever the law requires you to do, either you already had a conclusive reason to do it or you did not. If you did, then the law gives you no new reason. If you did not, then the law asks you to do what you have no conclusive reason to do. Therefore, you can never rationally treat the law itself as a conclusive reason for action. Yet, this is precisely what the law asks of you, Raz insists. Raz replies that acting on exclusionary reasons is, itself, rational and compatible with one's autonomy. It can, he thinks, be rational to obey the law just because it is the law, even if one would otherwise have conclusive reasons to act differently.

There remains, however, a puzzle about how authority, as Raz has described it, can be justified. Raz has his own answer, which I shall now explain. The major premise is that people sometimes fail to recognize the reasons that actually apply to them. Jim is heavily intoxicated, so he has a reason not to drive himself home. Failing to realize how intoxicated he is, he falsely believes that he can drive home safely. If he acts on what he believes to be his first-order reasons, then he will drive home—an imprudent and morally suspect decision. However, if he obeys the law, which forbids him to drive while intoxicated, then he will act on his actual first-order reasons. In other words, Jim is more likely to act on his actual first-order reasons if he obeys the law than if he acts on what he believes his first-order reasons to be. This entails, according to Raz, that the applicable law has justified authority for Jim (1986: 53).

If authority is justified in this way, then some laws have authority over some people, some of the time. However, law seems to claim more than this. According to some writers, law claims *general* authority: it demands that everyone always obey. In some cases this makes sense. The law does, indeed, "know better" than the intoxicated Jim. But in some cases, the law does not know better. In some cases, you are not more likely to act on your actual reasons by obeying the law instead of trying to act on your reasons directly. In such cases, Raz's theory does not entail that the law has authority for you. So Raz's theory entails that law has only piecemeal, rather than general, authority. I shall return to the duty to obey the law in Chapter 4.

10. The rule of law

"The rule of law" is a popular phrase with politicians, journalists, scholars, nongovernmental organizations, and others. The rule of law is celebrated as an ideal by nations in the developed world—a great, if incompletely realized, achievement of modern civilization. In recent decades, Western powers have advocated promoting the rule of law in foreign lands (Carothers 1998). But the rule of law is a concept with different conceptions, as is law itself (see sec. 1). As a concept, "the rule of law" refers to certain political ideals which a society might fulfill to a greater or lesser extent. For any conception of the rule of law we can ask questions such as the following. Under what conditions is it achieved? To what extent is its achievement possible? What, if anything, makes it valuable? Should societies aspire to it?

In this section, I shall distinguish a few popular conceptions of the rule of law and pose some of these questions. The main division separates *formal* from *substantive* conceptions. Formal conceptions specify forms and procedures of lawmaking and enforcement. Substantive conceptions include these formal criteria and also place restrictions on the content of laws. I shall begin with formal conceptions.

At a minimum, the rule of law entails the following ideas. First, the government should use law (as opposed to lawless violence, for example) to carry out its purposes. Secondly, everyone is subject to the law, bound by the law, and (in some sense) equal before the law. This includes the government itself and its officials as well as ordinary folk. Even public officials must obey the law, and when they change it they must do so via law-governed procedures. Third, there shall be a government of laws, not of human beings ("men").

Public officials shall not engage in arbitrary exercises of power without legal authorization. These ideas are found in an influential early discussion of the rule of law in the (1982/1885) work of the British jurist, A. V. Dicey (1835–1922). Dicey defines the rule of law in terms of three ideas: (1) regular law is supreme and superior to the arbitrary exercise of power; (2) all persons and classes, including public officials, are subject to, and equal before, the law; (3) constitutional law is a binding part of ordinary law. The phrase "a government of laws and not of men" appears in the Constitution of Massachusetts, in a statement drafted by John Adams,[4] and the idea was echoed by Chief Justice John Marshall of the US Supreme Court, who wrote that "the government of the United States has been emphatically termed a government of laws, and not of men" in the seminal 1803 case of *Marbury v. Madison*.[5]

The idea of a government of laws, not human beings, requires some interpretation. How is it even possible? After all, laws do not apply themselves. Only human beings (or other intelligent agents) can understand and apply laws, so government will always consist of human beings (Marmor 2004). Perhaps, the famous phrase really means, "a government not of human beings alone, but of human beings bound by laws."

But the rule of law has come to mean more than this. Recent discussions have emphasized conditions of *formal legality*. The American legal scholar, Lon L. Fuller (1902–78), suggests the following eight conditions on lawmaking and enforcement (1969):

(1) Cases must be decided based on general rules, not on a case-by-case basis.
(2) The rules must be publicized.
(3) The rules must be enforced prospectively, not retroactively.
(4) The rules must be intelligible to individuals, at least with the assistance of lawyers.
(5) The rules must be consistent with one another, not contradictory.
(6) The rules must not require conduct that is beyond the power of the affected party.
(7) The rules must not change too frequently.
(8) The rules must be applied as announced.

Formal legality conditions such as Fuller's represent a central aspect of the rule of law: the idea that laws should be written and implemented in such a way that they can actually guide human conduct (Marmor 2004; Raz 1979c; Hayek 1978; see also sec. 8 on the guidance function of laws). In other words, it should be possible for individuals to comply, and to comply *because* the law demands compliance. Most of the legality conditions above appear necessary to, or at least supportive of, this guidance function. Rules must be publicized because it is impossible to obey a rule of which one is unaware. Retroactive (ex post facto) laws are unacceptable for the same reason. Rules must be intelligible because it is impossible to obey a rule if one cannot understand what it requires. Rules must not contradict one another because otherwise no one could know which of the two contradictory rules to obey. Rules must not require you to do anything of which you are incapable. No one can be required to jump 2 meters in the air. A three-year-old cannot be required to read street signs.

Joseph Raz adds to Fuller's conditions several features that he sees as necessary, in practice, for the effective implementation of formal legality. These include an independent judiciary, open and fair hearings before unbiased magistrates, judicial review of legislative and administrative officials, and limitations on police discretion. The importance of an independent judiciary was emphasized centuries earlier by the Baron de Montesquieu (1689–1755).

Formal legality conditions are not all-or-nothing. Each can be satisfied to a lesser or greater degree. Some rules are publicized more effectively than others. Some are more intelligible than others. No one actually knows and understands every rule in a modern legal system. Lawmakers may even have reasons to keep some rules secret and to apply different rules than they announced (Dan-Cohen 1984). Complex legal systems inevitably contain a few unnoticed contradictions. Lawmakers change the rules, too, although if rules change too frequently then people become confused and disoriented.

Of Fuller's conditions, only the first—generality—is not directly connected to the guidance function. Consider the following norm: "Britney Spears shall shave her head at 12.00 GMT on January 1, 2015." This norm is not general in any sense—it addresses one individual and requires a specified act at a specified time. Yet, it is perfectly suited to guide Ms Spears, provided that the other legality conditions are met. There may be other reasons for lawmakers to formulate laws in general terms, but the guidance function is not one of them.

Fuller sees his formal legality conditions as reflecting what he called the "internal morality of law." He considers each to be necessary to the very existence of a legal system. He declares that "A total failure in any of these eight directions does not simply result in a bad system of law; it results in something that is not properly called a legal system at all" (Fuller 1969: 39). He also considers systems in which there is substantial, but less than total, failure with respect to one or more of these conditions. Foremost in his mind is Nazi

Germany, where there was a "general and drastic deterioration in legality" (Fuller 1969: 40).

Because Fuller considers certain moral attributes as necessary to the existence of a legal system, he sees himself as a kind of natural lawyer and opponent of the separability thesis (see sec. 8). But even if Fuller's conditions are not, in fact, necessary to the very existence of a legal system, they still reflect some basic requirements of the rule of law as we understand it today.

We can, however, ask questions about the value of the rule of law. Is it a good thing? The historian, E. P. Thompson, famously referred to the rule of law as "an unqualified human good" (1975: 266; criticized in Horwitz 1977). What is good about it? The rule of law seems to have at least some *instrumental* value—value as a means to an end. Formal legality is said to promote human autonomy and dignity by allowing individuals to understand the legal consequences of their behavior before they make decisions (Waldron 1989: 84–5). Legality is thought to be especially important in the area of criminal law, as a way of protecting criminal suspects from tyranny.

Fuller also argues that formal legality has a tendency to promote substantive goodness, although he recognizes that the former does not guarantee the latter. He suggests that a public commitment to the rule of law makes it harder for wicked rulers to carry out their purposes. Picture a dictator who wants to suppress political dissent. He would prefer to simply order the police to arrest and jail particular dissidents. But formal legality makes this more difficult for him. It requires that dissidents first be convicted of violating clear, intelligible, general laws that were publicized in advance. The dictator may be reluctant to publicize laws against political dissent. Doing so may actually encourage dissent, revealing him as the tyrant he is. Formal legality thereby encourages political leaders to allow political dissent, a substantively good result. Promulgation and publicity create political transparency and encourage public deliberation. This is another value that the rule of law might have.

Others emphasize that Fuller's conditions are strictly procedural, by design. They are "indifferent toward the substantive aims of the law" (Fuller 1969: 153), which means that even a legal system with very evil laws could, in principle, satisfy them. Consider laws that uphold slavery, segregate the races, oppress women, persecute religious minorities, or criminalize political dissent. Such laws do not offend Fuller's legality conditions if they are intelligible, consistent, stable, possible to obey, stated as general rules, publicized in advance, and faithfully applied (Raz 1979c). Chile in the years 1974–90, when led by General Augusto Pinochet (1915–2006), had an unjust legal system that arguably upheld the rule of law (Barro 2003). China and Iran might be other examples (Tamanaha 2004: 112). Some have suggested that the rule of law can even facilitate political repression in the wrong hands. This can happen, for example, if the public believes that, if their government maintains legality, then they are morally obligated to obey even its most unjust laws (Tamanaha 2004).

Theorists who see formal legality as an excessively "thin" conception of the rule of law try to incorporate into the rule of law many values they want to see in civil society: universal suffrage, free markets, social justice, freedom of expression, and so on (see, for example, Allan 1993). Some claim that the rule of law requires that certain individual rights be protected under law, at least in an unwritten constitution. The German constitution codifies a conception of the rule of law according to which the duty of all state authority is to respect and protect "human dignity" (German Basic Law, art. 1 sec. 1). Some argue that the rule of law requires a form of democracy, and that effective democracy presupposes the rule of law (Habermas 1996). The German sociologist, Max Weber (1864–1920), argues that the rule of law is necessary for capitalism to flourish (1967/1925). In some nations, political progressives insist that the rule of law requires social democracy or a generous welfare state (International Commission of Jurists 1959). Some conservatives, by contrast, argue that the rule of law is inconsistent with social democracy and the welfare state. The Austrian economist, Friedrich Hayek (1899–1992), originated the latter claim. He argued that progressive taxation and means-tested social programs treat people as unequal under the law, in violation of the rule of law (1978). Progressives have criticized his argument (Tamanaha 2004: 97–8).

Still other writers question any conception of the rule of law that includes substantive values beyond formal legality. They worry that the rule of law will mean less, and perhaps undermine itself, if we try to squeeze substantive values into it (Marmor 2004: 1–2; Tamanaha 2004: 113; Raz 1979a: 211). Consider, for example, conceptions of the rule of law that incorporate freedom of expression. Critics object that there is considerable disagreement about the scope and application of such values, in which case it will sometimes be difficult to establish to everyone's satisfaction whether a judge has complied with the rule of law, so understood. Judges may begin to use their own moral and political opinions to decide whether rights have been violated. This practice leads, in turn, to the politicization of the judiciary and the rule of human beings, not the rule of law.

> Concerns about political judging as a threat to the rule of law came into sharp relief in the United States during the contested presidential election of 2000. A vote recount was in progress in Florida when a Supreme Court majority, consisting of Republican appointees, halted it, effectively ensuring that the Republican candidate, George W. Bush, became president. Associate Justice John Paul Stevens (himself a liberal Republican appointee) wrote in dissent that the decision threatened "the Nation's confidence in the judge as an impartial guardian of the rule of law" (*Bush v. Gore*, 531 U.S. 98, 129 [2000]; see also Tamanaha 2006).

Another important question is what types of institutions and policies are necessary to maintain the rule of law, helpful to its maintenance, or even compatible with it? Formal legality conditions such as Fuller's are typically stated in terms of *rules*, as opposed to other legal standards (see sec. 6 on principles and policies). So the question arises, does the rule of law require that law consist entirely or mostly of rules? Several commentators, including Associate Justice Antonin Scalia of the Supreme Court of the United States (1936–), have suggested that it does (Scalia 1989; see also Alexander 1999; Schauer 1991). Only rules, these writers argue, provide the certainty and predictability demanded by formal legality. This conclusion leads some of these writers to question whether common-law decision-making, in which decisions sometimes precede the announcement of rules, is compatible with the rule of law (Scalia 1997; Schauer 1989; see also Chapter 2, sec. 9).

The rule of law has always had its critics. Some insist that legal rules are so indeterminate that the rule of law is impossible to achieve (criticized in Endicott 1999; Zapf and Moglen 1996; see Chapter 2, sec. 4). Formal legality is thought by some to be incompatible with administrative discretion and doing justice on a case-by-case basis, as considerations of *equity* demand (Solum 1994). Socialists suggest that the rule of law is an ideological commitment that serves capitalism (Sypnowich 1990), with the wealthy benefiting more from formal legality than do the poor. Even among supporters of the rule of law, some recognize that it can conflict with other values and should not be implemented to the highest possible degree (Marmor 2004).

Study questions

(1) What are Hart's major criticisms of Austin's theory of law? How might Austin defend his theory?
(2) Do you accept Dworkin's claim that judges use principles and policies as well as rules to decide cases? If Dworkin is correct about that, then must legal positivism be modified or abandoned?
(3) Distinguish between different kinds of connections between law and morality. Is there a necessary connection, or merely contingent connections?
(4) Which aspects of the rule of law, if any, should a legal system try to maintain?

Recommended reading

Alexander, Larry, and Emily Sherwin. 2001. *The Rule of Rules*. Durham, NC: Duke University Press.

Aquinas, Thomas. 1969. *Summa Theologiae*. Ed. Thomas Gilby. Garden City, NY: Image Books. Originally published, 1274.

Austin, John. 1995. *The Province of Jurisprudence Determined*. Ed. Wilfrid E. Rumble. New York: Cambridge University Press. Original edition, 1832.

Coleman, Jules. 2001. *The Practice of Principle*. Oxford: Oxford University Press.

Dworkin, Ronald. 1977. *Taking Rights Seriously*. Cambridge, MA: Harvard University Press.

—. 1986. *Law's Empire*. Cambridge, MA: Harvard University Press.

Finnis, John. 1980. *Natural Law and Natural Rights*. Oxford: Clarendon Press.

Fuller, Lon L. 1969. *The Morality of Law*. 2nd rev. edn. New Haven: Yale University Press.

Hart, H. L. A. 1994. *The Concept of Law*. 2nd edn. Oxford: Oxford University Press. Original edition, 1961.

Hayek, Friedrich A. 1978. *Law, Legislation and Liberty*. Vol. 1. Chicago: University of Chicago Press.

Raz, Joseph. 1979. *The Authority of Law*. Oxford: Clarendon Press.

Ross, W. D. 1930. *The Right and the Good*. Oxford: Clarendon Press.

Shapiro, Scott. 2011. *Legality*. Cambridge, MA: Belknap.

Tamanaha, Brian Z. 2004. *On the Rule of Law: History, Politics, Theory*. Cambridge: Cambridge University Press.

2

Courts and Legal Reasoning

Legal reasoning is one type of reasoning that takes law as its object. Not all reasoning about law is legal reasoning. This book contains much reasoning about law, but only some of it is legal reasoning. This book contains mostly *legal-philosophical* reasoning. What makes legal reasoning distinctive is that it aims to reach legal conclusions. These include conclusions about someone's legal rights, powers, and duties (i.e. what someone is legally required, permitted, or forbidden to do) and conclusions about the validity of particular legal norms. *Norms*, you will recall, are rules or other standards of conduct.

Legal reasoning is the characteristic kind of reasoning that one finds in published court opinions and briefs submitted by parties to a case at law. Legal reasoning also appears in legal memoranda circulated within law firms and in legal scholarship. It is the kind of reasoning that a lawyer offers in order to convince another lawyer that a certain conclusion is legally correct. Lawyers sometimes say that the purpose of studying law is not so much to "learn the law" as to learn to "think like a lawyer." They mean that studying law teaches competent legal reasoning. Those who are skilled at legal reasoning are able to construct, analyze, and challenge legal arguments.

This chapter examines how lawyers, judges, and other public officials reason about the law and defend legal conclusions. Again, the questions asked are both descriptive (how do lawyers and judges actually think?) and prescriptive (how should they think?). We shall ask a number of overlapping, interlocking questions.

1. Is legal reasoning deductive?

The first question is: what goes on in a judge's mind when she decides a case? For the purpose of answering this question we can use the example of a trial judge in a hypothetical tort lawsuit (see Chapter 5, sec. 3 on torts). The judge hears the following evidence. Defendant agreed to walk a friend's dog (a pit bull). Defendant took the dog to a park without a leash and the dog proceeded to bite plaintiff, causing minor injuries. Plaintiff sued defendant for medical expenses and compensation for pain and suffering.

What is the thought process that leads the judge to her conclusion? One suggestion is that the judge first arrives at a conclusion regarding the facts of the case: she determines, based on the evidence, what the defendant did and what caused the plaintiff's injuries. Then she identifies the legal rules that apply to such cases. These are particular rules of tort law, which she might know by heart or need to research. After identifying the applicable legal rules, she *applies* them to the facts and reaches her conclusion. She decides whether defendant committed a tort against plaintiff and, if so, what remedy the law provides.

In the preceding story, legal reasoning is a rule-driven process. The idea that legal reasoning is rule-driven has been highly influential in the history of legal philosophy. Some have claimed that legal reasoning is *deductive*, akin to logic or geometry. Some characterize legal reasoning as *mechanical*, meaning that no distinctively human judgment is required.

The notion that legal reasoning is deductive or mechanical has some important implications. It follows that there is always at least one legally correct answer to a legal question, and many incorrect answers. It might follow that there is always one and only one legally correct answer (compare Ronald Dworkin's "right answer" thesis, sec. 8).

There is, in fact, a way to represent much legal reasoning as deductive (MacCormick 2005). Consider the following argument:

(1) Anyone whose negligent conduct causes injury commits a tort.
(2) Taking a pit bull to a park without a leash is negligent.
(3) Dirk takes a pit bull to a park without a leash.
(4) Dirk's conduct is negligent.
(5) Dirk's negligent conduct causes the pit bull to injure Pam.
(6) Therefore, Dirk commits a tort.

This argument is deductively valid, at least if we interpret it sensibly: if the premises (1–5) are true, then the conclusion (6) must be true. Insofar as this argument constitutes legal reasoning, there is a form of legal reasoning that is, indeed, deductive.

Many questions about legal reasoning remain. Law involves nondeductive forms of reasoning in addition to deductive forms. Consider the role of a *fact finder* in a trial: a jury or, in a bench trial, the judge playing a fact-finding role. Fact-finding is not deductive. Jurors hear evidence and testimony from witnesses whose credibility they must assess. This is not a purely deductive process. Then jurors must formulate hypotheses about what happened—again, not by deduction, but by observation and inference.

So fact-finding is not a purely deductive process. But what if we take certain facts as given (stipulated), as in the argument above where the facts are stipulated in 2–5? We can take the legal rule stated in premise 1 and apply it to these facts. Then we can deduce a legal conclusion: Dirk committed a tort. So deductive legal reasoning is possible if enough facts are established.

2. Legal realism

One interesting question, however, is to what extent judges actually think this way. Published judicial opinions often present arguments in deductive form. But do these documents accurately reflect the judicial reasoning process? Do judges really begin with facts, identify the applicable legal norms, apply norms to facts, and reach conclusions? Many writers have doubted the accuracy of this simple picture. According to one school of thought, known as *legal realism*, judicial decision-making is "fact-driven" rather than "source-driven." The typical realist believes that judicial reasoning proceeds as follows. First, a judge hears the facts of the case and forms a judgment about which party ought to win. This judgment is not necessarily based on legal rules. The judge may not yet have even considered any rules. Imagine a judge hearing Pam's case against Dirk. The evidence convinces him that Dirk brought his pit bull to the park without a leash and that the dog subsequently bit Pam. Just on the basis of the evidence, the judge may conclude that Dirk has "wronged" Pam. He now *wants* to rule in Pam's favor (assuming he wants to "right" the wrong). However, he knows that he is expected to write an opinion that supports his ruling on the basis of legal norms. So he consults legal norms and tries to write a legal argument that supports his conclusion on that basis. Rather than allowing his conclusion to be dictated by legal reasoning, the judge allows his reasoning to be dictated by his prior conclusion, according to the realist.

Legal realism emerged as a school of thought in the United States in the 1920s and 1930s. Realists believe that different judges respond to the facts of a case differently depending on their individual psychologies, personal backgrounds, social class, and political beliefs. These influences often work subconsciously. Different realists emphasize different factors. Some emphasize the effects of a judge's personality (Frank 1963/1930). Others emphasize his political commitments and allegiance to his social class (Radin 1925). But all realists agree that judges are influenced by factors other than legal rules.

The legal realists are also often said to have accepted the predictive theory of law, which holds that a legal statement is true if and only if it accurately predicts how courts would rule. The predictive theory, however, has been subjected to devastating criticism by H. L. A. Hart and others (see Chapter 1, sec. 5). The predictive theory cannot account for what Hart calls the "internal point of view." According to the predictive theory, to say that littering is illegal is simply to predict that a court will uphold a conviction for littering. But the proposition that littering is illegal must mean more than this. Individuals can treat the fact that littering is illegal as a reason not to litter, even if they are ignorant of or indifferent toward the likelihood of sanctions. They can, in other words, take the internal point of view with respect to the law. Not everyone is like the bad man. The centrality of the internal point of view becomes even clearer when we consider judicial deliberations. It is impossible for rational judges to treat the law as merely a set of predictions of judicial behavior. A judge is not trying to predict his own behavior. He is trying to decide what to do. The predictive theory cannot account for the function of law in guiding judicial decision-making.

Legal realists also championed the idea that law should advance the purposes of a developing society, and that judges have an important role to play in promoting the general welfare. According to many realists, judges can, do, and should make policy from the bench. Many realists urged courts to be more candid about their role as policymakers, and to employ the latest social science in their effort to make good policy. This dimension of realism survives to this day in various forms, including the law and economics movement (see Chapter 5, sec. 3.2).

A movement that arose in the United States partly in reaction to legal realism is the *legal process school*, which emphasized differences in the relative competences of courts, legislators, private parties, and administrative agencies (Hart and Sacks 1994/1958). The legal process school argued that, by considering the different capabilities and tendencies of these various parties and institutions, sensible answers to difficult legal questions could often be reached, notwithstanding the claims made by some realists that judicial decisions are, perhaps necessarily, not source-driven (see sec. 4 on indeterminacy and rule-skepticism).

3. Sources of law

Lawyers deal with various *sources of law*. Important examples include constitutions, acts of the legislature (statutes), case law generated by courts, and administrative regulations of various kinds. Let us focus for the moment on the difference between statutes and case law or *precedent*. Statutes do not typically refer to individual persons or acts, but to *classes* thereof. Consider the Scottish Licensing Act 2005, which regulates sales of alcohol. The Act does not read, "The Dreel Tavern must not serve Sally a beer before 10.00 in the morning." It reads, "a person commits an offence if, outwith licensed hours, the person . . . sells alcohol." Legislation aims to use general classifying words. Case law, by contrast, uses few general terms. A judicial opinion resolves the case decided and offers reasons, but it does not necessarily state rules that purport to cover a wide range of future cases. Yet, judicial opinions set precedents in common-law systems (see sec. 9). It is often more difficult to determine the rule established in a case than it is to understand the rule established by a statute. The reader of a case must determine for herself which facts were relevant to the court's decision if she plans to use the case to predict how a future court will rule in a related case. It is often unclear what rule a case stands for and how the rule should be formulated. Courts broaden and narrow rules in the ordinary course of business.

Statutes also require interpretation. Sometimes it is obvious to the reader if a given fact pattern falls, or does not fall, within the scope of a given statute. These are *easy cases* (*plain cases*). In *hard cases*, by contrast, it is not obvious to the reader if the fact pattern falls, or does not fall, under the statute. Hart refers to this phenomenon as the *open texture* of language (1994/1961: 123). Open texture is inevitable because human beings, including lawmakers, have limited knowledge and are not entirely sure what they want to accomplish by legislating. A lawmaker drafting a general rule has one or more *paradigm cases* before her mind. A city councilwoman drafts a rule prohibiting "vehicles" in the park. She is thinking of sedans and sports cars. She definitely wants to keep these automobiles off the grass, but she cannot think about all the possible cases. What about riding lawnmowers, bicycles, mopeds, motorized wheelchairs, golf carts, helicopters, ambulances, and so on? Is a moped a vehicle? The answer is not obvious. Assuming that a sedan is a vehicle, is a moped sufficiently similar to it? Of course, a moped has an engine and wheels, as does a sedan. But the moped has only two wheels, not four, and it carries only one passenger. It resembles the sedan in some ways, but not others.

How are we to decide if a moped is a "vehicle"? One method begins with a paradigm case, identifies some of its important features, and proceeds to treat these as both necessary and sufficient. The sedan, for example, has four wheels and an internal combustion engine. If we treat those as the two essential features of a vehicle, then mopeds do not count. This method is sometimes called *formalism* or *mechanical jurisprudence* (Pound 1908). It has the advantage of reducing uncertainty in the application of rules to cases, but it cannot eliminate uncertainty altogether. An automobile running on natural gas might or might not be said to have an internal combustion engine. What about a car that has three wheels on the road, plus a fourth that retracts like landing gear? Formalism can only reduce, but never eliminate, the implications of open texture.

Another problem with formalism is that it reduces uncertainty at the cost of arbitrariness. Consider our initial question: is a moped a vehicle? The formalist makes this question easier to answer by stipulating that a vehicle has four wheels and internal combustion. But that stipulation itself is arbitrary relative to the purposes of the law. An electric pickup truck has no internal combustion engine, but to allow it into the park would contradict the presumptive purposes of the statute.

The challenge of drafting good legislation is that we need rules that real persons can follow without official guidance, so they must be clear. Yet, we also need rules that are flexible enough to accommodate unexpected cases. There are always trade-offs between clarity and flexibility. In different areas of law the trade-off will be made in different ways, with lawmakers providing different degrees of clarity. In some areas of law, the legislature uses deliberately vague language (e.g. "fair rate," "safe system," "reasonable conduct") and delegates the details to administrative bodies or courts. Such norms are often called *standards* (Kaplow 1992), rather than rules (although "standard" is also often used as a general category including all legal norms). In other areas, lawmakers insist on less vagueness, as when they define serious crimes.

4. Indeterminacy

As noted earlier, traditional theories of legal reasoning see the process of judicial deliberation as rule-driven. Some writers reject this claim for making unrealistic assumptions about judicial psychology. Judges, they suggest, respond primarily to facts rather than rules. But there is another, more basic way to challenge the idea that legal reasoning is rule-driven. The *rule-skeptic* denies that rule-driven decisions are even possible. Legal rules, the skeptic claims, are to some degree *indeterminate*.

Philosophers distinguish between two ways of understanding claims about indeterminacy, corresponding to the traditional distinction between *metaphysics* (the study of what exists) and *epistemology* (theory of knowledge). Let us suppose that the law is *metaphysically indeterminate* regarding whether a moped is a vehicle under the statute. In that case, the proposition that the moped is a vehicle is not true, but the proposition that the moped is not a vehicle is also not true. There is, as philosophers say, *no fact of the matter* about whether a moped is a vehicle under the statute. That is metaphysical indeterminacy.

Metaphysical indeterminacy contrasts with merely *epistemological indeterminacy*. Suppose, now, that the law is not metaphysically indeterminate: there is a fact of the matter about whether the moped is a vehicle. However, the law could still be epistemologically indeterminate: the answer to the moped question would be unknowable to us. Lawyers and other practical folks often treat epistemological indeterminacy as tantamount to metaphysical indeterminacy because they are not interested in unknowable truths. But philosophers try to keep these types of indeterminacy straight (Leiter 1996).

Ignoring for the moment the metaphysical/epistemological distinction, we can say that *radical rule-skeptics* embrace global indeterminacy—that the law is indeterminate in all cases. This includes even paradigm cases: they deny that we can know whether the sedan is banned from the park, although a sedan seems like an obvious example of a vehicle and the lawmaker actually had sedans in mind. What can we make of such global indeterminacy claims? We have already seen that Hart rejects global indeterminacy, both metaphysical and epistemological. The statute prohibiting vehicles in the park does, indeed, ban sedans, according to Hart, and we can know this fact. The sedan is an easy case. Hart admits, however, that rules are open-textured, so the law is indeterminate in hard cases. He accepts a *moderate* rule-skepticism. In systems that accept the doctrine of *stare decisis* (see sec. 9), one implication of moderate rule-skepticism is that judges perform a lawmaking function in hard cases. The older view of judges as merely discovering the law, rather than creating it, is not entirely correct, according to Hart.

It is worth noting the logical relationship between indeterminacy and the realist thesis that judging is fact-driven, not rule-driven. If the rules are indeterminate with respect to a given case, then it is impossible for a judge to decide it on the basis of the rules. So indeterminacy entails that judging is not rule-driven. The converse does not hold: if judging is, indeed, fact-driven, that does not entail indeterminacy of any kind. It entails, at most, that judges are ignoring the rules or applying them incorrectly. The problem lies in the judges, not in the rules.

5. Indeterminacy and critical legal studies

In the 1980s and 1990s, a politically progressive movement of legal scholars known as Critical Legal Studies (CLS) became prominent, primarily in the United States. The *crits*, as they were known, were influenced by legal realism, Marxism, postmodern literary theory, and other schools of thought. They were especially concerned to expose ways in which legal systems, and mainstream legal scholarship, work systematically to the advantage of the privileged, wealthy, and powerful at the expense of others. The law presents itself as a legitimate (neutral, impartial, objective, apolitical) arbiter of disputes between free and equal citizens. It purports to protect boundaries between public and private spheres of life for the benefit of everyone. The crits argued that this self-image is at least partially a myth. The content of the law reflects political power and contested value judgments. The law creates and polices boundaries between the public and private spheres, rather than respecting preexisting boundaries. Throughout history, courts have crafted legal doctrine to serve the evolving preferences of the privileged few.

CLS is often associated with the view that law is radically indeterminate (see Kress 1989), although there is some dispute about which crits endorsed the radical view. For the crits, the main point of indeterminacy is that judges foster the impression that their decisions are dictated by the law, when in fact they are making choices every day, often ones that reflect their own political preferences. The radical indeterminacy thesis was widely criticized and largely withdrawn. One of the leaders of CLS, the Brazilian legal scholar, Roberto Mangabeira Unger (1947–), rejects radical indeterminacy (1996). CLS has largely disappeared as a movement (Sunstein 2001), although its influence continues. The current consensus is that most mandatory rules of law are not radically indeterminate, and that even partially indeterminate rules can guide judges.

Some crits object that their position on indeterminacy was misunderstood. They do not deny that, in the vast majority of cases, lawyers agree about the correct result and can accurately predict judicial rulings (Balkin 1991). The crits' point is that this convergence simply reflects the fact that lawyers and judges are mostly heterosexual, white males from the same socioeconomic class. Legal reasoning that seems obviously correct to them would not seem obviously correct to someone with a different background (Kennedy 1997).

6. Hart on rule-skepticism

Hart considers another form of rule-skepticism, reflecting the idea that "the law is what the courts say it is"—a quotation attributed to Chief Justice Charles Evans Hughes (1862–1948) of the US Supreme Court. This argument for rule-skepticism begins with the observation that, after a case has been appealed to the highest court with jurisdiction, its decision is final and can be overturned only by legislation. In constitutional cases only a constitutional amendment can reverse the highest court. The court's decision *is* the law until lawmakers change it. This is so even if the court's ruling is outrageously mistaken in everyone else's judgment. Nor are judges punished or sanctioned for their incorrect decisions. From these facts, rule-skeptics conclude that judging is not rule-guided. After all, a court is always free to ignore the rules and its decision will still be enforced as law.

The flaw in this argument, Hart claims, is that it ignores the distinction between (1) what a rule requires and (2) who has final authority to decide what a rule requires. Compare a referee who makes a bad call in a sporting event. She has final authority. Nevertheless, her call was bad. She was supposed to apply the rules correctly but failed to do so. The authority to decide under a rule is not the authority to rewrite the rule. We can *imagine* a sport in which referees are given no rules to follow, but real sports are not like this. Similarly, we can imagine a statute that authorizes judges to decide cases without providing any standards to apply, but real statutes are not like this. Judges and referees have final authority, but it is still possible for them to follow the rules or depart from them. They are expected to follow rules and are properly criticized when they do not. Therefore, it is a mistake to infer from the fact that judges have final authority to the skeptical conclusion that judging cannot be rule-guided.

Hart admits that judges could collectively start rewriting the law at whim, just as referees could collectively start ignoring the rules of sports. This behavior would certainly change the legal system dramatically. But the mere possibility that a legal system could be so transformed does not convert it today into that sort of system.

The very idea of rule-guidance raises many important philosophical questions. What does it mean to say that someone has been "guided" by a rule? A simple theory holds that someone is guided by a rule only if she consciously reflects upon the rule while making her decision. But there are other, less restrictive, ways to understand rule-guidance. For example, Hart holds that obeying a rule does not entail consciously thinking about it while acting. One obeys a rule, according to Hart, if one appeals to it when one's act is challenged.

7. Theories of law versus theories of adjudication

Legal philosophers distinguish between theories that tell us what the law says (theories of *legal content*) and those that tell us how courts should decide cases (theories of *adjudication*). Ronald Dworkin (see Chapter 1) addresses both questions in one theory, which he calls *law as integrity*. Dworkin's theory is rich and intricate, so I must be selective.

For Dworkin, what the law says depends on how an ideal judge would rule. And Dworkin has specific views on how an ideal judge would go about deciding cases. Dworkin develops his theory in contrast to two other theories of adjudication that oppose both one another and his. The first theory—*conventionalism*—holds that judges should identify and apply rules that have been validated by the law-determining conventions of their legal system. In England, these include conventions such as the following: decisions by the House of Lords bind the lower courts; Acts of Parliament are law; and so on. Conventionalism is a form of legal positivism (see Chapter 1). One implication of conventionalism is that a hard case has no legally correct answer. In a hard case, the law-determining conventions fail to dictate a unique answer. Therefore, judges in hard cases must decide by looking outside the law, often "making new law" in the process.

The second theory opposed to Dworkin's—*pragmatism*—holds that judges should decide cases so as to bring about the best consequences overall, as they see it. In any given case, a pragmatist judge may decide that following established rules will, in fact, have the best consequences, in which case she will follow them. What makes her a pragmatist, however, is that she gives no extra weight to being consistent with past decisions (Dworkin 1986: 95). If she believes that departing from established rules will have better consequences, then depart from them she does.

Dworkin's theory opposes both conventionalism and pragmatism. Unlike the pragmatist, Dworkin believes that judges should give some weight to consistency with past decisions for its own sake. Unlike the conventionalist, Dworkin wants judges to look beyond the conventionally validated, and hence uncontroversially valid, rules. At the heart of Dworkin's alternative is his idea of *constructive interpretation*. Constructive interpretation is a particular way of interpreting something: a novel, for example, or a complex social practice such as a legal system. Constructively interpreting something involves ascribing a purpose to it in order to see it in its best light—to see it as the best possible example of its genre. Dworkin illustrates constructive interpretation with the example of a *chain novel*. This is an unusual kind of novel that is written sequentially by multiple coauthors. Each author drafts her assigned chapter before handing off the project to the next author. Each has the job of writing his chapter so as to make the novel as a whole the best it can be. Each therefore makes an overall judgment about the novel as he writes it. He adopts a working theory of the novel's characters, plot, genre, themes, and point. One can assess each of these judgments on two dimensions. First, the author considers the dimension of *fit*. She reads the partially completed novel and formulates one or more possible interpretations. In so doing, she imputes a certain aim to the partially completed novel as a whole.

Our novelist may have her own ideas about what makes for a good novel. But as a coauthor of a chain novel, she may not simply impute to it anything she chooses. She may not ignore large parts of the existing text simply because they conflict with her preferred aim. Rather, she must be able to imagine that a single, rational author could have written substantially the text so far with her suggested aim in mind. She can dismiss some details of the text as errors, but if she does this too frequently, then she has abandoned the original novel and started a new one.

In some unhappy cases, the novelist may conclude that her predecessors did a lousy job. She may be unable to find any interpretation that fits the text. In that case, she must give up and conclude that the novel makes no sense. More often, however, she will find herself with multiple interpretations, each of which fits the text to date reasonably well. In that case, she turns to the dimension of *quality*. Of the interpretations that fit the text reasonably well, she must choose the one that makes the work in progress the best it can be. At this point, she may appeal to her own aesthetic judgments about what makes for a better novel. She can nevertheless claim to be engaged in constructive interpretation of the text because the options from which she chooses are themselves constrained by the text.

According to Dworkin, judges should see themselves as playing a role analogous to the chain novelist's. Some of the "story" has already been written by others—previous lawmakers and judges. The judge should first attempt constructive interpretation. She should try to identify a set of principles that largely fits existing legal materials, including statutes, reported cases, and (if applicable) constitutions. This involves imagining that all legal rights and duties in her jurisdiction were created by a single authority, which one might think of as a personification of one's community. (This is fictional, of course—in a modern legal system there is no single individual or group who created the law.) In this respect, Dworkin's judge is no pragmatist.

The most important aspect of this fictional authority is that we envision it as possessing a unified, coherent conception of justice and fairness. Let us spend a moment on the idea of a *conception* of justice and fairness. Any *concept*, such as the concept of music, can have several corresponding conceptions (see Chapter 1, sec. 1). On a traditional *conception*, music must be tonal, which excludes a drum solo or rap lyric. On another conception, music is sound deliberately organized by human beings, which includes the drum solo and rapping, but excludes birdsongs and ambient noise (as in John Cage's silent composition, 4' 33"). On a still broader conception, even the latter would count as music.

The concepts of justice and fairness also have different conceptions. On some conceptions, for example, justice requires that resources be distributed to all on an equal basis. On other conceptions, justice requires that resources be distributed on the basis of individual productivity, and so forth. (These brief statements should not be confused with complete conceptions of justice, which can fill many pages; see Kymlicka 2001.) Constructive interpretation involves determining which conception of justice and fairness most closely reflects the actual legal practice of the system.

If the judge identifies more than one conception, each of which fits the legal materials reasonably well, then she must choose between them. The judge, as does the chain novelist, tries to make the "story" the best it can be, although the judge takes the perspective of political morality, rather than the novelist's perspective of literary aesthetics. She chooses the conception of justice and fairness that she considers the best and imputes it to the system as a whole, subject as always to the constraint of fit. So Dworkin's judge is not a conventionalist, either.

This is what constructive interpretation entails for the theory of adjudication. As noted, however, Dworkin presents his theory simultaneously as a theory of legal validity and content. He writes that "propositions of law are true if they figure in or follow from the principles of justice, fairness, and procedural due process that provide the best constructive interpretation of the community's legal practice" (Dworkin 1986: 225).

8. Right answers

Dworkin intends for law as integrity to support his best-known claim, the *right answer thesis*, which holds that in a developed legal system such as ours, there are right answers—legally correct answers—in almost all hard cases. Positivists reject the right answer thesis: they believe that there are no legally correct answers in hard cases. In hard cases, positivists think that courts must create new law. Their answers can be morally better or worse, but never legally incorrect.

The right answer thesis is easily misunderstood as stronger than it is. Dworkin does not claim that the right answer is always obvious, or that judges will always agree about it, or that it is always possible to demonstrate that the right answer is right (1986: viii–ix). The thesis just states that a right answer almost always exists. This is a metaphysical claim, not an epistemological claim (see sec. 4). Whether a real judge will find the answer or not is another matter.

Nevertheless, if the right answer thesis is true, then there must, in principle, be a way to identify the right answer. To illustrate, Dworkin asks us to imagine a character named "Hercules"—a judge of extraordinary intellect and patience who accepts law as integrity. Hercules decides cases in the following way:

(1) He identifies the legal question posed by the case before him.
(2) He makes a list of candidate doctrines, any one of which would resolve the case if it were part of the law. He invents these doctrines, but he does not formulate them on the basis of his own preferences. His goal is to anticipate which doctrine he will, in fact, discover in the applicable precedent, which he has not yet studied. A doctrine makes his list only if he thinks that there is a reasonable chance that the case law will turn out to support it.
(3) With this list of candidate doctrines in hand, he studies the reported cases that are most similar to the case before him.
(4) He rules out any candidate doctrines that conflict directly with reported cases.
(5) He rules out candidate doctrines that do not represent principles of justice or fairness at all (i.e. doctrines that represent ad hoc compromises or merely economic priorities).
(6) If more than one candidate remains, then Hercules gradually "fans out" from the most relevant precedents, which he has already examined, to more remote precedents (i.e. cases that are progressively less similar to the case before him).
(7) From the remaining candidates, Hercules chooses the doctrine that is supported by the largest, most factually diverse set of cases in his legal system.

Dworkin admits that there is no guarantee that Hercules will find a clear winner. Hercules may discover that, no matter how many cases he takes into account, two or more candidates always tie for first place. But Dworkin thinks that such occasions will prove rare in a highly developed legal system such as ours that has so much precedent to consider. When Dworkin insists that there is almost always a right answer, he means that Hercules could almost always settle on one answer using the method just described.

Many legal philosophers are critical of Dworkin's right answer thesis. Some object that the thesis is empty because real judges are not Hercules and have neither the patience nor the intellect to engage in constructive interpretation of so much law. Some suggest that two judges with Hercules' capabilities might often disagree about the right answer.

Critics also argue that Dworkin's method unjustifiably defers to the principles that happen to be imbedded in precedent, even if they are morally deficient. Dworkin incorporates moral reasoning into legal reasoning, but he does so in a strangely constricted way. Hercules does not decide cases on the basis of his own best understanding of justice. Rather, he decides cases on the basis of his best understanding of the conception of justice that happens to be imbedded in the precedent of his legal system. Therefore, the critic concludes, Dworkin's method has neither the advantages of methods that defer to clearly stated rules of law, nor the advantages of methods that make direct appeals to justice (Alexander and Kress 1995).

9. Precedent

Most legal systems in the English-speaking world—the United Kingdom, United States, Canada, Australia, and New Zealand—are known as *common-law* systems, as opposed to *civil-law* systems. The latter are more common in continental Europe and Latin America. In both systems, a court usually publishes a written opinion describing the facts of the case and explaining its reasoning. But there is a major difference: in common-law systems, but not in civil-law systems, published judicial opinions serve as *precedent* for future decisions.

This is not to say that courts in civil-law systems ignore past decisions. The reasoning of another court may be informative, and thus worth consulting, as are legal scholarship and the opinions of overseas courts. But scholarship does not bind courts, nor are Canadian judges expected to follow the Japanese judiciary. In civil-law jurisdictions, the published opinions of domestic courts have similarly limited weight. Precedents are *persuasive* but not authoritative. Civil-law courts do not see themselves as bound by precedent.

Imagine a judge in a newly formed legal system. He hears the case of an impoverished, elderly woman whose wealthy son refuses to support her. She is suing her son for a modest stipend. Because it is a new legal system, there are no controlling sources of law on this issue—no statutes or previous cases on point. This makes it a *case of first impression*. Courts in common-law jurisdictions sometimes proceed cautiously in cases of first impression: they decide the case, and may hope that future courts will be persuaded by their reasoning, but they have no expectation that future courts will follow their lead, any more than a civil-law court would have such an expectation. However, courts in common-law jurisdictions follow the doctrine of *stare decisis et non quieta movere* ("to stand by decisions and not disturb the undisturbed") or *stare decisis*, for short. When they decide cases of first impression, they usually expect future courts at or below their level to follow their lead.

Stare decisis is one of many court-crafted doctrines of adjudication, not typically found in any statute or constitution. The doctrine entails that precedents, themselves, are sources of law. The doctrines of the English common law—including tort, contract, and property—were created and refined by courts over the centuries, one precedent after another. Cases construing statutes and constitutions also set precedent in common-law jurisdictions.

Some precedents are easier to follow than others. Some opinions have obvious implications for future cases. Other opinions require interpretation. Lawyers distinguish between the *facts* of a case, the *question presented*, the court's *reasoning* or *ratio decidendi* (*ratio*, for short), and the *holding*.

Published opinions usually contain assertions and reasoning that do not form part of the ratio decidendi. These are known as *obiter dicta* (*dicta*, for short). It is sometimes said that the ratio of a case includes only the reasoning that was necessary in order to support the holding, the rest of the opinion being dicta. This formulation is problematic because it is often difficult to determine whether an assertion was "necessary" to the holding, but it remains a widely used formulation of the idea.

Courts are organized into hierarchies, with trial courts at the bottom, one or more levels of appellate courts above them, and a high or "supreme" court at the top. A case constitutes a *vertical precedent* for a court if it was authored by a higher court (Schauer 1987). If the US Court of Appeals for the Seventh Circuit publishes an opinion, then a federal judge in the Northern District of Illinois, which falls in the Seventh Circuit, is expected to treat it as a binding precedent, even if she disagrees with it. Courts that deviate from vertical precedent risk being reversed (and publicly chastised). They almost never admit that they are doing so.

A *horizontal precedent*, by contrast, is a case from a court at the same or lower level. Deviating from horizontal precedent is not itself grounds for reversal. If a federal judge in the Northern District of Illinois disagrees with an opinion authored by another judge in the Northern District (or by a judge in the Southern District of New York), then she might or might not follow his lead. She might state that she believes the previous case to be mistaken, or she might just decline to cite the case. Similarly, a judge on the Court of Appeals for the Seventh Circuit is required to follow precedents set by the Supreme Court of the United States, but not necessarily precedents from the Seventh Circuit.

Theorists have different ideas about how stare decisis requires courts to treat precedent, vertical and horizontal alike (Alexander 1989). I shall illustrate by returning to the fictional case of the elderly mother suing her son. To continue the story, the judge makes the decision that he thinks best, all things considered—he rules in favor of the mother. Subsequently, another judge on the same court hears an identical case of another elderly mother suing her wealthy son for support. Let us assume that there is no doctrine of stare decisis in this legal system. Nevertheless, the second judge decides in favor of the mother. The second judge might do so for reasons having nothing to do with the previous case. He might rule for the mother because he believes that she is morally entitled the support, or because he dislikes her son. He does not follow precedent at all, but simply treats the case as though it were a case of first impression.

Now stipulate that the second judge does not agree with the decision in the first case. He does not believe that children owe anything to their parents as a matter of justice. If he had been assigned to decide the first case, then he would have ruled in the son's favor. If he rules in favor of the son in the second case, then he is not following precedent. Again, he is treating it as a case of first impression.

Precedent really only enters the scene if the second judge, who disagrees with the first decision, nevertheless treats it as a reason to rule for the mother. He might reason that *comparative justice* (see Chapter 3, sec. 2.4) favors treating the second case as the first case was treated. Or he might suspect that the mother in the second case relied, perhaps reasonably, on the result in the first case, such that it would be wrong to frustrate her expectations by ruling against her (see Chapter 5, sec. 5). Either of these could be a reason for him to follow the precedent. All theories of precedent hold that courts have pro tanto reasons to follow precedent that are based on comparative justice and reliance.

Stare decisis is usually understood to mean more than this, however. On one account, horizontal courts have a reason to follow precedent in addition to the reasons of comparative justice and reliance mentioned earlier. On this account, the mere fact that a court has made a decision is an independent reason for a horizontal court to follow it, a reason that civil-law courts do not have. This is to say that the prior court has the *authority* to set precedent and that horizontal precedent, as such, has authority (see Chapter 1, sec. 9).

Even those who agree that courts have a reason to follow horizontal precedent, as such, can disagree about the strength of the reason. One view is that courts are absolutely bound by horizontal precedent. The more common view is that they have only a pro tanto reason to follow it—one that can be outweighed by other reasons (see Chapter 1, sec. 6 on pro tanto reasons). A judge might decide to follow precedents that she considers moderately unjust, but depart from precedents if their injustice exceeds a certain threshold.

Before we can ask how much weight to give to a precedent, we need to interpret it. There are two main methods. One method sees cases as announcing, following, or refining general rules. According to this method, a case sets a precedent only insofar as it announces a general rule. How does one go about identifying the rule announced in a published opinion? If one is lucky, then the court stated the rule explicitly. The English case of *Hadley v. Baxendale* announces the following rule:

> Where two parties have made a contract which one of them has broken, the damages which the other party ought to receive in respect of such breach of contract should be such as may fairly and reasonably be considered either arising naturally, i.e., according to the usual course of things, from such breach of contract itself, or such as may reasonably be supposed to have been in the contemplation of both parties, at the time they made the contract, as the probable result of the breach of it.[1]

This rule is fairly clear as rules of law go. But courts are not always so explicit. Often we must "read between the lines" in order to determine which rule the court believed it was following. For any given result, there are always multiple rules that could support it (Wittgenstein 1967; Quine 1964). Interpreters will disagree about which rule to attribute to the court and treat as the precedent established.

Consider another famous English case, *Priestley v. Fowler*:[2]

In 1835, Charles Priestley, a servant of Thomas Fowler, was injured in a wagon accident due to the negligence of another employee of Fowler's. A jury awarded Priestley monetary damages from Fowler to cover his medical expenses, but the Court of Exchequer reversed on appeal. *Priestley* has since been cited as the origin of the fellow-servant doctrine, which states that an employee may not hold his employer vicariously liable for another employee's negligence. Recent scholars, however, have argued that the court never intended to announce such a rule (Stein 2003).

Puzzles can arise even if the rule announced is perfectly clear. Courts sometimes misapply their own rules. The court in *Hadley*, for example, held for the defendant despite the fact that the damages suffered by the plaintiff were entirely foreseeable, such that the plaintiff should have won under the stated rule. Subsequent courts followed the announced rule, but an argument could be made for substituting a rule that would have supported the result actually reached.

To understand precedent in terms of rules is to hold that courts are bound only by the rule that the case announces, either explicitly or implicitly. On this view, the court's reasoning—as opposed to the rule—does not bind subsequent courts. This view also entails that the facts of the case should not inform the interpretation of the precedent. Proponents of a rule-based theory of precedent argue that their method provides superior guidance to courts and supports the rule of law (see Chapter 1, sec. 10).

Some scholars, however, find the rule-based theory of precedent unrealistic and too restrictive. They advocate an *analogical* approach (Brewer 1996; Sunstein 1993; Levi 1949). Analogical reasoning—reasoning by analogy—is the most prevalent type of legal reasoning in common-law jurisdictions. Analogical reasoning begins with a description of a case and a premise about its proper resolution. A second case is then described that has certain features in common with the first case. It is then argued that the similarities between the first and second cases warrant resolving the second case as the first was resolved.

Analogical reasoning keeps one in close contact with the particular facts of cases, always on the lookout for differences and similarities (Dancy 2004; criticized in Ridge and McKeever 2006). Critics of analogical reasoning argue that it proceeds in an ad hoc, unprincipled way. Its defenders dispute the charge. Analogical reasoning, they insist, makes use of principles, just as other forms of reasoning do. Analogical reasoning strives for consistent resolution of cases. If analogical reasoning supports resolving one case as another was resolved, then we should eventually be able to state a principle that supports both results and makes reference to the relevantly similar features of the cases. Analogical reasoning contrasts with rule-driven reasoning, however, in that the principles that justify results are not stated in advance or used as the basis for the decisions. Rather, the decision is made on analogical grounds, with any principles emerging only after the fact. Furthermore, the emergent principles are relatively low-level principles. They do not presuppose comprehensive theories of justice or value.

Consider the case of a twelve-year-old boy whose mother forces him to attend a religious school against his will. He sues his mother for the right to attend a secular school, but he loses in court. Thereafter, the court hears the case of a thirteen-year-old girl who is suing her father to prevent him from forcing her to receive an influenza shot against her will. Assume that the court believes either that the first case was decided correctly, or that it is bound to decide similar cases similarly. The court decides that the two cases are similar in the relevant respects, so it rules against the girl. Although the first court stated no principle in support of its holding, the second court suggests that the first case stands for the following principle:

> Parents have discretion to take reasonable measures in the best interests of their children, without the child's consent.

This is, indeed, a principle, but it operates at a relatively low level. It does not articulate any general theory of welfare, autonomy, the rights of children, or how these values interact. It makes no commitment to any first principles at the level of consequentialism or nonconsequentalism (see Chapter 3, sec. 2). It leaves unresolved many issues about the treatment of minor children. Can parents discipline their children by whipping them with a leather strap? Restrict their children to a vegan diet? Subject children to therapies designed to "cure" homosexuality? Two individuals who disagree about the answers to these questions might nevertheless agree on the principle stated above. They might also agree that the court correctly ruled in favor of the parents in the first two cases mentioned. The parental discretion principle above is a *mid-level* principle. Analogical reasoning trades in low-level and mid-level principles.

A major difference between rule-based reasoning and analogical reasoning about precedent is that the latter involves ever-closer scrutiny of particular facts, whereas the former deliberately abstracts from the particulars. Analogical reasoning treats the facts of previous cases as relevant to a fuller understanding of what constitutes a "reasonable measure." For example, if one wants to know whether requiring the girl to get a flu shot is reasonable, one might compare and contrast her case with that of the boy who wanted to change schools. Are the two cases sufficiently similar in relevant ways to warrant similar treatment?

By contrast, rule-based reasoning would not treat the facts of the first case as relevant to what constitutes a reasonable measure for parents to take. Rule-based reasoning still has to answer this question, but this could be done on another basis. The court could use its own judgment or consult contemporary community standards, or what have you.

Study questions

(1) Is there a sharp boundary between easy cases and hard cases, or a gradual shading of one category into another?
(2) To what extent is the law indeterminate? Does indeterminacy threaten the rule of law?
(3) Do you agree with Dworkin that courts should see themselves as analogous to coauthors of a chain novel? What are the virtues and flaws in this analogy?
(4) Could there really be right answers to difficult legal questions? How could we discover them?
(5) Should judges in common-law jurisdictions always follow precedent?

Recommended reading

Alexander, Larry, and Ken Kress. 1995. "Against Legal Principles." In *Law and Interpretation: Essays in Legal Philosophy*, ed. Andrei Marmor. Oxford: Clarendon Press. 279–327.

Alexander, Larry, and Emily Sherwin. 2008. *Demystifying Legal Reasoning*. New York: Cambridge University Press.

Altman, Andrew. 1990. *Critical Legal Studies: A Liberal Critique*. Princeton: Princeton University Press.

Dworkin, Ronald. 1986. *Law's Empire*. Cambridge, MA: Harvard University Press.

Frank, Jerome. 1963. *Law and the Modern Mind*. Garden City, NJ: Doubleday. Original edition, 1930.

Hart, H. L. A. 1994. *The Concept of Law*. 2nd edn. Oxford: Oxford University Press. Original edition, 1961.

Kennedy, Duncan. 1997. *A Critique of Adjudication (fin de siècle)*. Cambridge, MA: Harvard University Press.

Kress, Ken. 1989. "Legal Indeterminacy." *California Law Review* 77: 283–337.

Leiter, Brian. 1996. "Legal Realism." In *A Companion to Philosophy of Law and Legal Theory*, ed. Dennis Patterson. Malden, MA: Blackwell. 261–79.

Levi, Edward. 1949. *An Introduction to Legal Reasoning*. Chicago: University of Chicago Press.

Posner, Richard A. 2008. *How Judges Think*. Cambridge: Harvard University Press.

Schauer, Frederick. 1987. "Precedent." *Stanford Law Review* 29: 571–605.

Sunstein, Cass R. 1993. "On Analogical Reasoning." *Harvard Law Review* 106: 741–91.

Weinrib, Ernest J. 1996. "Legal Formalism." In *A Companion to Philosophy of Law and Legal Theory*, ed. Dennis Patterson. Malden, MA: Blackwell. 332–42.

3

Making, Justifying, and Evaluating Law

Every legal system has its own laws about which various questions can be asked. One question is: what is the content of these laws? In other words, which actions do they permit, forbid, and require? Once we understand the content of a particular set of laws, questions of *constructive interpretation* arise (see Chapter 2, sec. 7). Can we understand these laws as implementing a consistent set of values and principles? If so, then which values?

Finally, we can ask prescriptive or evaluative questions. Which laws should be enacted and enforced? Which laws are the best ones to have? Which values and principles should our laws implement? Should the status quo be maintained?

All of these questions are asked by private parties and legal commentators. They are also asked by lawmakers, including legislators, executive branch officials, and judges when they play lawmaking roles. Chapter 5 asks questions of constructive interpretation, which also arise in Chapters 7 and 8. This chapter introduces prescriptive and evaluative questions, which we will continue to pose at various points in the remainder of the book. Defending answers could involve most of moral and political philosophy, so I must be selective in this chapter.

1. Making law

What laws should lawmakers make? One possible answer is: none. Political anarchists defend the abolition of government and law, at least as an ideal (Rothbard 1978). But assuming that law is a good idea, what laws should we have? Let us begin by distinguishing our question from a different question of normative political theory: who should have the legal authority to make law? Dictators? Oligarchs? Representative legislatures? The citizens themselves? Our question assumes that the question of lawmaking authority has been answered. The basic structures of government are in place: we have lawmakers and established procedures for lawmaking. Given that someone is authorized to make law, we ask: what reasons should they take into account in doing so?

You can always avoid giving real answers to prescriptive questions about law by responding that lawmaking is a lawmaker's job, not yours. For the purpose of asking prescriptive philosophical questions about law, however, you should put yourself in the position of a lawmaker. In fact, you should imagine yourself as an influential lawmaker, secure in your office, who sincerely wishes to make good policy. What laws would you support and why? How would you justify your choices to someone else?

Of course, this is an idealization. Real lawmakers have to run for election, raise funds, and please constituents. Some give too much weight to their own interests and those of their friends. Put all that aside for now. Imagine that you have the power to enact whatever laws you wish, without fear of reprisal, and that you want to enact good laws for good reasons.

2. Normative concepts for justifying and evaluating law

When philosophers ask prescriptive questions about law, they use concepts such as *welfare, efficiency, rights, fairness, justice, equality, autonomy, liberty,* and *desert*. These concepts are related to one another in complicated ways. Philosophers have been thinking about them for centuries, resulting in many books. When a philosopher answers a prescriptive question about law, her answer is typically informed by one or more *normative principles*. Different principles have been proposed over the years, and philosophers continue to debate the merits of different principles. Principles favored by some philosophers are rejected by others. The most I can do here is give a brief overview.

2.1 Beneficence and welfare

The principle of *beneficence* plays a role in the thinking of almost every philosopher who asks prescriptive questions about law. Beneficence is simply the idea that lawmakers have at least a pro tanto moral reason to promote intrinsically good results and prevent intrinsically bad ones (see Chapter 1, sec. 6 on pro tanto reasons). In other words, unless they have a stronger reason to do otherwise, they should try to make the world a better place. This is an appealing idea in the abstract and not very controversial. However, much disagreement remains. How do we define "good results"? What does it mean to "promote" them? What, if anything, constitutes a good reason for lawmakers to refrain from promoting good results? There are many different answers to these questions.

Some legal philosophers understand "intrinsic good" in terms of human welfare—a position known as *welfarism*. Welfarism comes in three main versions. *Hedonists* believe that pleasure is the only intrinsically good thing in the universe and that pain is the only intrinsically bad thing. Other things are good only insofar as they increase pleasure and bad only insofar as they reduce pleasure or cause pain. This was the view of the English utilitarian, Jeremy Bentham (1748–1832), although Bentham also counted the pleasure and pain of nonhuman animals as good and bad, respectively. Hedonists disagree among themselves about how many different classes of pleasure and pain there are.

Some philosophers reject hedonism altogether. *Desire-satisfaction theorists* claim that it is good for a human being to have her desires satisfied, with or without pleasure, and bad for her to have her desires unsatisfied. Most desire-satisfaction theorists believe, however, that there are certain desires (e.g. desires based on false beliefs) that it is not good for one to satisfy.

There are also *objective list* theorists who believe that certain events and activities are good for an individual (e.g. freedom, knowledge, exposure to beauty), whether or not she desires them or takes pleasure in them. Finally, there are nonwelfarists who believe that things other than human welfare are also intrinsically good (e.g. beauty, trees, stars, God).

Without attempting to settle on one theory of intrinsic good, let us assume that some form of welfarism is correct. So beneficence requires promoting welfare. Now we must define "promote." One well-known definition states that promoting the good means creating a greater total of it—*maximizing* it. On this definition, beneficence entails that lawmakers have a pro tanto reason to make laws that increase total human welfare. This understanding of "promote" counts everyone's welfare and counts it equally. Some philosophers favor nonmaximizing theories, for example, by giving greater priority to raising the welfare of those with lower welfare (Nagel 1979).

As noted, most legal philosophers accept some version of the beneficence principle. *Consequentialists* believe that every lawmaker (and everyone else) has an all-things-considered moral reason to promote the good. *Utilitarianism* is the classic form of consequentialism, pioneered by the English philosophers Bentham, John Stuart Mill (1806–73), and Henry Sidgwick (1838–1900). Utilitarians are maximizing, welfarist consequentialists: they believe that we have an all-things-considered moral reason to maximize total welfare.

How might a utilitarian lawmaker go about deciding which laws to support? For simplicity, I shall imagine that she is being asked to decide between two bills. She must vote for one or the other. In theory, her process goes like this. First, she reads both bills and tries to predict the consequences of each for human welfare. If neither of the bills will create more welfare than the other, then it does not matter which one she supports. But if one of the bills will create more welfare than the other, then she votes for it.

In simple cases, the utilitarian lawmaker will not have trouble. In many real-world cases, however, she may not be able to determine with any confidence which of the bills will do more to promote human welfare. In that case, utilitarianism does not provide the guidance she needs. In the real world, utilitarian lawmakers employ various techniques to make their decisions more feasible. They often employ simplifying assumptions about human welfare. Two of the most popular simplifying methodologies are welfare economics and cost-benefit analysis. Welfare economics treats an individual's spending power, which is relatively easy to measure, as a proxy for her welfare. One outcome is more *efficient* than another if total spending power is greater in the former. Philosophers, including consequentialists, have raised many objections to the simplifying assumptions of welfare economics and cost-benefit analysis (Nussbaum 2000; Sen 2000). But consequentialist philosophers have not thus far managed to persuade utilitarian lawmakers to use a different theory of the good in place of welfare economics. Many lawmakers, of course, are not utilitarians in the first place.

The beneficence principle states that actors have at least a pro tanto moral reason to promote the good. Welfarism states that welfare is the only intrinsic good. Beneficence and welfare contrast with many other important value concepts, including rights, justice, fairness, equality, autonomy, liberty, and desert. These are *deontological* concepts. Some of the most interesting prescriptive questions about law require thinking about the relations between beneficence, welfarism, and various deontological concepts.

2.2 Rights

Of all the deontological concepts, *rights* play the most central role in law and jurisprudence. We shall need to distinguish several types of rights, but first let us examine what all rights have in common as rights.

In the central cases, rights are held by rational agents, such as ordinary adult human beings. There are interesting philosophical controversies about whether other entities have rights: human infants, dolphins, adults in persistent vegetative states, deceased individuals, corporations, groups of persons, and the like. For our purposes, we can think of right-holders as ordinary adult human beings.

A right is either a *claim* to something or a protected *option* to act. The fact that someone has a right can give someone else a reason to act or to refrain from action. If Minneh has a right to eat a kilo of wild strawberries that she has picked, then Aito has a reason not to take them from her. He has this reason independent of any other reason that he might have. Minneh's right also neutralizes certain other reasons that Aito might have to take the berries. For example, the pleasure that Aito would obtain from making a strawberry pie would otherwise constitute a reason for him to take the berries. Because Minneh has a right to the berries, however, Aito should not treat his prospective pleasure as any reason to take them at all—not even a slight reason. This is to say that rights provide *exclusionary reasons* (see Chapter 1, sec. 9).

Minneh's right to the berries has a correlated *duty* in Aito and in the rest of us who might want to take the berries. We owe that duty to Minneh, not to the world at large. Philosophers disagree about whether there are rights without corresponding duties (Perry 2009).

2.2.1 Hohfeldian analysis of rights

An American legal theorist, Wesley Newcomb Hohfeld (1879–1918), introduced a pioneering (1919) analysis of rights that is still in use. Hohfeld distinguishes four elements or *incidents*: *claims, privileges, powers,* and *immunities.* Each incident is a right on its own, but various incidents can also combine into more complex rights. I shall explain each incident in turn.

Ann holds a *claim-right* against Brad to wash Ann's scarf if and only if Brad has a duty to Ann to wash Ann's scarf. Brad owes this duty to Ann, in particular. His duty is "directed toward" her. In this case Ann, herself, will presumably benefit, but that need not be the case. If Ann holds a claim-right against Brad to wash Ann's sister's scarf, then Brad still owes this duty to Ann, not to Ann's sister. He owes this duty to Ann even if Ann hates both her sister and the scarf, although Ann probably has the power to *waive* her claim-right (see points 3(a) and 3(b) on p. 58). A claim-right always has one or more *correlative duties*. It can be a duty to act, as in Brad's case, or to refrain from action: Carol holds a claim-right against Dirk to keep off her grass if and only if Dirk has a duty to Carol to keep off her grass.

The absence of a duty is a privilege. Edna has a *privilege-right* to sing "Greensleeves" if and only if Edna has no duty not to sing "Greensleeves." A license to practice medicine gives one a legal privilege-right to do so.

Claims and privileges define all the actions that are forbidden, permitted, or required. The two remaining incidents (powers and immunities) are second-order incidents: they specify rights and duties regarding the creation, destruction, and modification of other incidents (see the discussion of secondary rules in Chapter 1, sec. 3). Forrest has a *power-right* under a set of rules if and only if those rules give him the ability to alter someone's Hohfeldian incidents (his own or someone else's). If Forrest is a police officer directing traffic, then the legal rules give him a power-right to alter, by means of a hand gesture, a driver's privilege-right to cross the intersection. If Ginger promises to cook Helen dinner, then Ginger exercises her power-right (under the moral rules of promising) to grant Helen a claim-right against Ginger to cook dinner.

The opposite of a power is an immunity. If Ivan lacks the ability to alter one of Josh's Hohfeldian incidents under a set of rules, then Josh has an immunity against Ivan with respect to that incident. Imagine that Josh is a teenaged minor child and Ivan is his father. Ivan orders Josh to mow the lawn every summer, which gives Josh a duty to mow the lawn. When Josh reaches legal adulthood, he acquires an immunity against Ivan's orders: Ivan loses the legal power to impose such duties on Josh by means of orders.

Hohfeld depicts the relationships between the incidents with two charts, which include some terminology that Hohfeld invented for the sake of logical completeness:

Opposites

If someone has a claim, then she lacks a nonclaim.

If someone has a privilege, then she lacks a duty.

If someone has a power, then she lacks a disability.

If someone has an immunity, then she lacks a liability.

Correlatives

If someone has a claim, then someone else has a duty.

If someone has a privilege, then someone else has a nonclaim.

If someone has a power, then someone else has a liability.

If someone has an immunity, then someone else has a disability.

As I mentioned, the incidents can combine into various complex rights, such as property rights. Mario's ownership of his car consists of the following:

(1) Mario has a privilege to use (or damage) his car. He has no duty not to use or damage his car.

(2) Mario has several claim-rights to his car: everyone else has a duty not to use or damage his car.

(3) Mario has various powers over these claim-rights:

    a. Mario can waive one of his claim-rights with respect to Danica by granting her temporary permission to use his car.

    b. Mario can waive his claim-rights permanently with respect to everyone by abandoning the car (this is *annulment* of his claim-rights).

    c. Mario can transfer his claim-rights to Danica by giving or selling his car to her.

(4) Mario has an immunity against others waiving, annulling, or transferring his claim-rights.

If Danica borrows Mario's car without his permission, then she *infringes* his right. If she is not justified in doing so, then philosophers would say that she does not just infringe his rights, but she *violates* them (Thomson 1990). If borrowing his car is, for special reasons, permissible, then she infringes his right but does not violate it. In such cases of justified infringement, Danica may owe Mario compensation for the use of his car or at least an apology.

2.2.2 Theories of rights

Philosophers have long argued about the function of rights. Traditionally, there have been two ways of understanding it: *will theory* and *interest theory*. Will theorists understand every right as including a power over a claim (Wellman 1997). To say that Mario has a right to his car is to say that he has the power to alter the duties of others with respect to his car as he sees fit—in accordance with his "will."

Interest theorists, by contrast, see rights as a means of advancing the interests of the right-holder (Raz 1986). To say that Mario has a right to his car, according to interest theory, is to say that his interest in the car is strong enough to give others a duty not to interfere with his use of it.

Will theory fits nicely with the universally recognized fact that rights can be waived. I can donate my entire retirement account to charity, even if this is a terribly imprudent decision that will leave me impoverished in old age. I have a right to make choices that are bad for me.

However, will theory has trouble accounting for even the concept of an inalienable right. Under the law, your right to life is inalienable. This does not mean that suicide is a crime, but it does mean that you lack the power to give someone else the legal right to kill you. Regardless of whether this is a good law, its existence proves that inalienable legal rights can exist. How can a will theory make sense of them?

Will theory also has difficulty accounting for the rights of infants and the mentally incompetent. An infant has no "will" to exercise or and is unable to alter the duties of others. Interest theory, by contrast, can accommodate the rights of infants: an infant has a right not to be subjected to physical pain if and only if her interests will be served by others refraining from subjecting her to pain. She needs no will in order to have rights, according to interest theory. Interest theory also may be able to accommodate inalienable rights: you have an inalienable right to life if and only if it serves your interests not to be able to waive that right. There is a further question whether having inalienable rights actually serves your interests, but at least the interest theory makes room for the possibility of inalienable rights.

2.2.3 Types of rights

With this conceptual framework in place, we can distinguish several types of rights. *Legal rights* are rights created by positive law. Eamon and Rowan execute a contract in which Eamon agrees to pay Rowan $200 for his bicycle and Rowan agrees to deliver the bicycle to Eamon the following week. After

Eamon pays Rowan, he acquires a legal right (a contractual right) to receive the bicycle. Legal rights are created by constitutions, statutes, common-law doctrines, administrative regulations, and so on.

In some legal systems, individuals also enjoy a special kind of legal right: *constitutional rights* or *charter rights*. Section 2 of the Canadian Charter provides a right to "freedom of thought, belief, opinion and expression." If Ontario tries to enforce a law that restricts someone's freedom of expression, he can challenge the law in court as a violation of his charter rights (see Chapter 9). Charter/constitutional rights are held by individuals or other legal persons such as corporations. They are held primarily against governments, but they can also be held against other private parties.

Unlike legal rights, *moral rights* are not created by law. Where they come from is something of a mystery. Moral rights include *natural rights*, which are understood today as rights that one possesses just in virtue of being a person. The English philosopher, John Locke (1632–1704), claimed that men have natural rights to "life, liberty, and property" (1988/1688). The American Declaration of Independence asserts that all men are "endowed by their Creator with certain unalienable Rights" including "Life, Liberty and the pursuit of Happiness." (Today we know that women also have these rights, if men do.)

Writers in centuries past always claimed that natural rights were given to men by God. Some people, theist and atheist alike, continue to believe that natural rights depend on God. Some theists insist that to deny God is to deny our natural rights. Some atheists agree, concluding that we have no natural rights. Natural rights, by definition, were not created by human beings. They are said to exist objectively, much as the laws of physics do. These metaphysical claims are too much for some philosophers to take. Bentham famously dismissed claims of natural right as "nonsense upon stilts" (Bentham 1962/1843: 489). Some philosophers since Bentham are no less skeptical of natural rights (Mackie 1977).

Despite ongoing controversies about natural rights, most philosophers today agree that we have *moral* rights, the content of which overlaps substantially with natural rights as traditionally conceived. Philosophers who believe in natural rights hold that our moral rights coincide with, or derive from, our natural rights. Those who believe in moral rights, but not natural rights, must offer a different account of the former. *Moral relativists* hold that one has a certain moral right if and only if there is a substantial consensus in one's community that one has it. In my community, there is a substantial consensus that individuals have a moral right not to be raped. Therefore, relativism entails that I have such a right, although it is not a natural right because there are no natural rights. If I lived in a community where few believed in a right against rape, then I would have no such moral right (Harman and Thomson 1996).

It is important not to confuse moral relativism with the proposition that our moral rights are created by law. Positive law almost always reflects some local moral beliefs, but relativism holds that widespread moral beliefs generate moral rights even if the law does not reflect them. People in my community agree that individuals with physical handicaps have a moral right not to be publicly mocked. Relativism entails that such a right therefore exists in my community, despite the fact that such mockery is legal. In what follows, I shall refer to our moral rights without specifying whether they should be understood as natural rights.

Moral rights figure prominently in our answers to prescriptive questions about law. Lawmakers must take our moral rights into account. They have at least a pro tanto reason to make laws that satisfy moral rights and not to make laws that infringe moral rights. If I have a moral right not to be beaten in the street, then the law might respond by criminalizing such beatings. If an impoverished infant has a moral right to be fed, then the law satisfies his right by providing him with nourishment. Lawmakers should consider which moral rights we have and how important they are. These questions arise, for example, in debates over the proper scope of the criminal law (see sec. 3).

2.2.4 Consequentialism and rights

Can consequentialists recognize moral rights? Philosophers have argued about this for decades (Pettit 1988). In a trivial sense, at least, the answer is "yes." The most familiar consequentialists—utilitarians—believe that everyone has a moral right to have his welfare counted along with everyone else's. But what about rights to life, liberty, physical integrity, self-expression, and so on? Utilitarians respond that promoting the good usually entails preserving all of these. To that extent, utilitarians can endorse these traditional moral rights, too.

Notice, however, that promoting the good entails respecting rights *usually*, but not always. The following case illustrates:

Paul owns a fancy speedboat. He has a moral right to control its use. Kelly asks Paul for permission to take nine of her friends out on the boat. Paul had no plans to use it that day, but he refuses her request. Kelly takes her friends on the boat anyway. They enjoy a wonderful afternoon. They clean the boat, fill the tank, and make some essential repairs, saving Paul some money. He is still annoyed, but his irritation is outweighed by the good that Kelly and her friends have produced. They have promoted the good, despite having violated Paul's moral right.

Most people believe that Kelly acts wrongly. Their judgment reflects the idea that Paul's right to control his boat (one of his property rights; see Chapter 5, sec. 2) functions as a *trump* (Dworkin 1977c: xi) on the promotion of the good, which is to say that violating his right is morally impermissible even if doing so promotes the good.

What do utilitarians say about this? Some "bite the bullet" and insist that Kelly does not, in fact, act wrongly, notwithstanding common beliefs. But most utilitarians try to justify trumping rights in utilitarian terms. They suggest that Kelly's actions could have negative long-term effects, or they retreat to indirect utilitarianism and argue that a rule allowing indiscriminate borrowing would not maximize welfare in the long run.

A consequentialist could respond, instead, by abandoning welfarism in favor of a theory that assigns more weight to losses than to gains and requires actors to minimize losses. When Kelly borrows Paul's boat without his consent, he incurs a loss. By contrast, if Kelly had not taken the boat, then no one would have incurred any loss: she and her friends would have been no worse-off than before. Kelly acts wrongly because she imposes an unnecessary loss—she fails to minimize losses, even as she maximizes welfare.

Nonconsequentialists object that this modification does not go far enough. There are cases in which even minimizing losses is impermissible. Here is my variation on a widely used example (Foot 1967):

> Dr Harris is caring for five patients in their twenties, each of whom is dying of organ failure. Two need kidneys, two need lungs, and one needs a heart. All will die within a week if they do not receive transplants. Unfortunately, there is an organ shortage. Dr Harris learns that no organs will become available in time to save these lives. But she happens to know of a healthy young man, Kazuo, also in his twenties, whose organs are compatible with these patients. She explains the situation to him and asks if he would be willing to give his own life to save five. Kazuo refuses. She follows him home. Before Kazuo knows what is happening, Dr Harris administers a general anesthetic, kills him painlessly, removes his organs, and transplants them into her patients. All the transplants are successful. She covers her tracks, so no one ever learns what she did. Dr Harris's patients go on to lead good, long lives.

Kazuo is innocent, poses no threat to anyone, and does not consent. Dr Harris violates his moral right to life, but she minimizes losses in the process. Although killing Kazuo costs him whatever welfare he would have accrued during the rest of his life, it prevents each of five patients from suffering a loss of comparable magnitude. Consequentialism therefore entails that Dr Harris's actions are morally permissible. Most people disagree.

How do consequentialists reply? Some bite the bullet again, denying that Dr Harris does anything wrong. But others look for a way to condemn Dr Harris in consequentialist terms. Some question whether she actually minimizes losses. Others suggest that treating the right to life as a trump against imposing losses is actually the most reliable way to minimize losses in the long run. This might be because actors are so fallible. Killing an innocent, nonthreatening person without his consent almost never minimizes losses. Fortunately, there is a widespread belief in a moral right to life that forbids killing the innocent, even to save lives. This belief discourages most of us from killing most of the time, which minimizes losses. To make an exception for cases such as Dr Harris's would be to abandon our belief in such a strong right to life. As that belief became less popular, homicides in general would increase, most of which would not actually minimize losses. Kazuo's case was exceptional. Therefore, although consequentialists themselves cannot sincerely believe in a right that is strong enough to protect Kazuo, they can endorse laws that cultivate a useful (although false) general belief in such rights. A constitutional bill of rights may have just this effect on our general beliefs.

Other consequentialists accommodate cases such as Kazuo's by adopting *rights consequentialism*, which permits actors to infringe rights only for the sake of preventing the violation of a more important right, or a greater number of similar rights (Scheffler 1994). Dr Harris acts wrongly, according to rights consequentialism, because no one was threatening the rights of her patients. Their organs failed for natural reasons. Rights consequentialism does not permit killing for the sake of preventing losses (e.g. saving lives).

Rights consequentialism does, however, permit infringing rights for the sake of preventing more infringements. A famous thought experiment that challenges rights consequentialism is the "frame-up hypothetical" (see Chapter 7, sec. 4.2). In this hypothetical, a sheriff imprisons an innocent man—infringing his right to liberty—for the sake of preventing a greater number of infringements of rights that are at least as important as the right to liberty. Rights consequentialism permits this, but many people believe it to be wrong. Those who believe that infringing rights is wrong, even for the sake of preventing more rights violations, understand rights as an especially strong kind of trump known as a *side-constraint* (Nozick 1974).

Cases such as Kazuo's and the frame-up hypothetical bolster nonconsequentialism because most people believe with great confidence that killing Kazuo is wrong and that framing someone for a crime is wrong. Consequentialists respond by describing other scenarios in which an actor infringes someone's rights in order to prevent harm, but we are not so confident that she acts immorally:

(1) Kelly and her friend are staying on an island in the middle of a large lake. Her friend falls ill and needs medical attention. The only way for Kelly to get her friend to a doctor is to borrow Paul's speedboat. She asks his permission, but he refuses. She takes his boat anyway.
(2) A patient has contracted an infectious disease. A public official quarantines him against his will.
(3) Israeli law requires all adult citizens to serve in the military (subject to various exemptions), even if they would much prefer to avoid service.

Infringing moral rights in these cases is not obviously wrong. Kelly could assert a "lesser-evils" justification under the criminal law (see Chapter 6, sec. 4.2). The law permits military conscription and quarantines under certain conditions.

Nonconsequentialists reply by clarifying their position: infringing rights is often, but not always, wrong. It depends on the right and what is at stake. Paul's right to control his speedboat is relatively unimportant, easily overridden by someone's need for medical attention. The quarantined patient's right to liberty is important, but must yield to public safety. Consequentialists ask why we do not say the same about the frame-up victim's liberty-right.

Consequentialists have also extracted concessions from nonconsequentialists using cases such as this:

> Terrorists have rigged a nuclear device to detonate in Paris, killing millions. It can only be disarmed via a remote control located in New York City. The terrorists have surgically implanted the disarming code in between the chambers of the heart of Job, an innocent New Yorker. The implant itself poses no risk to Job, but the only way to disarm the device in time is to remove it from Job's heart, killing him in the process.

Many people, even those who believe that Dr Harris is wrong to kill Kazuo, believe that killing Job is morally permissible because so many lives are at stake. This position is *threshold nonconsequentialism*, which holds that infringing rights is wrong unless necessary to prevent harm over a certain threshold (Alexander 2000). Most nonconsequentialists today are threshold nonconsequentialists.

2.3 Justice

Aristotle (384–322 BCE) distinguishes between *distributive justice* and *corrective justice* in his *Nichomachean Ethics*. Distributive justice concerns the allocation to individuals of initially unowned resources—one of the central concerns of contemporary political philosophy (Kymlicka 2001). Concerns of distributive justice arise in connection with tax policy, social welfare policy, health policy, education policy, international aid policy, the law of private property, and many other areas. Questions of distributive justice also arise in private law and criminal law. Different theories of distributive justice have different implications for law.

Corrective justice (also known as *rectificatory* or *restitutional justice*) concerns the compensation of individuals for wrongful losses by the responsible parties. Corrective justice applies mainly to the private law of tort and contract (see Chapter 5), although it also applies to international law (transitional justice, reparations; see Chapter 10).

Distributive and corrective justice both differ from *retributive justice*, which concerns the punishment of wrongdoers on the basis of desert (see Chapter 7). Retributive justice is mainly relevant to the criminal law.

What do consequentialists say about justice? Some believe that lawmakers should always promote the good, even at the expense of justice. Others agree that justice is important, but try to understand it in consequentialist terms, as they do with rights. Mill (1861) gives a famous consequentialist account of justice. Nonconsequentialists, by contrast, see each form of justice (distributive, corrective, retributive) as an independent value, irreducible to welfare or any other good. It is not always possible, they believe, for lawmakers to do justice while simultaneously promoting the good, just as it is impossible for Dr Harris to minimize losses without violating Kazuo's right to life (see sec. 2.2.4). Nonconsequentialists give at least some priority to justice over the good when the two conflict. For threshold nonconsequentialists, that priority is less than absolute.

2.4 Fairness

In law, "fairness" usually refers to yet another category of justice, known as *comparative justice* (or *formal justice*). If two cases are relevantly similar, then comparative justice requires treating them similarly. If you have two cookies and two children, then you should give one cookie to each, not two cookies to one and none to the other. If you give both cookies to one child for no good reason, then you treat the other unfairly. You offend both distributive and comparative justice. Imagine, instead, that you have one child and two cookies. You give the child one cookie and she asks for a second. When you refuse, she complains that you are being "unfair," but your decision does not offend comparative justice. There is no one else whom you are treating differently. Perhaps you are stingy, greedy, or cruel, but you are not unfair.

Comparative justice plays an important role in law. It requires determining whether two cases are relevantly similar and what would constitute similar treatment. We can distinguish between moral and legal similarity. Two cases can be legally similar but morally different or vice versa. The law does not take all morally relevant features of cases into account. Courts of law aspire to treat legally similar cases similarly. In common-law systems, this aspiration is reflected in the doctrine of stare decisis (see Chapter 2, sec. 9).

Matters are different when we turn to morality. Statutes often treat morally similar cases differently and morally different cases similarly. Zoning laws permit restaurants on one block but not on the next. The law allows someone to drive on his sixteenth birthday, but not the day before. Many acts of immoral deception and hurtful speech are perfectly legal. The law does not take notice of every moral distinction so many cases that are morally different are legally identical.

However, many modern legal systems include statutes or constitutional provisions that require governments to treat certain morally similar cases similarly. The Equal Protection Clause of the US Constitution has been interpreted to prohibit many laws that treat people differently on the basis of characteristics such as race, religion, national origin, and sex. Interpreting this clause has proven very difficult (see Chapter 9). The Charter of Fundamental Rights of the European Union (arts 20–3) likewise guarantees equality before the law.

2.5 Equality

This brings us to the concept of equality. Comparative justice simply requires treating similar cases similarly or "equally." But some conceptions of distributive justice require more or less than equal treatment. They require *substantive equality* rather than the *formal equality* of comparative justice. *Egalitarian* conceptions of justice require that people be provided with certain goods on an equal basis. Different egalitarian conceptions specify differently what must be equalized: opportunities, resources, welfare, capabilities for functioning, and so on (Daniels 1990). On some conceptions, for example, justice requires that every child be provided with an education of equal quality, regardless of his family background. Some conceptions of justice require that scarce resources be distributed on an equal basis. Other conceptions require that individuals with physical handicaps receive extra resources so as to bring their capabilities in line with the general population (Anderson 1999).

2.6 Liberty

Many different liberties or freedoms are important in modern law: freedom of conscience, religion, expression, movement, association, and so on. Most freedoms include freedom to act and freedom to refrain from action. Freedom of movement, for example, includes freedom to remain stationary. Freedom of expression includes freedom to remain silent. Freedom of religion includes freedom to renounce religious beliefs and practices.

Philosophers also distinguish between *negative liberty* and *positive liberty* (Berlin 1969). Negative liberty is an absence of external obstacles or constraints. Positive liberty involves the actual possibility of acting, including whatever internal or external resources are needed. If I tie your hands, or threaten to injure you, then I deprive you of the negative liberty to publish a blog that is critical of me. Whereas, if you do not know how to use a computer or you cannot afford one, then you have the negative liberty to publish your blog, but not the positive liberty to do so. Positive liberty is closely connected to autonomy (see next section).

Liberty is related to rights and justice. Most theories of rights entail that individuals have rights to various freedoms, which entails at least that it is wrong for others to curtail those freedoms. Distributive justice, on most conceptions, requires protecting various freedoms.

2.7 Autonomy

Modern legal systems also reflect the value of autonomy: the condition of being self-governing. A choice is made autonomously if and only it is made in a way that reflects the chooser's identity and values, independent of distorting influences. Ina is an adult woman who chooses not to eat on a particular

Tuesday. Is her choice autonomous? The answer depends on the background conditions and her mental state. Consider some fact patterns:

(1) Ina's doctor advises her to fast for 24 hours prior to a blood test (it is safe and medically indicated).

(2) Ina is a healthy gourmand whose friend bets her £50 that she cannot resist eating for a day.

(3) Ina is a prominent New Zealander who opposes the Chinese occupation of Tibet. She fasts in order to obtain publicity for her cause.

(4) Ina is an observant Muslim living in modern Britain. She chooses to fast during Ramadan, as her faith requires.

(5) As an adult, Ina joined a cult that convinced her that she will die a horrible death if she eats on Tuesdays.

(6) An enemy threatens to reveal an embarrassing secret about Ina unless she fasts for the day.

(7) Ina is destitute, with only enough food for her young son, so she gives it all to him.

(8) Ina suffers from anorexia nervosa which leads her to believe, falsely, that she is overweight.

(9) Someone has administered an appetite-suppressing drug to Ina without her consent.

(10) Ina suffers from a paranoid dissociative disorder that leads her to believe that someone is following her and poisoning her food.

In all of these cases, except possibly 6, Ina enjoys the *liberty* to eat. She faces no external physical impediments to eating, as she would if she were locked in a cell. Nor has anyone threatened her with force. Nevertheless, in some cases Ina's choice to fast is not autonomous, but *heteronomous* (not self-governed), most obviously so in cases 8–10. Her choice is most obviously autonomous in 1–4. Cases 5–7 are more difficult. Different philosophical theories of autonomy would offer different judgments about cases 5–7, which is where things get interesting.

Modern philosophers see autonomy as an important value that the law should respect and promote. Above all, laws should avoid compromising individual autonomy unless there is a good reason to do so. Throughout history, laws have compromised autonomy in many ways, often by misinforming individuals or depriving them of information that is relevant to their decisions.

The law should actively cultivate the conditions for autonomy and its exercise. It can do so by providing educational opportunities and information. The law can encourage individuals to deliberate thoughtfully, form their own values, make their own choices, and take responsibility for them. Laws regulate substances that are known to compromise individual autonomy.

Facilitating autonomy does not entail maximizing freedom. It entails increasing the likelihood that choices will be made on the basis of the individual's authentic values and judgment. Waiting periods before a divorce will be granted, for example, encourage married couples to deliberate carefully, rather than getting divorced when they are angry and not thinking clearly. These laws restrict liberty for the sake of cultivating autonomy.

The law can also protect individuals from threats to their autonomy. Laws require private parties to disclose relevant information, require parents to send their children to school, and require schools to expose children to certain facts. Laws protect freedom of association for adults, which limits the influence of parents on their adult offspring, thereby promoting autonomy. Many legal rights today can be understood in terms of respecting and promoting both autonomy and liberty. Debates over legal paternalism and moralism, addressed in the next section, concern both values.

3. Moral evaluation of the criminal law

Which sorts of conduct is it morally permissible for the state to criminalize? Which sorts of conduct should it criminalize, all things considered? The contemporary way of asking these questions is to ask what reasons the state may take into account in criminalizing behavior. There are various conflicting answers, corresponding to different *liberty-limiting principles* (Feinberg 1984) that philosophers variously defend. A liberty-limiting principle states "that a given type of consideration is always a morally relevant reason in support of penal legislation even if other reasons may in the circumstances outweigh it" (Feinberg 1990: ix). The best-known liberty-limiting principle is the

> Harm Principle: preventing harm to someone other than the actor is always a morally relevant reason for the state to coerce the actor.

Almost everyone accepts the Harm Principle, which is associated with John Stuart Mill. However, Mill also claims that the Harm Principle is the only liberty-limiting principle that is true. This claim is controversial. There are three other important liberty-limiting principles to consider:

> Offense Principle: preventing offense (as opposed to harm) is always a morally relevant reason for the state to coerce the actor.

> Legal Paternalism: preventing harm to the actor himself is always a morally relevant reason for state coercion.
>
> Legal Moralism: preventing inherently immoral behavior is always a morally relevant reason for state coercion.

The American philosopher, Joel Feinberg (1926–2004), defends a version of liberalism which holds that of all the liberty-limiting principles, only the Harm and Offense Principles are true. Each principle merits its own discussion.

Mill defends the Harm Principle on a utilitarian basis, claiming that its use would maximize happiness (although nonutilitarians can and do accept the Harm Principle). It is, of course, a serious matter for the state to coerce someone, but protecting other individuals from being harmed by him seems like a good reason. Police officers often use coercion to prevent harm to others. They are legally authorized to break up fights in progress, to rescue hostages, to recover stolen property, and so on. Surely they are morally permitted to do so. The state also punishes convicts, although the correct rationale for punishment remains a disputed subject (see Chapter 7). The Harm Principle could, perhaps, be used to support a crime control rationale for punishment (deterrence and incapacitation) or a defensive rationale.

3.1 What is harm?

Understanding the Harm Principle requires knowing what is meant by "harm." Harm includes, at a minimum, physical injury, physical pain, or lost use of one's property. In the broadest sense, to say that Jill harms Jack is just to say that she makes things worse for him—she reduces his welfare. But this understanding of "harm" is too broad: if Jill is an employer's first choice for a lucrative position that Jack badly wants, and Jack is the second choice, then she reduces his welfare by accepting the position, but she does not act wrongly. Therefore, she does not harm Jack for the purposes of the Harm Principle. Nor does a dentist harm Jack when she causes him pain. A surgeon causes at least temporary injury when he opens his patient's ribcage, but here as well there is no harm. In applying the Harm Principle, we should understand harmful conduct as *wrongful* conduct that reduces someone's welfare.

The law deals with many cases in which it is difficult to determine whether or not an event counts as harmful. Does George harm Martha if he defames her after her death, ruining her public reputation? Does a woman who abuses alcohol during pregnancy, causing birth defects, thereby harm her unborn child? Suppose Fred tricks Ginger into committing terrible crimes. She is never apprehended and feels no remorse. Fred wrongly causes Ginger to act wrongly, but does he harm her? These are difficult questions to which philosophers give different answers. We need answers before we can apply the Harm Principle to such cases.

And what about failures to prevent harm—can they be said to *cause* harm? When may the state use coercion against individuals for failing to prevent harm (see sec. 4, below)?

3.2 The Offense Principle

Harm is distinguishable from mere offense. Consider cases such as the following:

(1) X mocks Y to his face for being obese.
(2) X desecrates the flag of Y's country in front of Y, a patriotic citizen.
(3) X performs a Nazi salute in front of Y, who is Jewish.
(4) X uses profanity in front of Y and his children.
(5) X strips naked in front of Y on a public street.
(6) X consumes his own vomit in front of Y.
(7) X falsely informs Y that Y's beloved has died.

In each of these cases, X reduces Y's welfare without causing Y physical injury, physical pain, or depriving Y of the use of his property. X inflicts psychological injury on Y. This is harm in a broader sense, but there are different ways of understanding the Harm Principle. First, there is the question whether the action is wrongful. If it is not, then it does not cause harm for the purposes of the Harm Principle. But we must still decide which types of wrongfully inflicted psychological harm, if any, the Harm Principle covers. Most philosophers do not understand the Harm Principle as covering the actions described in 1–7. They classify these actions as *offensive*, but not harmful. Consider the

> Offense Principle: preventing offense (as opposed to harm) is always a morally relevant reason for the state to coerce the actor.

The Offense Principle is more controversial than the Harm Principle. No one believes that the state could properly criminalize offensive insults in general, even ones that cause emotional distress. Classical liberals such as Mill reject the Offense Principle altogether, but some modern liberals such as Feinberg accept a version of it that is limited to "serious offense." This position allows modern liberals to support, for example, laws against public nudity and seriously provocative speech ("fighting words").

3.3 Legal paternalism

One of the dividing lines between liberals and nonliberals is legal paternalism, which holds that benefiting the actor himself, or preventing harm to him, is always a morally relevant reason for state coercion. Liberals reject legal paternalism. Some nonliberals accept it. Consider the following:

(1) laws that require wearing seatbelts or motorcycle helmets;
(2) laws requiring wage-earners to contribute to a social security system;
(3) laws banning the purchase of marijuana, cocaine, and heroin;
(4) laws banning the sale of foods containing trans fats;
(5) laws banning the sale of any pharmaceutical until its effectiveness is scientifically demonstrated;
(6) laws criminalizing assisted suicide;
(7) laws authorizing civil commitment of individuals whom the state believes to pose a danger to themselves.

Such laws are usually defended in paternalist terms. The state requires you to wear a seatbelt in order to protect you from injury. But what if you prefer not to wear one? What if you would prefer to spend your earnings today and risk poverty in old age, instead of contributing to the social security system? What if smoking marijuana helps you to relax? What if you prefer the taste of donuts containing unsaturated fat with trans-isomer fatty acid ("trans fat"), which is unhealthy? What if you would rather take your chances with an unproven medicine? What if you think you would be "better-off" dead? The paternalistic state does not care. It limits your liberty for your own good, as the state sees it. If the state treats someone's own welfare as a reason to limit her liberty, then it acts paternalistically.

Lawmakers often have multiple reasons—paternalistic and nonpaternalistic—for enacting a particular law. A cigarette tax could be passed for the purposes of (1) protecting would-be smokers by discouraging smoking; (2) protecting the rest of us from secondhand smoke by discouraging smoking; and (3) raising revenue. The first of these, but not the latter two, is a paternalistic purpose. We should not say that a lawmaker acts paternalistically merely because she passes a law that happens to benefit someone whose liberty it restricts. Banning handguns may prevent would-be handgun owners from injuring themselves, but this is not paternalism if the purpose of the ban is protecting others.

We can distinguish further between pure and impure paternalism. Criminalizing the purchase of marijuana limits the liberty of the purchaser for her own sake. This is *pure paternalism*. By contrast, criminalizing the sale of foods containing trans fats (as opposed to their purchase) limits the liberty of the seller for the purchaser's sake. This is *impure paternalism*.

3.4 Weak and strong paternalism

Individuals sometimes act against their own interests because of factual ignorance or misunderstanding. Consider the case of medications that the state has reason to believe are dangerous—they pose a substantial risk of organ damage. The state bans the sale of such medications because it believes the following conjunction: (1) consumers would not purchase the drug if they understood its risks; and (2) some of them will fail to understand its risks. Such bans exemplify *weak paternalism*—they limit someone's liberty in order to compensate for presumed misunderstanding or ignorance of fact. Notice that such bans do not involve the state second-guessing a consumer's own ends. The state is simply helping consumers to better achieve their own ends. The state assumes that all consumers, including those who would purchase the drug if they could, would not purchase it if they were thinking clearly and understood its risks.

Strong paternalism is a different matter. Legislation is strongly paternalistic if the state limits someone's liberty for her own sake because it disagrees with her conception of her own welfare. Imagine a state concluding that the opera improves everyone's quality of life and for that reason requiring everyone to attend the opera. This requirement would apply even to those who have attended many operas and concluded that opera does not improve their welfare. This is different from the case of the banned drug. Few would purchase a drug if they understood it to be dangerous, whereas experienced operagoers who hate opera are not necessarily making a factual mistake. The opera-mandating state simply overrides their judgment about their own welfare, limiting their liberty for their own sake. This is strong paternalism, which is more contested and difficult to defend than weak paternalism.

In many interesting cases of paternalism, it is not obvious whether the law should be classified as strongly or weakly paternalistic. Supporters of bans on marijuana insist that this is merely a case of weak paternalism. Too many would-be marijuana users, they claim, fail to understand the lethargy and cognitive impairment that regular use causes. The ban simply compensates for this factual misunderstanding. Proponents of legalization object that law-makers are practicing strong paternalism—substituting their own judgment about what constitutes a good life for the equally reasonable judgment of citizens. Some reasonable individuals who understand well the effects of marijuana nonetheless relish a pot-smoking lifestyle.

3.5 Arguing about paternalism

Paternalism raises many important questions about the powers of government, individual rights, welfare, consent, and autonomy. An initial question is who bears the burden of proof: paternalist or antipaternalist? Paternalists restrict individual liberty, so they might seem to bear the burden. Yet they do so for the sake of benefiting individuals, so perhaps the antipaternalist bears the burden.

Mill believes that who bears the burden varies with the age of the person whose liberty is to be restricted: the burden falls on the antipaternalist if the person is a juvenile and on the paternalist if the person is an adult. The laws of English-speaking jurisdictions have always treated children in extremely paternalistic ways: they are forced to attend school and to receive medical attention against their will. Most importantly, the law requires children to obey any lawful order given by parents or guardians. There are interesting questions to be asked about the justification of paternalism toward juveniles, but most of the controversy surrounds paternalism toward adults, so I shall concentrate on that subject.

There are several arguments for rejecting legal paternalism toward adults. One antipaternalist argument is:

(1) The state should not adopt laws that always fail.
(2) Paternalistic laws (those that attempt to promote the interests of adults against their will) always fail.
(3) Therefore, the state should not adopt paternalistic laws.

Why might one accept the second premise? One might believe that paternalistic laws always fail because every adult is, at any given time, a better judge of his own interests than the state is. Activities and experiences that are good for you may not be good for me. The state cannot know you as well as you know yourself. In real legal systems, the state does not even attempt to tailor laws to individuals.

This argument is overstated. An adult does not always understand his interests better than the state does. Imagine an adult who gambles away her entire savings at a casino. While she was gambling, she would have resented anyone who tried to stop her, but she now admits that gambling was not in her interest. She wishes that the state or someone else had prevented her from gambling so much. If such a person exists, then the premise is false that every adult is, at any given time, a better judge of his own interests than the state is (assuming that her state believes that gambling away her savings does not serve her interests). Many individuals in the real world fit this description. A state that bans gambling engages in weak paternalism with respect to them.

The preceding paternalist argument infers from the premise that a certain individual would prefer to have been prevented from gambling to the conclusion that preventing her from gambling would have improved her welfare. Some antipaternalists reject the inference. They insist that restricting an adult's liberty against her will cannot, in principle, improve her welfare. Liberty, on this view, is a precondition on adult welfare. An adult gains more welfare, on this view, if she makes and acts upon her own choices, even if they are bad choices, than if she is compelled to make only good choices.

An antipaternalist need not make the implausibly strong claim that adults always know their own interests better than the state does. She can proceed with the more plausible claim that this is so, not always, but more often than not. This weaker claim is consistent with the proposition that at least some paternalistic laws raise welfare in some cases. However, all paternalistic laws also lower welfare in some cases. Most gamblers practice moderation, enjoy the excitement of gambling, and believe to the end that gambling increases their welfare. A ban on casinos lowers their welfare (not to mention the welfare of the few lucky gamblers who would strike it rich). The antipaternalist can argue that any paternalistic law produces a net loss of welfare, which is why paternalistic laws always fail, despite having some beneficiaries.

It is a complex question whether every paternalistic law produces a net loss of welfare. Paternalists concede that some paternalistic laws produce a net loss, but they insist that other paternalistic laws produce a net gain, and that lawmakers can tell the difference. Antipaternalists respond that lawmakers cannot, in fact, tell the difference.

Thus far I have been considering antipaternalists who accept welfarism (see sec. 2.1). Antipaternalists could also reject welfarism, as do many nonconsequentialists, including the German philosopher Immanuel Kant (1724–1804) and his followers. They can admit that some paternalistic laws maximize welfare, while insisting that welfare is not the only value. Paternalistic laws prevent or discourage individuals from acting on their own choices. Some antipaternalists see this as inherently wrong, even if the law maximizes welfare. Many Kantians, for example, allege that paternalistic laws fail to treat individuals as ends-in-themselves, using them merely as means to their own welfare.

Paternalists, too, can reject welfarism. A paternalist can hold that it is intrinsically good for individuals to make and act upon autonomous choices, regardless of whether doing so increases welfare. A paternalist who takes this position can argue that some restrictions on liberty actually increase the degree of autonomous choice and action in the long run. Consider bans on the sale of addictive narcotics such as heroin. Some individuals autonomously choose to take heroin. The law prevents them from acting upon their autonomous choice. Proponents of the law argue that it does so for the sake of future autonomy. The idea is that heroin addicts have severely compromised autonomy because their choices reflect their addiction rather than their essential selves. How to define an individual's essential self is an interesting question. The point is just that liberty-restricting laws need not be justified in welfarist terms. Most philosophers classify a law as paternalistic if it restricts an actor's liberty for the sake of preserving his own autonomy.

3.6 Legal moralism

Liberals and nonliberals also split over legal moralism, which holds that preventing inherently immoral behavior is always a morally relevant reason for state coercion. The reference to *inherently* immoral behavior is significant. Much immoral behavior also causes harm and/or offense to others and so provides a reason for coercion under the Harm and/or Offense Principles, respectively. An act is inherently immoral if its immorality does not derive from either harm or offense. Legal moralism holds that preventing immoral acts that cause neither harm nor offense to others is a reason for state coercion.

A legal moralist might begin by observing that all states criminalize actions that cause no harm or offense, such as unsuccessful attempts (see Chapter 6, sec. 6) and reckless driving. Liberals support criminalizing such actions by pointing out that such actions exhibit conscious disregard for substantial and unjustifiable risks of harm, although no harm results. Therefore, a broadly interpreted Harm Principle supports coercion to prevent actors from running such risks, whether or not harm materializes in a particular instance.

The real disagreement between liberals and moralists concerns actions that run no substantial risk of harm to others. Violations of sexual mores receive the most attention in the literature. Three interesting cases to compare are fornication, homosexual conduct, and incest, all of which were crimes for centuries and remain so to this day in some jurisdictions. Fornication is sexual intercourse between a woman and a man who is not her husband. Homosexual conduct is oral sex, anal sex, or manual stimulation of the genitals involving individuals of the same sex. Incest is sexual activity between individuals who are closely related to one another.

Any of these activities runs a risk of harm: sexually transmitted diseases or unwanted pregnancies, for instance. But even the broadly interpreted Harm Principle only supports coercion to prevent activities that run a *substantial* risk of harm. Even if we stipulate that fornication runs a substantial risk of harm, the risk is no greater than that of sexual intercourse in general, so it cannot be used to single out fornication.

A legal moralist argument, by contrast, does not rely on hypotheses about risk of harm, but only on a premise of immorality. Is fornication, homosexual conduct, or incest actually immoral? Many legal moralists, historically, have thought so. However, it is important to distinguish between legal moralism and moral condemnation of particular activities. Many civilized people today see nothing wrong with fornication or homosexual conduct, per se. They need not reject legal moralism in order to conclude that the state has no reason to criminalize these activities (see Dworkin 1999). However, they can still ask a philosophical question: if these activities *were* immoral, would that give the state a reason to use coercion? Legal moralists think so.

The case of incest is particularly fascinating. We must distinguish incest, per se, from sexual conduct between an adult and a minor child, which is criminal whether or not the parties are related. We must also distinguish incest, per se, from incestuous sexual activities that risk pregnancy and associated birth defects. Most modern jurisdictions criminalize incest between consenting adults even if there is no risk of pregnancy: for example, consensual sexual intercourse between an adult brother and his adult sister who has had a hysterectomy. In the Commonwealth of Massachusetts, two adult brothers who engage in consensual oral sex could receive a maximum sentence of 20 years in prison, although this activity creates no pregnancy risk and oral sex between unrelated men is legal.[1]

A liberal could take the position, upon reflection, that the state must not criminalize incestuous sexual activity between consenting adults (at least if pregnancy is impossible). But many liberals wish to avoid this revisionary conclusion. They can argue as follows:

(1) The fact that an activity creates a substantial risk of harm (including psychological harm) to others gives the state a reason to criminalize it.
(2) Consensual adult incest creates a substantial risk of psychological harm to other family members.
(3) Therefore, the state has a reason to criminalize consensual adult incest.

The second premise is plausible if the secret gets out. But many actions that liberal states permit also create substantial risks of psychological harm to family members. Think of adult children who abandon their parents' beloved religious faith or who insult and alienate their parents. Think of a woman who seduces her sister's fiancée. A liberal who accepts the first premise, above, may have to accept that the state has a reason to ban many activities that liberal states permit. The liberal might then argue that the state also has reasons *not* to ban seducing a sibling's fiancée, for example, whereas the state has no similarly strong reasons not to ban incest.

The moralist, by contrast, has a simpler argument:

(1) The fact that an activity is inherently immoral gives the state a reason to criminalize it.
(2) Incest is inherently immoral.
(3) Therefore, the state has a reason to criminalize incest.

It is interesting that the leading legal moralist of the twentieth century—Lord Patrick Devlin (1905–92)—does not actually support such a pure form of moralism. A bit of history puts Devlin's position in context. In 1954, the British Parliament appointed the Committee on Homosexual Offenses and Prostitution, chaired by Sir John Wolfenden, for the purpose of assessing British "morals laws." The report of the committee, known as the Wolfenden Report, endorsed a liberal view:

> It is not the duty of the law to concern itself with immorality as such. . . . It should confine itself to those activities which offend against public order and decency or expose the ordinary citizen to what is offensive or injurious. (*The Wolfenden Report* 1963: 143)

The Report accordingly recommended decriminalizing private, consensual, adult homosexual conduct. Devlin (1965), a judge on the High Court, challenged the Report in a 1958 lecture to the British Academy. Devlin does not make the pure moralist argument that the inherent immorality of homosexual conduct gives the state a reason to criminalize it. Instead, he argues that homosexuality poses an indirect threat to society. Every society, he suggests, is held together by its *public morality*—a set of moral beliefs that are widely and openly shared. Societies that do not maintain their public morality eventually disintegrate:

> For society is not something that is kept together physically; it is held by the invisible bonds of common thought. If the bonds were too far relaxed the members would drift apart. A common morality is part of the bondage. The bondage is part of the price of society; and mankind, which needs society, must pay its price. (Devlin 1965: 10)

Therefore, Devlin continues, a society has the right to use the criminal law to protect itself from threats to its public morality. Not only that, but certain actions condemned by public morality pose a threat to society even if performed in private. Devlin analogizes such actions to privately conducted activities aimed at subverting the government—such activities are properly criminalized before they cause harm or offense. An action violates public morality, according to Devlin, if and only if a "reasonable man" reacts to it with "intolerance, indignation, and disgust." In the Great Britain of 1958, he asserts, the reasonable man has such a reaction to homosexual conduct. Therefore, the state may continue to criminalize it.

As noted, Devlin's argument is not purely moralistic. He never asserts that homosexual conduct is, in fact, immoral. He never even asserts that a widespread belief in its immorality itself justifies criminalizing it. If that widespread belief could disappear without risking social disintegration, then presumably Devlin would not favor criminalization. To be sure, Devlin believes that British society *would* disintegrate if people stopped believing that homosexual conduct was immoral. But it is the risk of disintegration, not the moral beliefs themselves, that justifies criminalization. However, Devlin does not argue from the Harm Principle because he does not claim that homosexual conduct causes, or runs a risk of, direct harm to others.

No one denies that a society cannot survive with too little consensus on moral questions. Nevertheless, Devlin's argument has been widely criticized by liberals such as H. L. A. Hart, Ronald Dworkin, and Joel Feinberg (Feinberg 1990; Dworkin 1977a; Hart 1963). The question for Devlin is: how much consensus is needed? Surely not total consensus, as most thriving societies contain some moral disagreement. Devlin does not specify how much consensus is needed. The past two centuries are full of examples of societies in which the content of public morality changes over the course of two or three generations without social disintegration. Devlin is probably correct that a society will disintegrate if too much changes too quickly, but how much is too much? How quickly is too quickly? Devlin presents no empirical evidence that the integrity of British society actually depends on widespread disapproval of homosexuality. The fact that many Britons are disgusted by homosexuality lends at most very weak support to the hypothesis that decriminalizing homosexuality will cause social disintegration. Liberals also reject Devlin's analogy between homosexual conduct and subversive activity.

4. Punishing omissions: Bad Samaritan Laws

In many cases, someone has trouble with the law because of her *actions*: stealing property, punching someone in the jaw, taking pornographic photographs of children, publishing defamatory statements, removing one's clothing in public, or selling cocaine. Each of these cases involves a *bad act* of some kind. But one can also incur legal liability for certain failures to act (*omissions*). Contracts, for example, usually require the parties to perform certain actions on pain of breaching the contract. Parents are legally required to feed their children. Real estate owners must pay property taxes. Conscripted soldiers and jurors must report for duty. Firefighters must fight fires. In each of these cases, omissions can give rise to liability.

In most of the foregoing cases, the defendant voluntarily incurs a legal duty to act by taking certain prior actions. A party whose omission breaches a contract, for example, chose to execute the contract in the first place. Firefighters voluntarily take the job, understanding the associated duties. Virtually all parents voluntarily engaged in sexual intercourse leading to conception. In rare cases, however, an individual becomes a parent without taking any action leading to that outcome. His or her parental duties remain in force. Similarly, although most landowners voluntarily purchased their property, some people inherit land without taking any action. Nevertheless, they must pay taxes or take action to transfer the land. A conscripted soldier does nothing whatsoever to incur his legal duty to enlist.

Interesting questions have been asked about all of these duties to act. But legal theorists have paid special attention to a certain class of omissions: failures to assist someone in distress. Police officers are, of course, legally required to help people, as are emergency medical technicians, firefighters, lifeguards, and members of various other professions. Parents, legal guardians, teachers, and childcare providers are also required to help the children in their charge. In many jurisdictions, doctors are legally required to provide medical care in emergencies.

In most of the English-speaking world, however, the rest of us are not legally obligated to help strangers. If you walk along a stream and notice a child drowning, you are not legally required to rescue the child, or even to call for help. Only three of the United States (Rhode Island, Vermont, and Minnesota) impose any such obligation. So do several nations in continental Europe. Associated normative questions include the following:

(1) Should the law impose any obligation to assist strangers in distress?
(2) Under what conditions, if any, should the obligation apply?
(3) What level of liability should be imposed?
(4) Should the obligation be civil, criminal or both?

As noted, most English-speaking jurisdictions answer the first question negatively, following the position of an English statesman, Lord Macaulay (1800–59). Macaulay allows that certain omissions should be punished under law, but only if two conditions are met. First, an omission should be punished only if it causes harm, or is intended to cause harm, or is likely to cause harm. Secondly, an omission should be punished only if it is *otherwise* illegal. Consider, for example, a jailer who fails to feed his prisoner, which the law already requires him to do. If the prisoner dies of malnutrition, then the jailer is also liable for his death. There are similar cases of parents who fail to feed their children and nurses who fail to feed their patients. If a child (or patient) dies of malnutrition, then the parent (or nurse) is liable for the death because she had an independent legal obligation to feed the victim.

By contrast, Macaulay believes, bystanders with no prior legal obligation to act should not be held liable for harms they could have prevented. Is Macaulay correct? A lively debate has proceeded for generations, with writers arguing for and against a general legal duty to aid or rescue. I shall examine some of the arguments on either side.

Laws requiring bystanders to aid strangers in peril are known as *Bad Samaritan Laws* (or sometimes, confusingly, *Good Samaritan Laws*). There are several arguments for such laws.

4.1 Consequentialist defenses

I shall first consider consequentialist defenses. According to consequentialists, a Bad Samaritan Law (BSL) should be enacted if and only if it has better consequences than any alternative law. So we must consider the probable consequences of a BSL. The first question is whether good samaritan behavior actually produces good consequences. In some cases, it does.

> In January 1982, Lenny Skutnik, an office worker, rescued a struggling plane crash survivor by jumping into the icy waters of the Potomac River in Washington, DC. He saved a woman's life. Surely the freezing water was painful for Skutnik, who was wearing a short-sleeved shirt. His pain is a bad effect, but the woman's death would have been worse. If a BSL encourages other bystanders to do what Mr Skutnik did, then to that extent there is a consequentialist case for such laws.

In some cases, however, good intentions do not produce good results. Some samaritans accidentally injure the victims they try to help. Perhaps rescues should be left to professionals. Some rescue attempts fail, leaving no one better-off. And some failed rescue attempts also cost the rescuer her own life or limb, which is a worse outcome than if she had refrained from helping in the first place.

A BSL could also have other negative effects. It could encourage individuals to take foolish risks in anticipation of being rescued. It could discourage self-reliance. It could encourage bystanders to snoop on strangers, invading their privacy. It could reduce our quality of life by imposing a burdensome and unwelcome responsibility to keep one another safe. It could also encourage thieves and rapists to pose as people in peril, aiming to lure unsuspecting bystanders into their trap.

Another question that a consequentialist should ask is how many bystanders a BSL actually influences. As with many laws, there are individuals who would do what the law requires even if there were no law—some bystanders, such as Lenny Skutnik, will aid strangers in peril without any legal incentive to do so (there was no BSL in Washington, DC). On the other hand, there are bystanders who will not do what the law requires, despite the threat of sanctions. Few bystanders will enter a burning building, for example, even if the law requires them to do so (no actual BSL requires this). As usual, consequentialist lawmakers should concentrate on *marginal actors*—those whose behavior the law might actually affect. In the case of a BSL, these are bystanders who will assist strangers in distress, but only if the law requires it.

If there is no bystander whose behavior a BSL would influence for the better, then the BSL is not justified, according to consequentialism. But if even one such bystander exists, then we have a preliminary consequentialist case for a BSL. Whether the case is conclusive depends on whether the good effects of a BSL outweigh its bad effects, such as those mentioned earlier. These are difficult questions to answer.

4.2 Objections to Bad Samaritan Laws

Critics of BSLs have several other concerns. Rescuing an imperiled stranger sometimes requires enduring pain or endangering one's own safety, bodily integrity, or resources. Consider the following scenarios:

(1) The stranger is drowning in rough water.
(2) The stranger is trapped in a burning house that could collapse.
(3) The stranger is being attacked by a knife-wielding assailant.
(4) The stranger will die unless one of the bystander's kidneys is transplanted into her.
(5) The stranger will die unless she receives an expensive medical procedure that she cannot afford, although the bystander can.
(6) The stranger will die of thirst unless she drinks the bystander's only remaining water. (More water will not arrive for several days, leaving the bystander very thirsty, but still alive.)

The demands made of bystanders in the preceding scenarios seem excessive. Bystanders are not morally obligated to risk pain, injury, or death for the sake of strangers. Nor are they morally obligated to contribute large sums of money.

Excessive Demands Objection
(1) The law should not require anyone to make great sacrifices for the sake of a stranger.

(2) Aiding an imperiled stranger may require great sacrifices.

(3) Therefore, the law should not require bystanders to aid imperiled strangers.

Lord Macaulay accepts something like the Excessive Demands Objection. As a result, he concludes that the law should not punish failures to aid, except for those that are independently unlawful. A BSL of such limited scope makes no excessive demands.

Lawmakers share Macaulay's concern that BSLs will make excessive demands. But Macaulay's solution is not the only one. Consider Rhode Island's BSL:

> Any person at the scene of an emergency who knows that another person is exposed to, or has suffered, grave physical harm shall, to the extent that he or she can do so without danger or peril to himself or herself or to others, give reasonable assistance to the exposed person. Any person violating the provisions of this section shall be guilty of a petty misdemeanor and shall be subject to imprisonment for a term not exceeding six (6) months, or . . . a fine of not more than five hundred dollars ($500), or both.[2]

Rhode Island's statute limits the liability of bystanders in several ways. It applies only to bystanders "at the scene of an emergency," so it does not require anyone to help imperiled strangers whom he sees on a television news program. It requires a bystander to aid only "to the extent that he or she can do so without danger or peril to himself or herself or to others," so it does not require anyone to run into a burning building. And it requires only "reasonable assistance," which presumably means that no one is required to donate a kidney or empty her savings account for a stranger's sake.

Real BSLs include such qualifications so as to avoid the Excessive Demands Objection. Let us call such laws Minimal BSLs. There are, however, several remaining concerns about Minimal BSLs. First, the terms of these laws are vague. What constitutes an "emergency"? What constitutes "danger or peril" or "reasonable assistance"? Bystanders must know what is expected of them (see Chapter 1, sec. 10 on the rule of law). Defenders of BSLs note that these terms appear in other statutes as well and that fact finders (e.g. juries) can be trusted to apply these terms to particular facts.

A second concern about BSLs finds expression in slippery-slope arguments:

Slippery-Slope Objection

(1) Lawmakers should not do anything that makes them more likely someday to enact an Excessively Demanding BSL.

(2) If lawmakers enact a Minimal BSL, then they become more likely someday to enact an Excessively Demanding BSL.

(3) Therefore, lawmakers should not enact a Minimal BSL.

The fear is that once lawmakers embrace the notion that bystanders can be legally required to do *something* for strangers, they will gradually increase the demands on bystanders and eventually these demands will become excessive. Defenders of BSLs respond that this fear has not, in fact, materialized in jurisdictions with Minimal BSLs.

Another objection is that there is no intellectually consistent way to support a Minimal BSL without supporting a more demanding BSL. A consequentialist would require a bystander to make an emergency phone call to save a stranger's life because that life is worth more than the inconvenience to the bystander. But by the same rationale, it would seem that a bystander should be required to sacrifice an arm for a stranger's life. The stranger's life is worth more than the bystander's arm. Anyone who defends Minimal BSLs, but not Excessively Demanding BSLs, must articulate a moral principle that justifies the former, but not the latter.

4.3 Nonconsequentialist defenses

There are, in fact, nonconsequentialist arguments for a BSL. Consider the following:

Legal Moralist Argument for BSLs
   (1) Aiding imperiled strangers is morally admirable.
   (2) BSLs encourage aiding imperiled strangers.
   (3) Lawmakers should enact laws that encourage morally admirable behavior.
   (4) Therefore, lawmakers should enact BSLs.

This argument is logically valid, so we should examine its premises. The first premise is acceptable: aiding an imperiled stranger is usually a virtuous action, sometimes even heroic. The second premise is harder to assess. Lawmakers who enact BSLs surely intend to encourage good samaritanism, but it is an empirical question whether they succeed.

Another question is whether the legal moralist can answer the objection from inconsistency. Sacrificing one's arm for a stranger's life is morally admirable. The Legal Moralist Argument implies that lawmakers should enact BSLs that require such sacrifices. But that looks like an Excessively Demanding BSL. Perhaps, we should modify the argument:

Legal Moralist Argument for Minimal BSLs

(1) Giving reasonable assistance to imperiled strangers, if one can do so without danger to oneself or others, is morally obligatory.
(2) Minimal BSLs encourage giving reasonable assistance to imperiled strangers, if one can do so without danger to oneself or others.
(3) Lawmakers should enact laws that encourage morally obligatory behavior.
(4) Therefore, lawmakers should enact Minimal BSLs.

The preceding argument does not explicitly support Excessively Demanding BSLs, but neither does it answer the inconsistency objection. On what basis might one accept its first premise without also accepting a more burdensome moral duty to aid?

A similar problem arises for the following argument:

Retributivist Argument for Minimal BSLs

(1) Anyone who refuses to give reasonable assistance to an imperiled stranger, if he can do so without danger to himself or others, is morally culpable.
(2) Minimal BSLs punish anyone who refuses to give reasonable assistance to an imperiled stranger, if he can do so without danger to himself or others.
(3) Lawmakers should enact laws that punish morally culpable actors.
(4) Therefore, lawmakers should enact Minimal BSLs.

The retributivist argument fails to answer the inconsistency objection, just as the legal moralist argument failed. The question remains: is it consistent to support Minimal BSLs but not Excessively Demanding BSLs? Answering this question could require us to delve into philosophers' complicated debates about the extent of our moral duties to assist strangers (Schmidtz 2000). Many philosophers defend the commonsense view that you have some moral duties to help strangers although these duties are limited. Others argue that your duty to help strangers is limited only by your abilities. They might support Excessively Demanding BSLs.

At the other extreme are those who consider all BSLs, including Minimal BSLs, to be morally objectionable, even if it is taken as given that these laws produce more good than harm:

Responsibility Objection

(1) One is not morally responsible for harm that one does not cause.
(2) Bad samaritans who fail to prevent harm do not thereby cause such harm.
(3) Therefore, bad samaritans are not morally responsible for harms that they fail to prevent.
(4) The law must not punish someone because of something for which he is not morally responsible.
(5) Therefore, the law must not punish bad samaritans for harms that they fail to prevent.

Let us examine premises 1, 2, and 4. The truth or falsity of premise 2 depends on the nature of causation. This is a complex philosophical topic (see Chapter 5, sec. 4). A bad samaritan fails to prevent harm, knowing that harm will likely occur if he does not prevent it. On many popular theories of causation, however, the bad samaritan does not cause the harm. For one thing, the harm would have occurred even if the samaritan had not existed. And few of us are prepared to accept that one causes all the harms that one could have prevented. Such a theory seems to yield too many causes.

Premise 4 sounds plausible: in most cases, when a convict is punished for a harm that has occurred, there is at least a reasonable case to be made that he is morally responsible for it. But there are exceptions to this principle. Under the felony murder rule, for example, a conspirator can be punished for an accidental death that occurs during the course of a crime that he is committing (see Chapter 6, sec. 3.4). It is not obvious that the conspirator is morally responsible for this death, so the law does not seem completely committed to premise 4. Of course, some argue that premise 4 is true, nevertheless, and that the felony murder rule is unjust.

Finally, let us evaluate premise 1. It is dubious in its stated form. Consider a parent who fails to obtain readily available medical care for his child. The child suffers complications that proper care would have prevented. On many theories of causation, the parent did not cause the harm, but is nevertheless morally responsible for it. Parents supposedly have special, relationship-based moral responsibilities to protect their children. Some proponents of BSLs believe that everyone has some level of moral responsibility to protect everyone else, even without special relationships. Opponents of BSLs generally disagree. Without settling that dispute, we can conclude that premises 1 and 2 must be revised as follows:

> (1*) One is not morally responsible for harm unless (a) one caused it; or (b) one could have prevented it and had freely agreed to do so; or (c) one has a special relationship with the victim that entails a moral duty to prevent such harms.
>
> (2*) Bad samaritans who fail to prevent harm did not cause it, nor did they agree to prevent it, nor do they have special relationships with the victims.

Revised with these premises, the Responsibility Objection might be sound, but we cannot know without evaluating 1*, which I cannot do here.

Study questions

(1) What are the three main theories of intrinsic goodness? Which of these makes the most sense to use for the purpose of evaluating law?

(2) What kinds of rights, if any, can a consequentialist support?

(3) What is the difference between formal and substantive equality? Should the law promote one, the other, or both?

(4) How are liberty and autonomy similar? How are they different?

(5) What are the four basic liberty-limiting principles? Which of them do the laws of your jurisdiction seem to reflect most faithfully? Which of them should the law reflect?

(6) What are the best arguments for and against BSLs? Do you favor such laws, overall?

Recommended reading

Anderson, Elizabeth. 1999. "What Is the Point of Equality?" *Ethics* 109: 287–337.

Bentham, Jeremy. 1961. *An Introduction to the Principles of Morals and Legislation.* Garden City, NJ: Doubleday. Original edition, 1789.

Berlin, Isaiah. 1969. *Four Essays on Liberty.* Oxford: Oxford University Press.

Daniels, Normal. 1990. "Equality of What? Welfare, Resources, or Capabilities?" *Philosophy and Phenomenological Research* 50 (supp. vol.): 273–96.

Devlin, Patrick. 1965. *The Enforcement of Morals.* Oxford: Oxford University Press.

Dworkin, Gerald. 1999. "Devlin Was Right: Law and the Enforcement of Morality." *William & Mary Law Review* 40: 927–46.

—. 1988. *The Theory and Practice of Autonomy.* Cambridge: Cambridge University Press.

Feinberg, Joel. 1984. *Harm to Others*. Oxford: Oxford University Press.

—. 1990. *Harmless Wrongdoing*. Oxford: Oxford University Press.

Hart, H. L. A. 1963. *Law, Liberty, and Morality*. Stanford, CA: Stanford University Press.

Hohfeld, Wesley Newcomb. 1919. *Fundamental Legal Conceptions*. New Haven: Yale University Press.

Husak, Douglas. 2008. *Overcriminalization: The Limits of the Criminal Law*. New York: Oxford University Press.

Kagan, Shelly. 1998. *Normative Ethics*. Boulder: Westview Press.

Kymlicka, William. 2001. *Contemporary Political Philosophy: An Introduction*. 2nd edn. Oxford: Oxford University Press.

Locke, John. 1688. *Two Treatises of Government*. Ed. Peter Laslett. Cambridge: Cambridge University Press, 1988.

Mill, J. S. 1861. *Utilitarianism*.

Murphy, Liam. 2001. "Beneficence, Law, and Liberty: The Case of Required Rescue." *Georgetown Law Journal* 89: 605–65.

Raz, Joseph. 1986. *The Morality of Freedom*. Oxford: Clarendon Press.

Sidgwick, Henry. 1981. *The Methods of Ethics*. 7th edn. Indianapolis: Hackett. Original edition, 1874.

Wellman, Carl. 1997. *An Approach to Rights*. Dordrecht: Kluwer.

4
Law and Individual Obligation

The previous chapters concentrated on two perspectives from which the law is seen: the lawmaker's and the adjudicator's. In this chapter, I take up a third perspective: that of the individual legal subject or citizen. The central question is: what obligations, if any, does the law impose upon us?

1. The duty to obey the law

Do you have a duty to obey the law? That depends on what kind of duty is meant. It follows from the definitions of "law" and "legal duty" that everyone has a *legal* duty to obey the law: if the law requires you to salute the flag, then you have a legal duty to salute the flag. The interesting question is whether you have a *moral duty* to obey the law. The more general question is what moral reasons, if any, the law gives you. The traditional claim is:

> ### Duty to Obey the Law
> Everyone within the jurisdiction of a legal system has a pro tanto moral duty to obey every law of the system, just because it is the law.

A pro tanto duty is a duty that has some weight, but that can be overridden by stronger reasons (see Chapter 1, sec. 6). The Duty to Obey the Law claim

(DOL) therefore leaves open the possibility that stronger reasons could override one's duty to obey in the right circumstances.

DOL states that everyone has a duty to obey every law "just because it is the law." You do not get to pick and choose. According to DOL, the fact that a law is valid gives you a content-independent reason to obey it, whatever it says (see Chapter 1, sec. 9 on content-independent reasons). The fact that obeying the law is inconvenient or burdensome is not relevant.

To some philosophers (e.g. Ross 1930), DOL seems obviously true, but its truth is hotly contested to this day. Those who accept DOL usually conclude that the state is a *legitimate authority*. Those who reject DOL usually conclude that the state is not a legitimate authority—a position known as *philosophical anarchism*.

"Philosophical anarchism" sounds more radical than it is. You might assume that philosophical anarchists spend their time trying to overthrow governments. Not so. Philosophical anarchism should not be confused with *political anarchism*, which favors the abolition of the state (Rothbard 1978). Even political anarchists do not necessarily use force against the state. Some political anarchists use violence, but often they just try to persuade their fellow citizens peaceably to disband the state.

You might also assume that philosophical anarchists go around breaking the law whenever they wish: stealing, provoking fistfights, driving while intoxicated. Not so. For one thing, anarchists do not enjoy prison any more than the rest of us do. More surprisingly, an anarchist may decide not to break the law even if she knows that she will not be caught. A conscientious anarchist will not break a law if she thinks she has an independent moral reason to comply with it. One usually has an independent moral reason not to steal, provoke fistfights, or drive drunk, so one should not do these things, whatever the law says. Philosophers distinguish between *complying* with the law (doing what it requires, for whatever reason) and *obeying* the law, which is complying with the law for a special reason: because it is the law. Anarchists never *obey* the law, in this sense, but in reasonably just legal systems they *comply* with most laws, most of the time.

Although philosophical anarchism is less radical than it sounds, many philosophers who understand it perfectly are still convinced that it is false: they believe that legitimate states are possible. Some of them reject the premise that a legitimate state is one that imposes a moral duty to obey the law (Greenawalt 1987), but most of them accept the premise and defend DOL. In the remainder of this section, I shall examine some of the most influential arguments for DOL: arguments from consent, natural duty, and gratitude.

1.1 Consent

Perhaps the best-known argument for DOL is the argument from consent or "actual contract" (Grotius 2005/1625; Hobbes 1651). The major premise of the argument is this: if someone consents to obey the law, then she acquires a pro tanto moral duty to obey. Consenting can take the form of promising, agreeing, or contracting with the state.

Some individuals do, indeed, expressly consent to obey the law. When a foreigner becomes a naturalized citizen, she swears that she will obey the laws of her new nation. Public officials are often required to take similar oaths. These individuals acquire a consent-based duty to obey, at least on the assumption that they consented freely and had reasonably acceptable alternatives available to them.

Critics have long objected, however, that not all citizens expressly consent to obey (Hume 1965/1777). In fact, only a small fraction does so. Most Britons, for example, are natural-born citizens who never take an oath to obey the law. They have legal duties and are subject to sanctions for disobedience long before they reach the age of majority at which they are legally empowered to execute most contracts. Even in adulthood, most of them are never asked for their consent to obey. Yet DOL applies to everyone within the jurisdiction of the legal system. The classic response to the objection is Locke's (1988/1688) idea that anyone who voluntarily remains within the jurisdiction has "tacitly consented" to obey its laws. The moral force of tacit consent, however, is not obvious. Also, natural-born citizens are not legally permitted to leave their parents until they reach adulthood, and by that time they have formed extensive attachments to their native land. Emigrating would be extremely burdensome. Can they really be taken to have tacitly consented under these conditions? Some philosophers have recently tried to defend consent theory by arguing that certain widespread behaviors and intentions that fall short of express agreement can nevertheless generate obligations to obey. They suggest, for example, that thinking and speaking about oneself and one's fellow citizens in the first-person plural—as "We the People," for instance—may create moral obligations to one another that include an obligation to obey the law (Gilbert 2006).

1.2 Natural duties: Hypothetical contract

Instead of basing the duty to obey the law on consent, or any voluntary act, some philosophers base it on our natural duties—moral duties borne by each of us simply in virtue of being a person (see Chapter 3, sec. 2.2.3 on the related concept of a natural right). A rule utilitarian, for example, holds that everyone has a moral obligation to follow rules that, if widely followed, maximize utility. Rule utilitarians who support DOL argue that utility is maximized if everyone follows a rule that requires obeying the law (at least under most conditions). Utilitarianism faces various objections discussed in Chapters 3 and 6.

An alternative to utilitarianism is hypothetical contract theory. The American, John Rawls (1921–2002) was one of the most important political philosophers of the twentieth century. Rawls specifies our natural duties as those defined by principles that rational, self-interested agents would choose as the basis for social cooperation in an *original position*. The original position is a hypothetical situation in which no one knows his individuating characteristics, such as his sex, race, religion, talents, tastes, socioeconomic status, and so on. In this situation, Rawls argues, rational persons would choose principles that impose, among other things, a "natural duty to support and comply with just institutions" (1971: 115). Rawls does not claim that real people have consented to these principles, but rather that they would consent to them under the idealized conditions of the original position. Rawls argues that the fact that we would choose these principles in the original position supports his conclusion that they bind us in the real world. This is the essence of hypothetical contract theory. The moral force of a hypothetical contract can, however, be doubted (Dworkin 1973).

1.3 Natural duties: Fair play

In the past few decades, the natural duty that has drawn the most attention as a basis for political obligation is the *duty of fair play* (Rawls 1964; Hart 1955; see Chapter 7, sec. 6.2). Here is a fair-play argument for political obligation:

(1) If a group of individuals participates in a rule-based cooperative enterprise, and each member restricts his liberty in ways that produce benefits for everyone, then anyone who benefits from the enterprise owes everyone else a duty to submit to all of its rules, as well.

(2) Most people within the jurisdiction of a legal system participate in a cooperative enterprise based on legal rules and restrict their liberty in ways that produce benefits for everyone.

(3) Therefore, anyone who benefits from their obedience to legal rules owes them a duty to submit to all of the legal rules, as well.

The first premise is the *fair-play principle*, which captures the idea that benefiting from the efforts of others without contributing one's fair share is free riding and is intrinsically wrong. Critics of the fair-play argument challenge both the fair-play principle and its application to legal systems.

A famous objection to the fair-play principle originated with the American philosopher, Robert Nozick (1938–2002). Imagine a community of 365 residents, most of whom join together in an agreement to provide daily musical entertainment for the community over the public address system. Every resident, including residents who did not agree to do so, is assigned one day per year to operate the music system. Everyone enjoys the music that plays over the public speakers as they go about their business. But some individuals who did not agree to participate choose not to contribute when their day arrives. They enjoy the music, but they would prefer not to contribute, even if that meant no music at all. Nozick suggests that such individuals have no duty to contribute, despite having benefited from the scheme.

Some readers do not share Nozick's intuitive judgment: they believe that everyone has a duty to contribute, even if she did not agree to do so. But many defenders of the fair-play principle agree with Nozick that a member of the community has no duty to contribute if she did not *voluntarily accept* benefits (Simmons 1979). Merely walking across town enjoying the music does not constitute voluntary acceptance of benefits, but merely *passive receipt* of benefits. The fair-play principle becomes more plausible if we specify that "benefiting from the enterprise" means "voluntarily accepting benefits," not just passively receiving them. But this improvement creates a new problem for the fair-play argument. Imagine a woman, Soledad, who never voluntarily accepts any of the benefits of her legal system: she never calls the police, visits the public library, takes medicines developed with state-funded research, or the like. The fair-play argument seems not to entail that Soledad has a duty to obey the law.

A defender of the argument could bite this bullet and concede that loners such as Soledad have no duty to obey. More likely, the defender will point to other ways in which Soledad benefits from the legal system: police control crime, keeping her safe; the military protects her from foreign invaders; environmental regulators keep her air and water clean. Soledad receives these benefits even if she avoids receiving benefits from the state whenever she can.

The problem is that these *public goods* are precisely ones that Soledad cannot avoid receiving without extreme effort. She does not voluntarily accept them, she just passively receives them. So the improved fair-play principle does not entail that Soledad has a duty to obey. In response, some philosophers define a set of goods that can be presumed to benefit any rational person. These presumptively beneficial goods include police and military protection, clean water and air, and so on. We can modify the fair-play principle to state that anyone who passively receives presumptively beneficial goods from a cooperative enterprise has a duty to obey its rules. Using that version of the principle, the fair-play argument entails that even Soledad has a duty to obey the law (Klosko 1992). The remaining question is whether that version of the principle is true.

1.4 Gratitude

The argument from gratitude (Walker 1988) is one of the oldest arguments for DOL, dating back to Plato:

(1) If Benefactor benefits Beneficiary, then Beneficiary owes Benefactor a debt of gratitude.
(2) If Beneficiary owes Benefactor a debt of gratitude, and Benefactor asks Beneficiary to obey Benefactor's instructions as a way of discharging Beneficiary's debt, then Beneficiary is morally obligated to do so.
(3) The state benefits everyone in its jurisdiction.
(4) Therefore, everyone owes the state a debt of gratitude.
(5) The state asks everyone to obey the law as a way of discharging his debt.
(6) Therefore, everyone is morally obligated to obey the law.

This argument faces many objections (Klosko 1989). Suppose we accept the first premise: Beneficiary owes Benefactor a debt of gratitude. The second premise remains dubious: is obeying Benefactor's instructions really the only way for Beneficiary to repay his debt? Why not a thank-you gift of Beneficiary's choosing?

Accepting the third premise, we can question the fourth. Few of us want all of the benefits provided by the state, and an unusual citizen might want none of them (Soledad from sec. 1.3). Perhaps, Beneficiary owes Benefactor nothing for bestowing unwanted benefits upon him. Also, citizens pay taxes which the state uses to provide its services. They might be thought to owe the state no more than I owe a merchant whom I have already paid: words of thanks, perhaps, but not obedience. Finally, one might doubt that obeying the law can even function as an authentic expression of gratitude if the state uses coercion to obtain it.

2. Civil disobedience

Having considered some arguments for a pro tanto duty to obey the law, we now turn to unusual circumstances under which such a duty, if we have one, might be overridden. Civil disobedience is a form of civil resistance involving deliberate lawbreaking under special conditions. Defining "civil disobedience" has proven controversial, although there are widely recognized paradigm cases (see sec. 2.1). Civil disobedience raises several philosophical questions. How should it be defined? Under what conditions, if any, is it morally justified?

2.1 History

The term "civil disobedience" first appears in 1866 as the title of a classic essay by the New England transcendentalist, Henry David Thoreau.[1] Thoreau defends his decision to withhold tax payments in protest of slavery and the Mexican-American war. The most celebrated twentieth-century defense of civil disobedience is the "Letter from Birmingham City Jail," written in 1963 by the American minister and civil rights leader, Dr Martin Luther King, Jr.

The practice of civil disobedience, as opposed to the term, has probably existed since the dawn of state authority. It has received attention from such intellectual giants as Plato, Aquinas, Locke, Kant, Emerson, Tolstoy, Gandhi, Arendt, and Camus. The philosophical literature on civil disobedience grew rapidly in the 1960s and 1970s, with contributions continuing into the present.

Which actions actually constitute civil disobedience depends on how one defines it. Everyone would agree that some activities of the following groups qualify as civil disobedience. In recent years, civil disobedience has been practiced by abortion protesters; environmentalists and eco-saboteurs; animal-rights activists liberating laboratory animals; antinuclear activists; war protesters (especially during the Vietnam War); opponents of South African apartheid; anticolonialists (notably Gandhi's followers in India); American suffragettes; political dissidents in communist regimes; AIDS activists (notably the organization, ACT UP); and individuals seeking civil rights for African-Americans (famously Rosa Parks and King's followers). A newer form of civil disobedience, using computers, is known as "hacktivism" (Huschle 2002). Familiar examples from earlier centuries include Martin Luther's heresy and refusal to recant in 1521 (which was arguably unlawful at the time), and the Boston Tea Party of 1773 (although the colonists committed their crimes clandestinely, in disguise, and without submitting to punishment; see sec. 2.5.2).

2.2 Definition

Much controversy surrounds the definition of "civil disobedience." Rawls defines it as "a public, nonviolent, conscientious yet political act contrary to law usually done with the aim of bringing about a change in the law or policies of the government" (1971: 364). Carl Cohen defines it as "an act of protest, deliberately unlawful, conscientiously and publicly performed" (1971: 39). Both Rawls and Cohen note that civil disobedience must be "conscientious"—the individual must honestly believe that her actions are morally permissible, albeit illegal.

Civil disobedience differs in several respects from everyday lawbreaking. Most importantly, lawbreaking constitutes civil disobedience only if undertaken for certain reasons. One engages in civil disobedience only if (1) one deliberately performs an act that one sincerely believes to be unlawful (Rawls 1971: 365); and (2) one does so for some moral or political purpose. The second condition represents one sense in which the disobedience is considered "civil." Recognized purposes include inducing the state or other institution to change a law or policy that the lawbreaker considers unjust or inexpedient or to rectify a putative injustice. Some writers also include the purpose of interfering with the state's enforcement of a putatively unjust law (Haskar 2001: 138–54).

Some writers accept the two aforementioned conditions as also jointly sufficient for civil disobedience. Others add additional necessary conditions concerning ends, means, and/or circumstances. Some writers classify as civil disobedience only actions that are committed publicly (Cohen 1973: 16; Rawls 1971: 366), while others define civil disobedience to include some surreptitious lawbreaking.

Some writers characterize civil disobedience as essentially undertaken as a form of *protest* (Cohen 1971: 11). Rawls, for example, requires that the law-breaker "address the sense of justice of the majority of the community" (1971: 364). He defines civil disobedience as "guided and justified by political principles" not "principles of personal morality or . . . religious doctrines" or "group or self-interest" (1971: 365). He also limits his theory to "nearly just societies" with "legitimately established democratic" states (1971: 363). He requires that civil disobedience practitioners accept the legitimacy of the state and convey their acceptance by the manner in which they choose to disobey. Most other writers favor less restrictive definitions (Haskar 2001).

Civil disobedience is commonly distinguished from other forms of opposition and dissent, such as conscientious objection, lawful protests, and secession (see Chapter 10). Some writers require that an act of civil disobedience be intended as a form of dissent from particular policies. They distinguish civil disobedience from cases of disobeying a law because it requires conduct that one believes to be immoral, or forbids conduct that one believes to be morally permissible (Bayles 1970: 6). Others classify such lawbreaking as civil disobedience. Cohen, for example, distinguishes between moral and political disobedience but recognizes both as civil disobedience (1971: 56–75).

Rawls distinguishes civil disobedience from other forms of dissent, such as "legal demonstrations, . . . infractions of law designed to raise test cases before the courts . . . militant action and organized resistance" (1971: 363). He and others insist that civil disobedience cannot be motivated by "fundamental opposition to the legal order." Other writers classify even such "militant" actions as civil disobedience. Cohen, too, distinguishes civil disobedience from revolution, although he acknowledges that Gandhi, for example, practiced civil disobedience as a precursor to revolution (Haskar 2001: 112; Cohen 1971: 42–8).

For some writers, the term "civil disobedience" carries a positive normative connotation, such that an act of civil disobedience is, at least prima facie, morally justified. For others, it is a normatively neutral term, such that there are both justified and unjustified acts of civil disobedience. Questions of definition and justification are often confusingly intertwined in the literature.

2.3 Political obligation

Most discussions of civil disobedience presuppose that individuals bear at least a pro tanto moral duty to obey the law (see sec. 1). Having defended this assumption, Rawls describes the prospectively disobedient individual as facing a "conflict of duties" (1971: 363). However, many writers after Rawls, and some before him, deny that individuals bear even a prima facie moral obligation to obey the law as such (see, for example, Simmons 1979). For such writers, there is no conflict between a general duty to obey the law and one's other reasons, although there may still be reasons, often decisive ones, to obey the law in any given case. Some writers who defend a general duty to obey agree that it does not always apply in cases where civil disobedience is entertained, and that even where it applies, there are sometimes reasons for civil disobedience that outweigh one's duty to obey.

2.4 Justification

Two basic normative questions about civil disobedience are: (1) is it ever justified? and (2) if so, under what conditions is it justified and what types of it are justified? Legal, moral, and prudential justification must be distinguished. Civil disobedience is, by definition, legally unjustified, although a prosecutor might choose not to prosecute it, or a jury might acquit the accused, or a judge might decline to sentence the convict. I shall ignore the question of whether, and to what extent, the state should punish or otherwise respond to acts of civil disobedience. I shall concentrate on when one is morally permitted to engage in civil disobedience, ignoring the further question of whether one is ever obligated to do so. I shall also assume that the citizen's society is reasonably just. In unjust societies, greater latitude for disobedience may be appropriate.

In Plato's *Crito*, Socrates insists that, at least in a democracy, the citizen must always obey the law, even if the state threatens him with unjust execution. Some subsequent writers agree that individuals must always obey the law, at least in reasonably just societies, and therefore conclude that civil disobedience is never justified in such societies (see, for example, Green 1907). Most modern writers take a more permissive stance.

The most popular justifications for civil disobedience, historically, have invoked higher law or natural law, as in the writings of Aquinas, Grotius, Locke, Jefferson, and King (see Chapter 1, sec. 8). One who disobeys the law for conscientious reasons may claim to be obeying a higher law, typically divine in origin. When human laws conflict with divine laws, natural lawyers claim, the divine must prevail in conscience (Aquinas 1969/1274; King 1969).

Appeals to higher law confront epistemological concerns about how the content of that law is known to us. Instead of making a direct appeal to higher law, some defenders of civil disobedience simply appeal to the desirable consequences of civil disobedience (Singer 1973). A consequence-based defense of a particular act of civil disobedience will consider such factors as the following. How serious is the injustice protested? How much attention will the act bring to the injustice? How likely is the protest to be effective? Will the public understand the purpose of the protest? How much inconvenience and expense will the act cause the community? How probable is it that injury to person or property will result, indirectly, from the act? Will the act set a bad example or decrease respect for the law? Will it weaken the democratic process? These predictions are often difficult to make.

2.5 Methods and conditions

Two people who agree that a certain law is unjust might, nevertheless, disagree about whether civil disobedience is justified in opposition to it. Peter Singer (1973) supports civil disobedience in order to gain publicity for a viewpoint that has not received a fair hearing and to induce reconsideration of a decision. Rawls holds that civil disobedience is only justified in response to "instances of substantial and clear injustice," specifically serious infringements of equal liberty or fair equality of opportunity (1971: 372). He considers civil disobedience to be justified, for example, if ethnic minorities are denied the right to vote, to hold office, to own property, or to relocate, or if religious minorities are repressed. By contrast, he does not permit civil disobedience for unjust tax policies.

2.5.1 Direct and indirect

An act of civil disobedience can be *direct* or *indirect*. Direct civil disobedience involves breaking the very law or policy to which one is opposed, as when an African-American in the Jim Crow era sits on a public bus in a seat designated "whites only" by city ordinance. In many cases, however, direct civil disobedience is impractical or less effective than indirect civil disobedience, which involves breaking a law, not itself opposed, in order to protest another law or injustice, or to express opposition to a state. Most modern writers permit indirect disobedience, but they disagree about the conditions, if any, under which it is permissible. Justice Abe Fortas of the US Supreme Court, for example, denies that indirect disobedience is justified if society provides legal means of recourse (1968: 63).

2.5.2 Publicity and punishment

As noted, some writers define civil disobedience to exclude surreptitious law-breaking. For others the following questions arise. First, is surreptitious civil disobedience ever permissible? Secondly, is it ever permissible for lawbreakers to evade authorities, or must they always submit to arrest? Rawls holds that one who engages in civil disobedience must have "willingness to accept the legal consequences of [his] conduct" (1971: 366). Others deny that disobedients are obligated to accept punishment (see Greenawalt 1987).

2.5.3 Violence

The question of violent disobedience also generates controversy. Some writers make civil disobedience nonviolent by definition (see Bedau 1970). Some see it as a form of expression or address and believe violence to be incompatible with that function. Rawls claims that civil disobedience expresses fidelity to law "by the public and nonviolent nature of the act" (1971: 366). Others classify some violent lawbreaking as civil disobedience, but oppose it (Singer 1973: 134), and still others maintain that violent civil disobedience is morally permissible under certain conditions (Morreall 1976).

2.5.4 Exhausting other remedies

Some writers maintain that civil disobedience is justified only as a last resort, such that one must exhaust all other legally available remedies, including legal protests and demonstrations, before engaging in civil disobedience (Bayles 1970: 12). Other writers do not require that one exhaust all other remedies. Even those who generally require first exhausting legal means often recognize that there are cases of injustice so extreme that there is no need to use all available legal means before resorting to civil disobedience.

2.5.5 Other conditions

Several other questions of justification arise. Some are questions of prudent strategy and tactics. If success is unlikely, then civil disobedience may be imprudent. Some writers insist that it is also morally unjustified if success is too unlikely (Bayles 1970: 18). Protestors should take into account the risk of injuries to third parties. Morality may also require that protestors take care to ensure that the overall level of civil disobedience in their society stays below a certain threshold.

2.6 Objections to civil disobedience

There are several distinct arguments against all civil disobedience. Each identifies some important moral considerations. However, the defender of civil disobedience denies that any of these arguments shows that all civil disobedience is impermissible (Cohen 1971).

First, critics of civil disobedience often claim that the practice expresses unjustified contempt for the law. Defenders counter that civil disobedience can express great respect for the law, if performed publicly, conscientiously, and nonviolently, with nonrevolutionary intent and acceptance of punishment.

The second critical argument claims that anyone who engages in civil disobedience puts his own interests above those of society. In response, defenders observe that civil disobedience can be practiced for entirely altruistic purposes, although it may, in a particular case, also serve the disobedient's long-term self-interest, in which case her motives will surely encounter greater suspicion.

Thirdly, critics accuse civil disobedients of taking the law into their own hands. Defenders acknowledge that this is true in a certain sense. But to recognize the permissibility of civil disobedience is not to imply that lawbreaking for any reason whatsoever is permissible. One can hold that civil disobedience is sometimes permissible while denying that lawbreaking for the sake of pleasure, profit, or convenience is ever justified. Taking the law into one's own hands for such purposes is wrong, but civil disobedience is, by definition, not done for such purposes.

Fourthly, civil disobedience is said to undermine respect for the law. Defenders admit that it could, indeed, have this effect. But historically it has not, at least in reasonably just societies, when performed publicly, nonviolently, and with acceptance of punishment. Some injustices, moreover, are severe enough to warrant civil disobedience, even at the cost of undermining respect for the law to some degree. Some defenders have also emphasized that the existence of unjust laws, left unchallenged, may itself undermine respect for the law, in which case civil disobedience has a constructive role to play.

Fifthly, critics object that civil disobedience is self-defeating. Defenders acknowledge that in some cases it is. It can provoke resentment on the part of innocent bystanders whom it adversely affects and who might otherwise be sympathetic to the cause. However, civil disobedience properly performed has these effects to a limited degree and thus is not necessarily self-defeating.

Finally, critics contend that civil disobedience subverts the democratic process. This its defenders deny. An act of civil disobedience may, indeed, prove more effective in advancing a desired policy change than would any lawful form of political participation, but an act of civil disobedience is also far more costly to the individual. Unlike, for example, someone who secretly stuffs a ballot box, thereby amplifying his political voice at little cost to himself (and thereby arguably subverting democracy), disobedients who accept punishment bear a burden that very few citizens are prepared to bear for the sake of such amplification. The defenders of civil disobedience insist that, properly disciplined, the practice will never become widespread enough to pose a substantial threat to the democratic process as a whole.

Study questions

(1) If we do not have a duty to obey the law, in the philosopher's sense, then are we allowed to steal, assault, and deceive one another whenever we wish?

(2) What is the difference between philosophical anarchism and political anarchism?

(3) Do you consider yourself to have consented to obey the law? When and how did you do so?

(4) In Nozick's example of the musical entertainment community, do you believe that the holdout individual who does not want to participate is treating his neighbors unfairly? Why or why not?

(5) Do you believe that rational, self-interested individuals in Rawls' original position would choose principles of justice that included a duty to obey the law? How would this choice benefit them?

(6) What forms of civil disobedience, if any, do you support? Is it ever permissible to break a just law as an act of civil disobedience?

(7) Must civil disobedience be carried out in public? Is it wrong to try to avoid arrest and punishment? Is violent disobedience ever acceptable?

(8) Does civil disobedience threaten the rule of law?

Recommended reading

Bedau, Hugo A., ed. 1991. *Civil Disobedience in Focus*. New York: Routledge.

Brownlee, Kimberley. 2009. "Civil Disobedience," *Stanford Encyclopedia of Philosophy*. http://plato. stanford.edu/entries/civil-disobedience

Gilbert, Margaret. 2006. *A Theory of Political Obligation: Membership, Commitment, and the Bonds of Society*. Oxford: Oxford University Press.

Green, T. H. 1907. *Lectures on the Principles of Political Obligation*. London: Longmans.

Greenawalt, Kent. 1987. *Conflicts of Law and Morality*. New York: Oxford University Press.

Grotius, Hugo. 2005. *The Rights of War and Peace*. Ed. Richard Tuck. Indianapolis: Liberty Fund. Original edition, 1625.

Haskar, Vinit. 2001. *Rights, Communities and Disobedience: Liberalism and Gandhi*. New Delhi: Oxford University Press.

Hobbes, Thomas. 1651. *Leviathan*.

Hume, David. 1965. "Of the Original Contract." In *Hume's Ethical Writings*, ed. Alasdair MacIntyre. London: University of Notre Dame Press. Original edition, 1777.

King, Martin Luther, Jr. 1969. "Letter from Birmingham City Jail." In *Civil Disobedience: Theory and Practice*, ed. Hugo Adam Bedau. Indianapolis: Bobbs-Merrill. Original edition, 1963.

Klosko, George. 1992. *The Principle of Fairness and Political Obligation*. Lanham, MD: Rowman & Littlefield.

Lefkowitz, David. 2007. "On a Moral Right to Civil Disobedience." *Ethics* 117: 202–33.

Locke, John. 1688. *Two Treatises of Government*. Ed. Peter Laslett. Cambridge: Cambridge University Press, 1988.

Lyons, David. 1998. "Moral Judgment, Historical Reality, and Civil Disobedience." *Philosophy & Public Affairs* 27: 31–49.

Plato. 1997. *Crito*. In *Plato: Complete Works*. Eds. John M. Cooper and D. S. Hutchinson. Indianapolis: Hackett.

Rawls, John. 1964. "Legal Obligation and the Duty of Fair Play." In *Law and Philosophy*, ed. Sidney Hook. New York: NYU Press.

—. 1971. *A Theory of Justice*. Cambridge, MA: Harvard University Press.

Raz, Joseph. 1979. "A Right to Dissent? I. Civil Disobedience." In *The Authority of Law*. Oxford: Clarendon Press. 262–75.

Simmons, A. John. 1979. *Moral Principles and Political Obligations*. Princeton: Princeton University Press.

Singer, Peter. 1973. *Democracy and Disobedience*. Oxford: Clarendon Press.

Walker, A. D. M. 1988. "Political Obligation and the Argument from Gratitude." *Philosophy and Public Affairs* 17: 191–211.

1. Constructive interpretation of legal doctrine

Law presents objects for study at many different scales. Sometimes legal philosophers think about law in general. We have done a lot of that so far in this book. At other times we think about a particular legal system at a particular time—that of present-day Ireland, California, Tokyo, Ancient Rome, Nazi Germany, or the European Union. On still other occasions we focus on one department of law, such as the law of torts. In that case our focus may be geographically and temporally broad (e.g. tort law in the Anglophone world in the past century) or narrower (e.g. tort law in Victoria, Australia from 2000–09). We might focus narrowly within the department (e.g. the tort of defamation), or more narrowly still by jurisdiction (e.g. defamation in Victoria).

However, broadly or narrowly we focus our attention, there are different types of questions that we might ask, as our interests dictate. Any domain of law can be understood for various purposes. A resident of Victoria may want to know whether she has any legal recourse against a neighbor who accuses her of sympathizing with terrorists. Her lawyer and her accuser's lawyer want an answer to the same question and they should know how to find it. So should the trial judge who hears the case. Laypersons, lawyers, and judges usually just want to know how the law "works" or what the law "is" on particular legal questions. Competent lawyers can usually do this.

An experienced Australian jurist may be an expert on tort law in Victoria. If you describe the facts of a case, then she will predict the outcome of a corresponding lawsuit, at least if she has time to research the law. She can describe the law and predict outcomes accurately in a wide range of tort cases (see Chapter 2, sec. 2 on legal realism). Sometimes she gets it wrong, but her predictions are about as accurate as anyone's. She has a *lawyer's understanding* of tort law. A lawyer's understanding is a valuable commodity. Few law students aspire to any more than this kind of understanding.

However, there are other questions to ask about the law, even about something as narrow as defamation in Victoria. These questions presuppose a lawyer's understanding and go beyond it. The first question is: which historical events and decisions produced this body of law? A simple answer might reference people in Australia's past who believed that individuals whose reputations are unjustly damaged should receive compensation. A real historical answer would, of course, be more detailed, but this is the idea.

The first question is *historical-explanatory*. It mainly interests legal historians, but philosophers also take heed because it relates to another question that centrally occupies them. This is an *interpretive* question: once we understand how a particular body of law functions, what theoretical account of it can we give? Can we make sense of it as an implementation of a consistent set of values and principles? Answers to historical-explanatory questions often provide useful information for answering interpretive questions. If you find a mysterious machine and want to know what purpose it serves, it helps to learn what its engineers intended it to do. Analogously, if you want to know what values a body of law implements, you should consider what values its creators intended it to implement.

Of course, engineers sometimes fail, as do lawmakers. Laws can fail to implement their intended values. They can even be self-defeating. Also, a body of law was created by multiple individuals who might have had different values in mind. Even a single lawmaker might be conflicted about his values. Nevertheless, answers to interpretive questions should at least be informed by available answers to historical-explanatory questions.

There is another question that occupies legal philosophers—one that we first encountered in Chapter 3. This is the *prescriptive question*: what laws should be enacted and enforced? In practice, legal theorists tend to blend interpretive and prescriptive discussions in confusing ways. Sometimes it is difficult to tell if a writer is merely interpreting or also prescribing. The very distinction between interpretation and prescription is contested (see the discussion of Dworkin in Chapter 2, sec. 7). Some theorists insist that to interpret is always, in part, to prescribe. And, as noted above, interpretation should surely inform prescription. Even radicals should understand what they propose to revolutionize and be prepared to explain what is wrong with it.

This chapter discusses the *private law* of the common-law jurisdictions (the United Kingdom, United States, Australia, New Zealand, Canada, etc.). Private law is the part of the law that establishes civil liability for legal wrongs committed against private parties. It is distinguished from *public law*, in which the state takes the initiative to act on behalf of the people as a whole. Criminal law (Chapter 6) and (in some jurisdictions) constitutional law (Chapter 9) are the main branches of public law.

Private law originated as a body of common-law doctrines that developed in England centuries ago. Private parties (*plaintiffs*) bring lawsuits against other parties (*defendants*) in trial courts. The private law is divided into various departments, three of which are *property, tort*, and *contract*. The law of property specifies principles governing the acquisition of entitlements to real estate, personal property, intellectual property, and so forth. Tort law concerns the protection and use of property, including one's own person. Contract law deals with valid transfer of entitlements between persons. Each of these three departments receives its own section.

2. Property

Some philosophical questions about property are conceptual and metaphysical: what is property? Does it have certain essential elements? What types of property exist? What are the relations between property, acquisition, ownership, possession, and use? Does property depend upon law for its existence or could it exist without law? What property rights, if any, exist prior to law?

There are also fundamental questions about property that lie at the intersection of legal and political philosophy: what property rights, if any, should the law protect? How can one acquire rights to particular property? The

Pacific Ocean has no legal owner. Why should anything have one? Why, in particular, should anything have a *private* owner? British Railways was owned by the government for 50 years. Should governments own everything? What things should the law permit us to buy and sell (Satz 2010)? And if some things are privately owned, who should get what?

I shall ask some of these questions in this section. I shall also pose some descriptive and interpretive questions about the positive law of property in Anglo-American legal systems. The basic legal question is: what property rights does the law protect? The interpretive question is: what sense can we make of the property law of a specified jurisdiction? Does it reflect a consistent set of values? Which ones? The prescriptive question is: what rights *should* property law protect?

I cannot examine all of these questions, even briefly, in this book. I spend more time on questions that are specific to legal philosophy and less likely to be covered in political philosophy courses.

2.1 Justifying private property

How might one justify the general idea of private property? And how might one justify particular *distributive principles* that specify who gets what? Property rules of some kind are necessary for any resource that leads to conflict over access, use, and control. There have never been property rights in air because there have never been conflicts over its use. Even companies that use tons of air to manufacture purified oxygen do not need anyone's permission. They leave plenty of air for the rest of us (and the oxygen eventually returns to the atmosphere). If the day ever comes when there is not enough air on earth to satisfy everyone's desires, then property rights in air may be introduced. If humans ever colonize Mars, then Martian law may provide property rights in artificial air.

Property can take three main forms: common property, collective property, and private property. A public park is *common property*: anyone can use it, although there may be rules that keep it open and usable for all.

Consider, by contrast, the headquarters of the US Defense Department: the Pentagon. Access to this building is highly restricted. It is, however, *collective property*. The people of the United States collectively own the Pentagon and, through their elected representatives, collectively decide how to use it.

Finally, there is *private property*—the main subject of property law. Private property rules assign resources to different private owners, each of whom has exclusive control over his property. Private owners need not consult with anyone else in deciding what to do with their property. If you own a restaurant, then you may close it down as you wish, even if doing so disadvantages your waiters and loyal customers. However, even private property can be subject to use restrictions. Zoning ordinances prevent me from running a commercial hair salon in my home. Hotels in the United States cannot refuse to rent rooms on the basis of race. Historic preservation laws prevent the owner of the Whitechapel Bell Foundry in London from destroying it without permission from the local planning authority. But for the most part, owners may do as they wish with their property.

There have been primitive societies without private property in which people's desires are modest relative to available resources. But all modern societies include private property along with common and collective property. Political decisions sometimes convert what was private property into common or collective property, or vice versa. Some factories and apartments are owned by governments, some roads and prisons by private firms.

A basic moral argument for private property is that it makes people better-off than any other system. Picture a cornfield held as common property—anyone can harvest from it. The problem is that no one has an incentive to sow seed or irrigate the *commons* because he cannot be confident that he will reap what he has sown. The field is overharvested and soon lies barren. Dividing it into private plots creates incentives to cultivate, leading many people to do better under privatization (Hardin 1968). It is, however, implausible that privatization literally improves everyone's well-being and is thus, as economists say, *Pareto-optimal* (see sec. 3.2). After all, some lucky individuals do very well overharvesting the commons and fare less well under privatization. But it is often claimed that privatization increases *aggregate* well-being. Private property facilitates a market economy with employment opportunities for those who otherwise might go hungry. It might even help the worst-off to do better than the worst-off would do in a commons (Rawls 1971).

So the law protects rights in private property. But do these rights always generate Pareto improvements? If a homeless man trespasses on your field to gather corn, then you can call the police on him. They will remove him even if you have plenty of extra corn and he is very hungry. They will use public resources to remove him, rather than billing you individually. For both of these reasons, legal protection of private property still stands in need of moral justification.

Rather than being held privately, a cornfield could be held as collective property, with the state planting and harvesting the corn and distributing it to everyone, perhaps on an equal basis or on the basis of need. But privatization also has an advantage over collectivization. Some people would prefer to plant wheat or apples. Each individual is typically in the best position to know what will enhance his well-being. Private property allows individuals to decide for themselves how to use resources: wheat in your plot, apples in hers, corn in his. In a complex economy there are simply too many decisions to be made about how to use resources for a centralized social decision process to handle them all as efficiently and effectively as the decentralized market (Hayek 1978).

For these reasons, private property improves the well-being of many people. In most nations around the world much property is privately owned. Nevertheless, some people do very poorly in private property systems. How might we justify the system to *them*? There are several possible responses.

2.1.1 Utility

Utilitarians hold that policies should maximize the total quantity of well-being in the world (see Chapter 3, sec. 2.1). Although some individuals fare worse under a private property system than they would under any alternative system, others fare better. If total amount of well-being is higher under private property, then a utilitarian supports it. So this is one way to justify private property even to those who fare poorly.

However, many philosophers argue that it is unjust to maximize the total quantity of well-being without regard for its distribution. They insist that we cannot justify a system under which one person fares very poorly simply by noting that it enables someone *else* to do very well. Individuals, they claim, are separate from one another. Policies must be justified to each of them, individually (Rawls 1971). This is a common objection to consequentialist theories (see Chapter 3, sec. 2.2 and Chapter 7, sec. 4).

2.1.2 Desert

Another defense of private property appeals to the idea that different individuals *deserve* to receive different resources. The major premise is that resources should be distributed on the basis of desert. The minor premise is that a private property system does this more accurately and/or effectively than the alternatives.

The truth of the minor premise depends on the correct theory of desert. Consider the claim that those who work harder deserve more. It is true that private property enables some hardworking people to do better than they would under the alternatives: a lone inventor toils for years, finally creating a device that earns him a fortune in a market economy. In a more egalitarian system, his efforts go unrewarded. But there are also individuals in market economies who find themselves with money for which they have not worked at all: some stumble upon crude oil; others are born with beautiful faces that sell magazines; many others inherit wealth. Millions of less fortunate individuals, whose skills and attributes have little market value, do grueling work every day just to survive.

What, then, can we conclude about private property as a system for getting individuals what they deserve? Assuming, for now, that *individual effort* is the sole basis for desert, does private property do a better job than the alternatives? We cannot reach a conclusion without a lot more information and reflection.

Of course, other theories of desert do not identify it with individual effort. Perhaps, whoever most deserves a resource is whoever *needs* it the most, or whoever took first possession, or whoever added the most value to it, or whomever the gods favor. Private property is more defensible on some theories of desert than on others. The important point is that no feasible property system allocates resources perfectly on the basis of desert, however we understand desert. The question is: which imperfect system outperforms the other imperfect systems?

2.1.3 Virtue and personality

There are still other arguments for private property, in addition to arguments from utility and desert. Some writers argue that private property cultivates *virtues* such as prudence, industry, and self-control and discourages the opposing *vices* of imprudence, laziness, and incontinence. Their idea is not that those who display these virtues deserve more. Rather, the idea is that these virtues are intrinsically good and that private property gives individuals an incentive to develop and exercise them.

Others emphasize that private property enables individuals to "make their mark" on the world in a tangible way (Hegel 1991/1821). When someone opens a restaurant, records a love song, invents a better mousetrap, or designs her investment portfolio, she changes the world in a way that reflects and actualizes her unique personality. Private property can facilitate creativity and self-expression.

2.1.4 Liberty

Finally, there are well-known arguments for the thesis that private property facilitates, or is even necessary for, political freedom. The idea is that individuals who privately hold enough resources will be able to form and express their opinions freely, without fear that their government or their adversaries will retaliate. Privately owned media outlets safeguard political dissent. The internet is an extreme example: some owners of private websites use them to publicize political corruption and to express unpopular opinions. This would be impossible if all websites were collectively owned or held in common (Hayek 1978).

2.2 Understanding property law

Like it or not, every legal system today protects private property. The rest of this section (sec. 2) addresses questions about private property in Anglo-American law. Some of these questions are descriptive and conceptual. What are the basic concepts of property law? What does "ownership" mean in law? What can be legally owned? There is also the question of distribution, which can be asked either interpretively or prescriptively. The interpretive question is: what distributive principles does Anglo-American property law embody? On what basis does it distribute property to owners? The corresponding prescriptive question is: what distributive principles *should* our property law embody?

2.2.1 What can be owned?

The law of property, at a minimum, covers the ownership of things by people, where "things" should be understood broadly. People own land and buildings (*real property*). To own a plot of land is to have certain rights with respect to a region of the earth's surface. People own physical objects such as helicopters and pencils (*personal property* or *chattels*); natural resources such as water, fossil fuels, forests, and wild game; farm animals and cultivated crops such as wheat. Human beings were owned in earlier times as slaves, but no more under law. Today, everyone owns his or her own body and body parts.

You can also own intangible items. I own the funds in my savings account, but they are not particular gold coins. You can own *intellectual property* (a copyright, patent, or trademark). I own a hardcover copy of *Harry Potter and the Goblet of Fire*. I may use, rent, sell, or destroy it at will. The author, J. K. Rowling, owns the copyright to the book, which includes the right to print copies of the book and to license others to do so. I do not have that right.

You can own the air rights above certain land, whether or not you own the land itself. You can own a *chose in action*: a debt, commercial paper, negotiable instrument (which is both a chattel and a chose in action), document of title, or contract. Creditors, for example, often sell debts to collectors who buy the right to pursue the debtor. This is the sale of a chose in action.

You can own stocks and shares in companies. You can own the income from a business without owning the business itself. You can own the interest on an account without owning the principal.

2.2.2 Ownership

But what does it even mean to say that someone *owns* something? The language of "ownership" has different meanings in different contexts. Owning a motorcycle gives you different rights than owning a patent. Two motorcycle owners have different rights if one financed his purchase and carries a balance while the other owns her cycle outright. Just knowing that you own something does not tell me what rights you have.

The dominant theory of ownership conceives it as a *bundle of rights*. What does this common slogan mean? Ownership has three main *incidents*: liberty of use, right to exclude, and powers of transfer. First, an owner of x has no obligation to use or to refrain from using x in a certain way. She has the right to occupy, use, modify, consume, or destroy x as she wishes (although, of course, she cannot use it to violate someone else's rights). Secondly, no one but an owner of x has these rights. Others are obligated to refrain from occupying, using, modifying, consuming, or destroying x without the owner's permission (see Chapter 3, sec. 2.2.1).

Of course, an owner's permission changes this. She can transfer some or all of her rights, temporarily or permanently. She can lend you her book (*bailment*), rent you her sailboat (*lease*), or give you permission to graze your sheep on her field (*easement*). She can also transfer property to another owner by gift, sale, or bequest.

2.2.3 Possession

Property law covers more than ownership. Possession is neither necessary nor sufficient for ownership. This is most obvious in cases of unlawful possession. If you take my wristwatch off my wrist and put it in your pocket, then you possess it. If you do not have my permission, then you possess it unlawfully. You certainly do not own it. If I gave you permission to take my watch to the repair shop then you possess it lawfully, but you still do not own it. I own it but do not possess it. Similarly, you lawfully possess a borrowed library book but do not own it. The library owns it but does not possess it.

2.2.4 Distribution

We arrive now at the question of initial distribution: who owns what in the first place? There are two basic ways of thinking about it. One approach holds that the question needs no answer. On this view, a property system can be morally justified even if the initial distribution is entirely arbitrary. This position is associated with the great Scottish philosopher, David Hume (1711–76). Hume assumes that human beings have always competed for resources, using violence and intelligence against one another. At some point, however, a person may decide that, although more would always be nice, he has enough resources that it is not worthwhile to continue trying to take possessions from others. If enough individuals in the vicinity reach the same conclusion, then a stable *equilibrium* emerges around the existing distribution. Many people benefit from the stability, which makes markets possible and frees up time and energy for more productive pursuits. This is not to say that the distribution that prevails in this equilibrium is just. It is largely arbitrary. But Hume denies that the justice of the initial distribution should concern us. The property system itself can be just even if the initial distribution is not.

In opposition to Hume's position, many writers believe that the property system is not just unless the initial distribution is just. These writers disagree, however, about what makes an initial distribution just. Some believe that it must be the subject of a collective decision across the entire society. Others believe that the actions of independent individuals can generate justified entitlements. The first approach is credited to Jean-Jacques Rousseau (1712–78); the second to John Locke (1632–1704).

In general, the law assigns initial ownership rights to first occupants, but thereafter the law perpetually redistributes property. Subsequent owners usually acquire title by voluntary transfers such as sales, gifts, and bequests that are enforceable in court. But the state also practices involuntary redistribution. The state taxes Jack's income and uses the funds to purchase goods or services from Jill. Courts award monetary damages in lawsuits. In the United Kingdom, the state executes *compulsory purchases* (known as *takings* in the United States) of private land for public use (Epstein 1985). The state also regulates private property in various ways. For example, the state might prevent a homeowner from building an addition to her historic home—one that would increase its market value. It is an interesting question whether the state thereby "takes" some of the owner's property or "redistributes" property. Less commonly, states engage in land reform, as the State of Hawaii did in 1967 in order to break up long-standing real estate oligopolies by forcing landlords to sell homes to renters. Land reform is controversial.

2.3 Intellectual property in digital music

Volumes have been written on the property-related topics already mentioned. I shall now turn to a special case from the modern world that raises interesting philosophical questions: intellectual property in digital media.

2.3.1 What is intellectual property?

Intellectual property (IP) is one type of nonphysical property (choses in action being another, see sec. 2.2.1). IP includes copyright, patent, and trademarks. Almost any nonphysical property could constitute IP if it was produced, in some sense, by a human being. The American painter, Jasper Johns, owns the copyright in the likeness of his famous series of lithographs depicting the digits 0–9. He created these images and has not transferred his copyright. He does not, of course, own the number nine. Numbers are nonphysical entities, but no one created them. Whereas physical objects that no one created (e.g. wildflowers) can be owned, no one can own nonphysical entities that no one created.

Although IP is nonphysical, by definition, our interactions with it require physical manifestations. The Museum of Modern Art in New York owns some of Johns' lithographs, which are physical objects. Johns has no rights in these lithographs. He cannot control access to them, move them, alter them, or transfer them. However, he owns the copyright in the images. We must distinguish the physical lithograph, 3, sitting in the museum, from the corresponding nonphysical image, which is copyrighted. The image, itself, is a kind of idea or pattern. You might think of copyright as giving Johns legal control over the creation of images that look very much like his lithograph, 3. Anyone who wants to create an image that looks very much like that lithograph—to "copy" it—may legally do so only under conditions specified in the law of copyright. The law gives Johns substantial control over who can create and/or distribute physical manifestations of his copyrighted images. If you want to sell posters that are indistinguishable from 3, then the law requires you to obtain Johns' permission (which he might give you for a fee).

2.3.2 Justifying intellectual property

Unlike physical property, IP is *nonrivalrous*: your ability to read your copy of the novel, *Twilight*, is not compromised if the publisher sells more copies. Of course, your copy of *Twilight* is physical property, not IP. As such, it is *rivalrous*: your ability to read it is compromised if others squeeze in front of you.

Because IP is nonrivalrous, we can imagine a smoothly functioning legal system that does not protect it. A laissez-faire regime would allow everyone to copy, transfer, sell, and perform creative works without restrictions. But real legal systems protect IP. There are three main arguments for IP rights, which roughly correspond to the arguments for property rights in general (see sec. 2.1). Utilitarian arguments for IP rights rely on the claim that protecting IP creates incentives for socially beneficial creativity. Desert arguments assume that the creators of IP deserve to control it because of their talent and labor. Personality theories characterize IP as a form of self-expression. The force of these arguments varies with the type of IP. I shall examine each argument from section 2.1, as it applies to a specific type of IP—copyright in digital recordings.

2.3.3 Copyright

I shall concentrate on the US law of copyright. Copyrights are granted only in original works that have a physical manifestation. You cannot copyright a poem that you have written in your head until you write it down or dictate it into a recording device. Copyright applies to written words, music, architecture, visual art, computer software, photography, maps, and film. Theories, concepts, and ideas themselves cannot be copyrighted, no matter how original and valuable they may be, although distinctive verbal formulations or pictorial representations can be copyrighted.

US law protects the rights to reproduce, adapt, distribute, display, and perform copyrighted works. Copyright owners can rent, donate, or sell these rights in any combination and with various limitations, as they please. Sony/ATV Music Publishing owns copyrights to all the songs written by the Beatles, music and lyrics. Sony/ATV could give you the right to perform "Yellow Submarine" in public, but only in Moscow and only on January 13, 2015.

US copyrights expire permanently 70 years after the death of the author. Those who purchase copies of a copyrighted work may sell, transfer, rent, or lend their copies to others. There is also an exception to copyright known as *fair use*, which is a limited right to copy, perform, or imitate someone else's copyrighted work for certain specified purposes, including scholarship, commentary, parody, criticism, journalism, and education. I am legally permitted to quote the sentence, "We all live in a yellow submarine" in this book. I copied it from the Beatles and it is unmistakably their lyric, copyrighted by Sony/

ATV. However, it is a short phrase and I am using it for scholarly and educational purposes, so it falls under fair use. If I wanted to include the entire song lyrics, then I would need permission from Sony/ATV.

2.3.4 Digital audio recordings

By the 1990s, recorded music was a multibillion-dollar industry. A few large corporations owned the copyrights in most commercially available recordings, including all of the most profitable ones. Compact discs were the unrivaled format of choice. Most consumers wanted to own more music than they were willing or able to buy. Many consumers regularly recorded cassette tapes or CDs that they had borrowed or rented. The music industry always considered this practice to be a copyright violation, and a few courts agreed, although it was virtually impossible to stop. Fortunately for the industry, there were technological limits at the time: copies of cassettes suffered from reduced sound quality, which worsened substantially within a few "generations." But technology improved. By the late 1990s, consumers were copying CDs onto their computers, using free software to compress the tracks into formats such as MP3, and sharing them with one another. The volume of sharing grew exponentially with the advent of internet-based sharing sites, the most famous of which was Napster. The music industry lost revenue and fell into a crisis from which it has never fully recovered.

The music industry maintains that online sharing of copyrighted recordings without the copyright owner's permission and downloading them for personal use—*piracy*—is illegal under US law. The courts agree. The prescriptive question is: should lawmakers protect the right of copyright owners to forbid online music-sharing? The answer may depend on the rationale for copyright.

2.3.5 Rights

One rationale for copyright is desert-based. Locke argues that individuals enjoy a natural right of self-ownership, which supports a right to control things with which they "mix" their labor. When the Rolling Stones record "Satisfaction," they mix their labor with the recording, reflecting their original ideas, talents, and efforts. This is much clearer in the case of original music than it is, for example, in the case of someone who happens to find gold, having exerted no special effort or skill. Locke concludes that creators deserve to control the products of their labor.

There are some serious objections to Locke's argument. "Mixing" labor is merely a metaphor. How can the Rolling Stones "mix" their labor with a recording, which is an abstract object? The recording is really a pattern that can be manifested in an infinite number of physical media, or in none. How can the Stones' labor mix with an abstract object, any more than it can "mix" with the number seven? Remember, the Stones are not asking simply for control of the master tapes, which are undeniably their physical property. They want the law to prevent others from making recordings of recordings of "Satisfaction," thousands of miles away. These activities do not affect the Stones or interfere with their possession of their master tapes. The Stones must argue that their labor is mixed in with the musical pattern itself and travels with it across the internet as copies of copies of MP3s are made. Current law does, in fact, choose to reward the Stones' creative efforts by giving them this legal control over the behavior of distant others. But why should the law do so? The law could reward the Stones in an infinite number of more limited ways. For example, the law could require that anyone who copies a recording of "Satisfaction" must label the recording "'Satisfaction' by the Rolling Stones." That seems like a fitting reward, giving credit where it is due. Of course, it is not a reward that the Stones can readily convert into money, but perhaps that it as it should be. When you copy "Satisfaction" to your computer, you do not make the Stones any worse-off than they would otherwise have been. They can claim that you have *unjustly enriched* yourself, but you have not done so at their expense. True, they would be better-off *if* you paid them to copy the recording. But likewise, you would be better-off if they sent you a copy for free, or even paid you to listen to it. That is no reason for the law to require them to oblige you, so why should the law require you to reward them for their labor, just because they want you to do so? No one, including you, ever forced the Stones to record songs.

Perhaps, the Stones would not have recorded songs had they not expected to control the recordings. But even if so, that is only a reason for the law to protect copyright in recordings that were made while such expectations were reasonable. It is not a reason for lawmakers to protect copyrights in future recordings.

2.3.6 Personality

Instead of arguing that they deserve to control the reproduction of their recordings, the Rolling Stones might argue that the law should give them this control as a means of self-expression. The Stones' definitely express themselves in their recordings. Their personalities are manifested in an audible form. If they were prevented from recording music to share with the world, their lives would be much poorer and less fulfilling. We would know much less about them and they might know less about themselves. For this reason, the law should protect their right to record music. Perhaps, it should also prevent others from misrepresenting the Stones, for example, by altering a recording of "Satisfaction" and presenting it to the public as the Stones' work.

However, this reasoning does not seem to apply to the case of simple music piracy, in which the copy of the recording is intact and used just as legally purchased copies are used. Hearing a pirated copy of "Satisfaction" is the same experience as hearing a purchased copy. The Stones' ability to develop and express their personalities is not impeded in any obvious way.

2.3.7 Utilitarianism

Finally, there is a ubiquitous utilitarian argument for banning music piracy. Interestingly, the Copyright Clause of the US Constitution (Art. I, sec. 8) has a preamble that explicitly references a utilitarian rationale:

> The Congress shall have power . . . [t]o promote the progress of science and useful arts, by securing for limited times to authors and inventors the exclusive right to their respective writings and discoveries.

Applying this principle to recorded music, the idea is that allowing artists to control their recordings creates incentives for them to record music that consumers will want to hear. From a utilitarian perspective, such laws are desirable if and only if the benefits to society outweigh the costs. So we must answer an empirical question, comparing the real world to an alternate world. In the real world, piracy is illegal, which makes it relatively expensive for consumers to obtain desired recordings. However, artists have a substantial incentive to make recordings that others will want to hear because they will have considerable control over the market.

In the alternate world, piracy is legal. Consumers can obtain desired recordings much less expensively than in the first world. With the internet, each song costs as little as a minute of time to download, plus the negligible space it requires on a mass storage device. However, artists have less incentive to make marketable recordings in the first place because they cannot profit as much from their efforts.

It is an empirical question what effect legalizing piracy would have. Because piracy has always been illegal in the internet era, some speculation is necessary. Perhaps legalizing piracy would discourage artists from recording the type of music that is currently popular, such that consumers would become less satisfied, overall, with the artistic merits of the recordings that continued to be made. However, consumers might be more satisfied, overall, with this state of affairs. If piracy were legal, then music would be virtually free. Maybe we face a societal choice between a world of relatively expensive recordings that we like a lot, and a world of virtually free recordings that we like less. Some would also suggest that there is no positive correlation between the artistic merits of a particular recording and the role played by profit in the motivations of the artist. Perhaps the "best" artists are not the ones who care the most about money. It might be good for society if legalizing piracy drove out the most profit-driven artists. On the other hand, recording music costs time and money. Even the most talented artists might choose not to record if they doubted that they could at least recover their investment in the market.

It is a philosophical question how much good exists in a given world, once the facts are known. Utilitarians favor rules that maximize total happiness, so the question for them is: which world contains more happiness? Utilitarians do not believe that artists have a moral right, based on desert or considerations of personality, to legal protection against piracy.

3. Tort

A *tort* is a type of harm—physical, mental, pecuniary, or otherwise—for which someone can be held responsible in a civil lawsuit. *Tort law* is the associated department of law. Torts are private wrongs that generate disputes between private parties. The judicial branch adjudicates the dispute, but the state is not a party. Many lawsuits brought by individuals or private organizations against other individuals or organizations are tort claims. There are many other types of lawsuits, such as breach of contract (see sec. 5), unjust enrichment, lawsuits brought pursuant to statutes, and so on.

Tort law is messy and complicated. It consists of thousands of individual decisions, yielding myriad doctrines of greater and lesser specificity. It can appear ad hoc. The interpretive project for theorists of tort law is to try to make sense of it as manifesting a consistent set of values and principles. This is a huge undertaking. Most contributions are limited in scope, attempting to explain only some portion of tort law.

The basic elements of a tort lawsuit are as follows. Plaintiff claims that (1) defendant owed her a certain duty of care under the law; (2) defendant acted wrongfully, violating that duty; and thereby (3) caused in fact; and (4) proximately caused; (5) her injury (see sec. 4, on legal causation). Plaintiff usually demands compensation from the defendant (the *tortfeasor*) for her wrongful loss, although in some cases she might seek an *injunction*—a command from the court that the defendant stop what he is doing.

We can divide torts into *intentional* and *unintentional*, depending on the mental state of the defendant (see Chapter 6, sec. 3 on mental states). In Anglo-American law, unintentional torts—what laypersons call "accidents"—are mostly governed by negligence liability, with strict liability applying in specific situations. In the United States, for instance, manufacturers are strictly liable for harm caused by their products, when used as directed.

3.1 The purpose of tort law

What purposes does tort law serve? One possible answer is that tort law serves to enforce part of ordinary morality. The idea would be that when someone's rights are unjustly violated, she acquires a moral right against the wrongdoer to compensation and the wrongdoer bears a corresponding moral duty. Perhaps, tort law simply gives legal force to these moral rights and duties. However, tort law diverges from ordinary morality in several major respects (Postema 2001).

3.2 Law and economics

Another approach sees the goals of tort law as entirely public, not private. The American judge, Oliver Wendell Holmes, Jr (see Chapter 1, sec. 5), argues that tort law has two purposes: to deter behavior that harms others and to compensate victims of such behavior. Tort lawsuits, he suggests, are simply efficient ways of achieving these purposes. We should not understand them as vindicating the moral rights of plaintiffs or as forcing defendants to discharge moral duties. Holmes thus advocates an *instrumental* approach to tort law (and law generally). The American legal realists (see Chapter 2, sec. 2) also adopt an instrumental approach, as do the theorists of *law and economics*, who use microeconomic analysis (mainly welfare economics) to understand and evaluate legal rules. Economic analysis of tort law was pioneered by Ronald Coase, Guido Calabresi, William Landes, and Richard A. Posner.

Law and economics has emerged as the most influential theoretical approach to tort law in the United States and is increasingly studied elsewhere. Before considering its application to tort law, we need to understand some basic features of the approach. The economist suggests a single objective for tort law—to maximize something. Usually economists treat *wealth* as the object of maximization, although some use *social welfare*. From there, the analysis can take either an explanatory or a prescriptive form. The explanatory version examines existing rules, and the major precedents that established them, and tries to show how these rules advance a maximizing objective. The prescriptive version of law and economics tries to identify the optimal rules—the maximizing ones—and advocates adopting these, whether or not the law currently incorporates them. A theorist can pursue both explanatory and prescriptive projects. She can explain in economic terms whatever existing rules she can, while advocating that we change rules that fail to promote her economic objective.

Law and economics is a *consequentialist* theory (see Chapter 3, sec. 2.1). This means that if an economist wants to evaluate a set of legal rules, she asks: "what consequences would this set of rules have, in the long run, if they were adopted, publicized, and enforced?" This is the only question that matters to a consequentialist. Consequentialists evaluate rules exclusively in terms of their tendency to promote states of affairs that are independently defined as good.

Law and economics is also a *maximizing* theory: it defines one state of affairs as better than another insofar as the former contains a greater total quantity of value than the latter. The best rules are the ones that promote the best states of affairs, so defined. Utilitarians treat well-being as the only intrinsically valuable thing, so they advocate rules that produce the greatest possible quantity of well-being. Economics can be seen as an attempt to approximate a utilitarian moral ideal. However, economists have difficulty using the concept of well-being in practice. They need numerical representations of well-being that they can compare across persons. For example, if a rule affects both Bart and Lisa, then we must determine how much well-being it adds to Bart and how much it takes from Lisa before we can conclude whether it maximizes aggregate well-being. So we must measure their well-being on a common scale. This may be possible, in principle, but it is surely difficult and labor-intensive. This is the problem of *interpersonal utility comparisons* (Elster and Roemer 1993).

Economists circumvent the problem of interpersonal utility comparisons by substituting the concept of *economic efficiency* for the concept of maximum aggregate well-being, using the ideas of Italian economist Vilfredo Pareto (1848–1923). Consider a society inhabited only by Bart and Lisa and compare two states of affairs: A and B. Bart enjoys the same level of well-being in both A and B. He is *indifferent* between them. But Lisa enjoys more well-being in B than in A. Therefore, B is *Pareto superior* to A: no one is worse-off in B than in A and at least one person is better-off. A state of affairs is *Pareto-optimal* if and only if no state of affairs is Pareto superior to it. This is one way to understand the concept of economic efficiency.

Pareto ranking provides a way to compare states of affairs without doing bothersome interpersonal utility comparisons. The law could try to promote Pareto-optimal states of affairs. Although achieving Pareto optimality does not guarantee that aggregate well-being is maximized, it is the best we can do without making interpersonal utility comparisons.

The Pareto test would make sense in a world in which all human interaction was voluntary. In such a world, the law could simply enforce voluntary transactions, each of which would move society through successively Pareto superior states of affairs toward the optimal state. Imagine that Bart has the last watermelon of the season. Lisa has $5, but would prefer the watermelon, so a sale makes both Bart and Lisa better-off, while no one else is affected. If all human interactions were voluntary, then the law could limit itself to contract enforcement (see sec. 5).

Unfortunately, individual behavior in the real world has adverse effects on third parties with no say in the matter. When Lisa eats the watermelon in her backyard, it attracts a bumblebee that stings her neighbor, Maggie. So the sale to Lisa makes Maggie worse-off and is not Pareto superior, after all. Lisa's purchase creates a *negative externality* (or "social cost") for Maggie—a cost that is born involuntarily by Maggie, not Bart or Lisa. Because of negative externalities, few transactions in the real world are, in fact, Pareto improvements. Transactions usually have third-party losers as well as winners.

Legal economists address this problem by modifying Pareto efficiency into *Kaldor-Hicks efficiency.*[1] One state of affairs, B, is Kaldor-Hicks superior to A if and only if the winners in B could, in theory, compensate the losers so as to produce a state of affairs that is Pareto superior to A. Imagine that Bart would actually be willing to take $3 for the watermelon and pay Maggie $2 to compensate her for the bee sting (if that were a condition of the sale), and that Maggie would agree to be stung in exchange for a $2 payoff. In that case, the sale of the watermelon to Lisa for $5 is *Kaldor-Hicks efficient.* The important point is that Kaldor-Hicks efficiency does not require *actual* compensation, merely hypothetical. After the bee stings Maggie, she does not benefit from the fact that Bart *could* pay her $2 in compensation if he does not actually do so. Kaldor-Hicks efficiency thus strikes many philosophers as a poor proxy for utilitarianism (White 2008), but it dominates the law and economics literature.

In contemporary law and economics, the most influential defense of Kaldor-Hicks efficiency as a prescription is found in the work of Richard A. Posner (1939–), a federal judge on the Seventh Circuit Court of Appeals in the United States. Posner consider an outcome to be efficient—*wealth-maximizing*—if and only if each resource is controlled by the individual who is willing to pay the most for it. Legal rules should be designed to generate such allocations (Posner 2010).

With this basic understanding of what economists want the law to maximize, consider a simple scenario involving unintentional harm. Peter owns a paint factory that dumps toxic runoff into an adjacent pond belonging to his neighbor, Paul. Paul is breeding six fish in the pond that he plans to sell as pets. For each can of paint that Peter manufactures, one of Paul's fish dies. In order to focus attention on the common law, you should assume that no statutory environmental regulations are in place. How should the law respond?

3.2.1 Internalization

A simple proposal from the English economist, Arthur Pigou (1877–1959), is for the law to transfer money from Peter to Paul, by means of either a tax or a liability rule. Assume that Peter earns a profit of $10 for his first can of paint, $8 for his second, $6 for his third, and so on. Paul earns a profit of $11 for his first fish, $9 for his second, $7 for his third, and so on. So when Peter manufactures his first can of paint, one fish dies and Paul loses $1. According to Pigou, the law should transfer $1 from Peter to Paul. Peter still makes $9 profit, so he will still manufacture the first can. When Peter manufactures a second can, a second fish dies and Paul loses $3. The law should transfer $3 to Paul, but Peter still makes $5 profit. Peter manufactures a third can, a third fish dies, and the law transfers $5 to Paul. Peter still makes $1 profit. But Peter will not manufacture the fourth can because he only stands to make $4 on it and he knows that the law would transfer $5 to Paul.

So we arrive at a state of affairs in which Peter manufactures three cans of paint, killing three of Paul's fish. Peter compensates Paul a total of $9, which is what Paul could have earned from the sale of three fish. Peter sells three cans, netting $24–9 = $15. This is Pareto superior: Peter is better-off and Paul is no worse off. The law has forced Peter to *internalize* the social costs of his activity. If the law limits Peter to manufacturing three cans but does not actually require him to compensate Paul, then the state of affairs is Kaldor-Hicks efficient but not Pareto superior.

3.2.2 Coase theorem

Most lawyer-economists no longer view internalization as the best way to promote efficiency. This is largely because of a (1960) article published by the American economist Ronald Coase (1910–), a Nobel Laureate in Economics. Coase makes two basic points. First, he argues that the pursuit of efficiency does not actually require the law to identify the "cause" of the harm. Our previous discussion assumed that Peter's factory was the sole cause of death for Paul's fish. In fact, Peter and Paul are both "but-for" causes (see sec. 4.1) of the harm: Paul's fish die because Paul chose to breed fish in his pond *and* because Peter chose to manufacture paint. The law, according to Coase, should not try to single out one actor as the "true" cause of the harm.

Secondly, Coase argues that under certain conditions the government need not determine optimal activity levels, such as how much paint Peter should manufacture. Instead, the government can simply define legal entitlements and enforce private transactions. These transactions will, in turn, find an efficient outcome. This claim is the *Coase Theorem*. Suppose the law gives Paul a right to an injunction against Peter. This allows Paul to sue Peter to prevent his manufacturing any paint at all. (If Peter violates the injunction, then he will go to jail.) After the law gives Paul that legal right, he and Peter can negotiate their way to an efficient outcome. Peter will offer to pay Paul somewhere between $9 and $24 for the right to manufacture three cans of paint. Everybody wins.

Notice that the efficient outcome can be reached regardless of who receives initial legal entitlements. Instead of giving Paul the right to an injunction, the law could give Peter a legal right to manufacture as much paint as he wants. Under this rule, Paul will offer to pay Peter somewhere between $9 and $27 to limit his manufacture to three cans. Again, everybody wins and the government need not determine anyone's optimal activity level.

The Coase Theorem relies on some assumptions. First, it assumes that the government enforces private agreements and assigns *alienable* property rights to the parties—rights that they can freely trade in whole or in part. More importantly, the Coase Theorem assumes that the parties can locate one another and negotiate at sufficiently low cost. This is the assumption of *low transaction costs*. It does not hold for all parties in all situations. Sometimes transaction costs are high, as when parties cannot easily communicate. But the Coase Theorem is sound where its assumptions hold.

3.2.3 Deterrence

The Coase Theorem has led most lawyer-economists to abandon the idea that the law should pursue efficiency by determining who should internalize social costs. Where transaction costs are low, the law need not concern itself with social costs. Where transaction costs are high, however, there is still a role for tort law: deterring inefficient behavior. This is the function that economists today usually emphasize. Consider the frequent cases in which someone accidentally injures a stranger. Neither party could have predicted the accident and negotiated a deal, so transaction costs are prohibitively high. Accidents almost always have costs, monetary and otherwise. In principle, any accident could have been prevented. If you never ride in vehicles, then you will never have a car crash. But precautions always cost something that can be assigned a monetary value: time, effort, or money itself. The law could prevent all car accidents by banning driving altogether, but this cost is too great. The law requires people to take some, but not all possible, precautions. So which precautions does the law require? Except in some special situations, the law of accidents applies a *negligence* standard. It requires you to exercise "due" or "reasonable" care. Under a doctrine of negligence liability, a defendant who exercises reasonable care is not liable, no matter how much damage she causes. The question is: what constitutes reasonable care for a particular type of activity?

Economists suggest that the law should define reasonable care in such a way as to minimize the sum of the *expected costs* of accidents and the costs of taking *precautions*. The expected cost of an accident is the cost of the loss, if it occurs (L), times its probability of occurring (P): $P \times L$. Following convention, I shall represent the cost or "burden" of taking precautions as B. With these variables we can state a famous formula that represents one conception of reasonable care: $B < PL$. This is known as the *Hand Formula* after the American judge, Learned Hand, who stated it in the 1947 case of *U.S. v. Carroll Towing*.[2] The Hand Formula means that you fail to exercise reasonable care, and are therefore negligent, unless you invest in precautions costing at least as much as the expected costs of accidents associated with your activity. To illustrate, let us suppose that Peter and Paul do not negotiate in advance. Peter manufactures five cans of paint for a profit of $30, killing five of Paul's fish and costing Paul $35. Let us assume, however, that Peter could have disposed of his waste safely for $20. The Hand Formula entails that Peter was negligent because 20 < 35, so Peter would have to pay Paul $35 in damages. This rule gives Peter an incentive to dispose of his waste safely, which is the cost-minimizing decision.

This is a very simple case, in which only one party has the ability to take precautions, and the precautions are all-or-nothing. Economists have refined the Hand Formula to cover more realistic situations. Usually both parties have the ability to take precautions, and precautions can be taken to greater or lesser degrees. But the basic structure of the Hand Formula remains.

In the United Kingdom and other Commonwealth countries, tort law virtually disregards the cost of precautions, focusing almost entirely on PL. Courts in these nations ask if the risk was "reasonably foreseeable." If it was, then they ask what precautions a reasonable man would take in the face of such a risk. If the risk is "substantial" as opposed to small, then defendant is liable no matter how costly precautions would have been—even if B > PL. The cost of precautions matters in these nations only if the risk was very unlikely to materialize.[3]

3.2.4 Objections to economic analysis

The analytical resources of economics have proven powerful and economic analysis has flourished. From the beginning, however, many scholars have challenged it, both as an explanation of the law as it has developed and as a prescription for how it should be.

Ronald Dworkin (see Chapter 2, sec. 7), in an early challenge to Posner, rejects wealth-maximization as the basic goal of the legal system (Dworkin 1980). It can be unjust from the standpoint of distributive justice (see Chapter 3, sec. 2.3) to allocate resources to those who are willing to pay the most for them. Efficiency is surely a value, but it is not the only value that the legal system ought to pursue.

Some also dispute the claim that tort law can effectively encourage efficient behavior. Deterrence only works if actors have reasonably accurate information about the expected costs of their decisions. Peter may not know until after the damage is done how many of Paul's fish his factory is going to kill, the price of those fish, or the cost of safely disposing of his waste. Economic models also assume that individuals respond to economic incentives in rational, self-interested ways (see Sunstein 2000). Economists recognize these objections, but argue that, in the long run, people such as Peter will invest in the relevant fact-finding.

Another objection to deterrence theories is that the Hand Formula seems unfair as a prescription. It permits some defendants to inflict harms on plaintiffs without any compensation. For example, if it would cost Peter $36 to safely dispose of his waste, then the Hand Formula entails that he is not negligent if he fails to do so, despite the fact that his actions cost Paul $35 (Epstein 1985).

Economic theory is also offered as an interpretation of existing tort law. Many scholars argue that it fails in this capacity. The most prominent objection is that there is no plausible economic explanation for the structure of tort law as concerned with private, two-party interactions. A tort lawsuit is brought by a plaintiff against a defendant. The plaintiff seeks compensation from the particular individual whom she believes has caused the harm. If the goal were just to deter inefficient behavior, then such a system would not seem to be the best way to achieve it. Instead, the state could simply fine those who engaged in inefficient behavior, deposit the fines into a public fund, and use it to make payments to those who suffered accidental losses. This is not how tort law has ever actually worked. A necessary condition for a judgment of tort liability is that the defendant *caused* harm to the plaintiff (see sec. 4, on causation). The plaintiff and the defendant must be linked in this way, and the payment must flow along this linkage (Stone 2001; Wright 1995; Coleman 1992; Weinrib 1989).

3.3 Noneconomic approaches to tort law

Philosophers have been especially active in challenging economic analysis and in offering alternative theories of tort law. These alternatives have become quite sophisticated since 1980. Most of these alternatives ground tort law in conceptions of justice. Although economic efficiency itself is a conception of distributive justice, it has become common to contrast economic theories of law with "justice-based" theories. A few words about theories of justice are therefore needed.

The distinction between corrective and distributive justice dates back to Aristotle (see Chapter 3, sec. 2.3). Aristotle writes that *distributive justice* is "manifested in distributions of honor or money or the other things that fall to be divided among those who have a share in the constitution" (1130b). Aristotle believed that these goods should be distributed according to "merit," but modern philosophers consider other bases of distribution (e.g. need, humanity). A strictly egalitarian conception of distributive justice, for example, requires that goods be distributed equally to all. Philosophers have developed many competing conceptions of distributive justice (see Kymlicka 2001).

Whereas distributive justice concerns fair initial allocation of goods in society, *corrective justice* concerns transactions between individuals that depart from the initial allocation. In a voluntary transaction, such as a sale,

Aristotle thinks corrective justice requires that the items exchanged have equal value (1130b–1131a). We need not concern ourselves with this claim. Our subject is involuntary transactions, such as theft, physical injury, and homicide. In such transactions (which constitute torts under modern law), Aristotle's conception of corrective justice requires that something be taken from the offending party and given to his victim so as to restore "equality" between them. Modern conceptions of corrective justice deemphasize equality, but take from Aristotle the basic idea of doing justice between a wrongdoer and his victim, without regard for whether the background distributions were just. Suppose that Donald has inherited a fortune while Nancy is a diligent, working-class woman with no savings. Nancy carelessly breaks Donald's finger while cycling. Corrective justice might require her to compensate him, even if their wealth disparity violates distributive justice. In this regard, corrective justice is said to be at least partly independent of distributive justice (Benson 1992; Coleman 1992).

Notice that corrective justice reflects the structure of tort law in just the ways that economic theories do not. Corrective justice links Nancy to Donald and assigns moral significance to causal facts (e.g. that Nancy caused Donald's fracture). For this reason, many philosophers think corrective justice theories are more promising as interpretive theories of tort law. I discuss some representative theories in the following sections (secs 3.3.1–3.3.5).

3.3.1 Weinrib

Tort theorists advance several competing conceptions of corrective justice. One of these is based on the theories of the Immanuel Kant and G. W. F. Hegel (1770–1831), which the Canadian legal scholar, Ernest Weinrib, develops in a Kantian spirit (1995). Private law, Weinrib claims, regulates interactions between actors and their possible victims in a way that respects everyone's moral status as a free and self-determining agent. An individual's person and property embody his will, and any interference with one's will by another is wrongful. This makes sense of the wrongness of torts against person and property. Weinrib claims that the negligence doctrines of Anglo-American law reflect his conception of corrective justice more closely than does the Hand Formula popular in the United States (1995: 152).

Weinrib's theory raises a difficult question for any corrective justice theory of torts: how to justify the legal requirement that tortfeasors pay monetary damages? Weinrib's critics object that his theory only explains why tortious acts are wrong (Gardner 1996; Perry 1992). It does not justify any specific response on the part of tortfeasors. The fact that interfering with someone's will is wrongful does not entail that one must do anything in particular to make up for it. One might, for example, simply apologize to one's victim, or make a generous charitable donation to a third party, or even commit suicide. Yet, the law does not require tortfeasors to do any of these things, nor does it accept any of these actions as substitutes for paying monetary damages to the victim. Weinrib's Kantian position does not explain why such payments are the wrongdoer's uniquely appropriate response.

3.3.2 Fletcher

Also inspired by Kant, specifically the Kantian social contract theory of John Rawls (1971), the American legal scholar, George P. Fletcher (1939–) sees tort law as implementing a specialized form of distributive justice, applied specifically to the domain of risk imposition (1972). Unlike Weinrib, who emphasizes the actor's wrongdoing, Fletcher emphasizes the victim's loss. Fletcher's background principle is one of equal security: "we all have the right to the maximum amount of security compatible with a like security for everyone else" (1972: 550). Fletcher claims that free and equal individuals would agree to live under this principle if they had to choose a principle in advance, without knowing whether they would find themselves as injurers or victims in the future. Consider a population of highway motorists, all careful drivers. Each imposes risks on other drivers who expose her to similar risks. The risks to which they expose one another are *reasonable* only if each gains more from exposing others to risks than she loses from having those risks imposed upon her. Everyone gives up an equal amount of freedom, gains an equal amount of security, and gains more in security than she loses in freedom. Recovery of damages, Fletcher contends, is warranted only if a driver harms another by an action that imposes a nonreciprocal risk on her—a risk of a different degree and character than those that the plaintiff imposed upon the defendant.

Fletcher has a problem similar to the problem facing economic theory: how to account for the importance of causation in tort law? If the goal is fairly distributing security, then why not require everyone who engaged in excessively risky behavior to compensate victims, regardless of whether his behavior actually culminated in harm (Keating 2001; Perry 1996)?

3.3.3 Perry

Stephen Perry advances a corrective justice theory of tort law (Perry 1992). His first premise is that everyone is morally responsible for the consequences of his actions. If an individual chooses to act, then he becomes entitled to the benefits of his actions, and also responsible for any harmful consequences. It would be unfair to make others bear losses resulting from your conduct. However, as Coase emphasizes (see sec. 3.2.2), the actions of both parties are always necessary for harm to occur. Why hold only one of them responsible? Perry's answer is that the party responsible for the outcome is the one for whom the outcome was foreseeable, and hence avoidable.

Even if precautions were not feasible, the party for whom the outcome was foreseeable could have simply refrained from the harmful activity. This makes him responsible where others, who could not have foreseen the harm, are not. However, Perry recognizes that this argument does not entail that anyone must pay monetary compensation. But of the risks that one could avoid, there are some that one *should* avoid, such that taking them constitutes negligence. If you take such a risk and it results in harm then, Perry concludes, it is reasonable to require you to pay full compensation.

The key question is how to determine whether a defendant "could have" foreseen the outcome. One possible test is whether she did, in fact, foresee the outcome. But most actual defendants did not, so that test would insulate all but intentional tortfeasors from liability. Perry suggests that the proper test is not whether the defendant actually foresaw the outcome, but whether she, with her individual characteristics, had the *capacity* to foresee and avoid it. This position raises deep philosophical questions about statements of the form, "She *could have* done better" (see Chapter 6, sec. 5.3). What does it mean to say this of someone who insists that she was "trying her best"? Perry distinguishes his theory from less demanding theories that hold one responsible only if one actually had some awareness of the outcome as a possibility. But he also distinguishes it from strict liability theories that hold one responsible for harms that she causes, even if she lacked the individual capacity to foresee and avoid the harm (see sec. 3.3.5).

3.3.4 Coleman

A conception of corrective justice also underlies Jules Coleman's theory of tort law (2001, 1995, 1992). Coleman sees corrective justice as the principle that those who are responsible for wrongful losses suffered by others have a duty to repair them. It has three basic aspects. First, corrective justice applies only to losses that human beings bring about, not to natural disasters or acts of God. Secondly, a claim of corrective justice is made by a victim, not against the world at large, but against the particular party who has injured him. Finally, claims of corrective justice call for rectification or repair of a wrongful loss by the wrongdoer, not just fair distribution of losses. Corrective justice is a public practice involving state coercion that manifests a kind of political fairness between free and equal citizens.

Coleman has an especially sophisticated view about the relationship between the content of corrective justice and the content of tort law. He denies that tort law must simply answer to preexisting, objective standards of corrective justice. Instead, he claims that the details of tort law themselves partly determine what corrective justice requires. Of course, not every possible set of tort law rules would satisfy corrective justice. But within certain limits, what corrective justice demands of actors in a particular legal system at a particular time depends on what the tort law of that jurisdiction requires. Corrective justice has some content even in a state of nature, but it acquires additional content in a well-ordered legal system.

3.3.5 Epstein

The American legal scholar, Richard A. Epstein (1943–), is the most famous proponent of a general strict liability approach to tort law as a substitute for negligence liability (1995, 1973). Epstein's theory is unabashedly revisionary and prescriptive—it does not attempt to describe current law. Epstein argues that a defendant should be strictly liable in tort for harms caused, regardless of whether she was negligent. However, he greatly limits the liability implications of his view with an unorthodox theory of legal causation. Epstein would treat a defendant as the legal cause of harm only if she caused it by means of force, fright or shock, compulsion, or by creating dangerous conditions.

4. Causation

Causation plays a role throughout public and private law (Moore 2009), but it looms especially large in criminal and tort law. Causation is almost always an element of a tort, so it makes sense to address causation in this chapter.

Causation is one of the basic categories of the understanding (Kant 1998/1787). We use causal notions constantly in everyday life whenever we think with transitive verbs such as "cause," "damage," "create," "change," "affect," or "eliminate." You might assume that you already know everything there is to know about causation. In fact, causation is a tremendously difficult and confusing subject. Our topic here is *legal* causation—the concept or concepts of causation that figure in legal reasoning, especially in attributions of legal responsibility.

Lawyers distinguish between *cause-in-fact* and *proximate cause*. An event or condition constitutes the legal cause of an effect if and only if it is both a cause-in-fact and a proximate cause. I shall discuss each idea in turn.

4.1 Cause-in-fact

A tennis ball knocks a wine glass to the floor where it shatters. The ball is a cause-in-fact of the glass breaking. More precisely, you might say that "the ball striking the glass at 10 kilometers per hour" is a cause-in-fact. There are actually many other accurate ways to describe the event. Notice that I have written "*a* cause-in-fact," not "*the* cause-in-fact." This is because any given event has many causes-in-fact—an infinite number, perhaps.

There are three main theories of cause-in-fact: *but-for theory*, *NESS theory*, and *scalar theory*. Each deserves attention.

4.1.1 But-for theory

But-for theory classifies only necessary conditions as causes-in-fact. The theory states: a prior event, c, is a cause-in-fact of a later event, e, if and only if it is the case that, if c had not occurred, then e would not have occurred (Mackie 1974). Assume that Sophia threw the ball. Had she not done so, then the wine glass would not have broken. So her throwing the ball is also a cause-in-fact of the glass breaking.

But-for theory is simple and elegant. However, it does not always yield intuitively acceptable conclusions. Suppose two snipers independently shoot large bullets through a victim's brain stem, either of which would suffice to kill him. Although he dies, the but-for theory entails that *neither* sniper caused his death. That seems incorrect.

Or imagine that Mr and Mrs Suarez plan to bake a cake, requiring both eggs and flour. Mr Suarez forgets to buy eggs. Mrs Suarez forgets to buy flour. But-for theory entails that neither Suarez is responsible for the outcome (no cake for them). Intuitively, however, both are responsible.

4.1.2 NESS theory

Problems such as these have persuaded some theorists (Wright 1985) to adopt a broader theory of causation-in-fact. This theory holds that c is a cause-in-fact of *e* if and only if *c* is a Necessary Element of a Sufficient Set (NESS) of preconditions on *e*. Consider the state of affairs in which there is only one sniper at the scene. A sufficient set of conditions for the victim to die includes his location, the timing of the shot, the fact that his head was exposed, the correct operation of the rifle, and many others. The sniper's action is a *necessary* element of that set—if all the other conditions hold, but the sniper does not fire, then the victim does not die (assuming, for the moment, that the other sniper does not exist). Therefore, on the NESS theory, the sniper's shot remains a cause-in-fact of the death, even if we bring the other sniper back into the picture. Either sniper's shot, combined with other jointly sufficient conditions, would have sufficed for the death. That is what makes each shot an independent cause-in-fact, just as we intuitively believe.

The question remains: how do we know that a given set of conditions is sufficient for the victim's death? The NESS test relies on *empirical generalizations* to answer this question. When certain types of conditions are present, deaths *usually* occur. Some critics of NESS theory object that, in the real world of human affairs, such generalizations are unreliable.

4.1.3 Scalar theory

A third major approach to causation is called "scalar" or "quantitative" (Moore 2009; Stapleton 2008). On these theories causation is a matter of degree: a cause can contribute to an effect to a greater or lesser extent. Scalar theories hold that *c* is a cause-in-fact of *e* if and only if *c* is a "substantial factor" in the occurrence of *e*. Fanny pours ammonia down the kitchen drain while Leroy independently pours chlorine bleach down the bathroom drain. Neither chemical alone is volatile, but they combine in the pipes and explode. A scalar theory treats both Fanny and Leroy as causes-in-fact of the explosion. Both contributed, although neither action alone risked an explosion. The law, similarly, holds defendants responsible when they are one of the causes of a harmful outcome, even if not the only cause. When an effect has multiple causes, scalar theories also have the virtue of allowing us to rank them based on extent of contribution. Modern tort law parallels this idea with a doctrine known as "comparative negligence" in the United States and "contributory negligence" in the United Kingdom.

Critics object that scalar theories themselves require a theory of causation in order to understand what it means to "contribute" to an effect. But advocates of scalar theories respond that causation is, at this level, a primitive concept that cannot be further analyzed (Moore 2009).

4.2 Proximate cause

Cause-in-fact is an indispensible concept, but it cannot be the whole story about legal causation. Each effect has too many causes-in-fact to count. Recall Sophia throwing the tennis ball that hits the wine glass. If she had stayed in bed today, then she would not have thrown the ball, so her getting out of bed is also a cause-in-fact of the broken glass. So is the fact that Sophia's parents conceived her, that their parents conceived them, and so on. But in our ordinary thinking we would hardly consider Sophia's great-grandmother a cause of the broken wine glass.

Thus far I have only considered *events* as causes-in-fact. If we widen our gaze to consider other conditions, then the universe of causes-in-fact grows still larger. Take the fact that no one kidnapped Sophia this morning. This is a condition—a state of affairs—but it is not an event. Rather, it is the absence of an event. If such conditions can be causes-in-fact also, then Sophia's "non-kidnapping" is a cause-in-fact of the glass breaking, since she would not have thrown the ball had she been kidnapped. The same goes for the fact that no one moved the glass before it was struck. The question whether nonevents can be causes is philosophically controversial (Moore 2009).

Whether or not we consider nonevent conditions (absences) to be causes-in-fact, the basic problem remains: there are too many causes-in-fact, stretching back in time, for the law to take notice of them all. The law is only interested in those that are also *proximate* causes, variously known as "adequate," "direct," "effective," "operative," "legal," or "responsible" causes. Causes that are not proximate may be called "remote," "indirect," or "legally inoperative." So the law must somehow limit the set of causes-in-fact that will concern it.

One limitation is that only legal persons—human beings or institutions granted legal personhood—can be proximate causes. Tornadoes, stampeding stallions, and runaway trains can wreak havoc, but they are not *legal* causes whatever they do.

The other limitations are more complicated. In the most influential treatment of legal causation, H. L. A. Hart and Tony Honoré (1959) claim that c is not a proximate cause of e if a certain type of subsequent event, s, occurs. Suppose Abe spills gasoline in the forest. Thereafter Ben, not having seen Abe, drops a lit cigarette on the same spot. The cigarette would have extinguished but for the gasoline, and the gasoline would have dissipated but for the cigarette. But together they start a forest fire. Abe and Ben are both causes-in-fact of the fire, but only Ben is a proximate cause. Ben's dropping of the cigarette is a *subsequent voluntary intervention*. Such events "break the causal chain" initiated by Abe and begin a new causal chain starting with Ben.

Other types of subsequent events can also break the causal chain on Hart and Honoré's theory. Carol pushes Debra off the sidewalk and into the street. A second later an overhead scaffold collapses. Falling debris injures Debra, who would have been safe on the sidewalk. This is a *coincidence*. Carol is a cause-in-fact of Debra's injury, but not a proximate cause. Paraphrasing Hart and Honoré, we can define a coincidence as a conjunction of two or more events, close to each other in space and time, where the following conditions are satisfied:

(1) The two events happening close to one another in space and time is very unlikely; and
(2) the conjunction contributes causally to an effect; and
(3) the two events occur independently; and
(4) no one arranged for the events to happen together; and
(5) neither event constitutes a preexisting condition.

Let us apply these conditions to our hypothetical. The two events are Debra stumbling into the street and the scaffold collapsing. First, it is very unlikely that two such events would occur close to one another in space and time. By contrast, there is no coincidence if Carol pushes Debra into a busy street and Debra is struck by a car. Cars are common on busy streets.

Secondly, the conjunction is a cause-in-fact of Debra's injury (see sec. 4.1). Thirdly, the one event did not make the other more likely. By contrast, if Carol shoves Debra into a mechanical lever that releases the scaffold, then the events are not independent and Carol is a proximate cause of Debra's injury. In the original scenario, however, the events are independent.

Fourthly, no one arranged for the events to occur together. What if the nefarious Carol had known that the scaffold was about to collapse and pushed Debra in order to put her in the path of the debris? In that case, Carol would be a proximate cause of Debra's injury.

Finally, neither event constitutes a preexisting condition. For the sake of contrast, let us remove the scaffold from the scene and imagine that Debra has a weak heart and is easily frightened. She is terrified at being pushed into the street and goes into cardiac arrest as a result. Debra's medical history and mental constitution are preexisting conditions. Although Carol had no idea, she is a proximate cause of Debra's heart attack (whether she is *liable* at law is a further question).

Many theorists have followed Hart and Honoré's theory of proximate cause. But there are many difficult questions to be answered. The criteria are challenged as too vague. What does "very unlikely" mean? What constitutes a "preexisting condition" as opposed to an event? What makes an intervention "voluntary" (Feinberg 1966)? To critics, these do not even look like factual questions. The whole idea that there are facts about proximate causation appears naïve to them. Instead of defining proximate causes as though these terms had precise meanings, they think we should simply ask whether it makes sense as a policy matter to hold someone liable under various circumstances.

Critics also question whether Hart and Honoré's theory is fair. Someone who is momentarily careless and unlucky can find herself the proximate cause of an extremely costly accident (Waldron 1995). The preexisting condition criterion creates similar worries. Recall the scenario where Debra has a heart attack. Although the criminal law should certainly find Carol guilty of misdemeanor assault for shoving Debra, some consider it unjust to hold her accountable for Debra's unexpected cardiac arrest.

4.2.1 Probability

Another way to understand proximate cause uses the notion of probability. The idea is that an event is a proximate cause of an effect if and only if events of that type significantly increase the objective probability of effects of the type that occurs. If Carol pushes Debra into the street where a car hits Debra, then Carol is a proximate cause because one could have known in advance that pushing Debra significantly increases the risk of that type of accident. Being struck by a car in the middle of a busy street is said to be "within the risk" of being pushed into a busy street. But if Carol pushes Debra into the street and the scaffold collapses on Debra, then Carol is not a proximate cause because one would not have thought in advance that pushing Debra would significantly increase the risk of that type of accident. Being struck by a collapsing scaffold is *not* within the risk of being pushed into a busy street. This theory has strong support in both criminal and civil law (Keeton 1963; Williams 1961; Seavey 1939).

4.2.2 Remoteness

Finally, some theorists claim that causal chains gradually weaken over space and time. An event, they insist, should not be seen as a proximate cause of a much later and/or very distant effect, even if all the other criteria of proximate causation are fulfilled. Their objection is illustrated with the famous case of *Palsgraf v. Long Island Railroad Co.*:[4]

> Mrs Palsgraf was standing on a railroad platform as a train pulled away. A passenger carrying a package ran ahead to catch the train as it left. He nearly fell, so two railroad employees attempted to help him, giving him a final push from behind to get him onto the train. This push caused the passenger to drop his package. Unbeknownst to the employees, the package contained fireworks that exploded when the package hit the ground. As a result of the explosion, some scales at the other end of the platform fell and struck Mrs Palsgraf. She sued the railroad (which is responsible for injuries tortiously caused by its employees in the course of their employment). A jury found in favor of the plaintiff, Mrs Palsgraf. The verdict was affirmed on appeal, but reversed by the high court of New York in an opinion authored by Justice Benjamin Cardozo.

If we accept Hart and Honoré's theory of proximate causation, then it would seem that the railroad employees' actions are the proximate cause of plaintiff's injuries. Their pushing the passenger is a but-for cause of the package dropping, which is a but-for cause of the explosion, which is a but-for cause of the scales falling, which is a but-for cause of Mrs Palsgraf's injuries. There is no subsequent voluntary intervention or coincidence. You might think it is a "coincidence" that the package had fireworks in it, but that is not so according to Hart and Honoré: the existence of the fireworks is not an "event" but a condition that existed prior to the pushing of the passenger. Of course, the whole thing is an extraordinary piece of bad luck, but that does not matter to proximate causation.

Palsgraf challenges Hart and Honoré in two ways. First, if you believe that the railroad should not, as a matter of justice, be held liable, then Hart and Honoré have to explain to you how their theory would not, in fact, impose liability.

More importantly, from a lawyer's perspective, the high court of New York does not appear to have accepted Hart and Honoré's theory of proximate causation. Instead, Justice Cardozo holds that Mrs Palsgraf's injuries did not "fall within the risk" of the railroad employee's action, which suggests a different theory of legal causation.

4.2.3 Further questions about proximate causation

Some writers suggest that proximate causation is really a normative matter, not a causal one. To say that an action is the proximate cause of an effect is, they think, just to say that the law *should* hold the actor responsible. There is no additional factual, scientific question to be answered once it is established that the action is a cause-in-fact.

It is important to remember that in determinations of civil or criminal liability for harm caused, the law usually requires more than proximate causation. Being the legal cause of harm is neither necessary nor sufficient for legal responsibility. The defendant's conduct must be something that the law recognizes as unlawful. Nora slowly backs out of her driveway, checking her rearview mirror. She hits a neighbor's small dog, which she could not have seen from the driver's seat. Nora is a proximate cause of the dog's injury, but she is not liable because tort law applies a negligence standard in such cases and she was not driving negligently.

Most legal rules require also that the defendant acted with a certain mental state or *mens rea* (see Chapter 6, sec. 3). This can require, for example, that the harm be foreseeable. Foreseeability is not a causal notion at all. It concerns, rather, what the actor, or a reasonable person of some description, could be expected to anticipate.

The harm, moreover, must be one that the law recognizes. Ricardo sees some wild blueberries and gets excited about making jam tomorrow. When he returns to pick them he is disappointed to discover that Numa has picked them all. Numa is the proximate cause of Ricardo's disappointment, but disappointment is not a legally recognized type of harm, so Numa owes Ricardo nothing under law, not even a spoonful of jam.

Proximate causation is not sufficient for liability. Nor is it necessary. A defendant who is not the proximate cause of harm may still be liable. Many criminal offenses are not harm-based in the first place so the issue of harm-causation does not arise (see Chapter 7, sec. 6.1). Possession of contraband and attempted murder are examples of serious crimes that are not harm-based. But even if harm is a necessary element—as it always is in tort law—a defendant who is not its proximate cause might still be liable. Nannies who fail to prevent little children from injuring themselves can be liable in tort because they have a duty to care for the children. A defendant might also be liable if she influences others and harm results: she advises, encourages, assists, permits, coerces, deceives, or misinforms someone with the result that someone suffers harm. Finally, a defendant might be liable if she provides an *opportunity* that motivates or enables someone to cause or suffer harm. In none of these cases is the defendant a proximate cause of the harm, but she is liable on a different theory of liability.

5. Contract

Contracts are everywhere: between employers and employees, merchants and suppliers, pop stars and record companies, authors and publishers, home-builders and subcontractors, and so on. Even marriages are a type of contract under law. This section (5) will review the elements of contract before considering some major theories of contract law.

5.1 Elements of contract

Nonlawyers usually think of a "contract" as a paper document, but it is better thought of more abstractly—as a type of mutual commitment. Any contract can be committed to paper and many are. In fact, the law requires certain contracts to be "reduced to writing" if they are to be enforceable (e.g. the *Statute of Frauds*). But some verbal contracts are also binding and enforceable at law. Think of a contract as a set of commitments that the parties have a legal duty to fulfill.[5]

The details of contract law vary from one jurisdiction to the next, but the basic elements are uniform throughout the English-speaking world. A valid or "enforceable" contract requires (1) competent parties, (2) bargain, (3) offer, (4) acceptance, (5) consideration, and (6) intent. Let us examine each of these.

Most adults and other legal persons (e.g. businesses) are legally *competent* to form contracts. Minor children are not, except in special circumstances. Competence is also compromised when a *fiduciary* (a trusted person such as an attorney, clergy member, or relative) inappropriately influences someone to form a contract. Contracts made by minors or adults under undue influence are *void*—courts will not enforce them.

A contract cannot form until one party makes an *offer*, letting the other know that she is willing to enter the bargain and inviting him to *accept* it.[6] The parties must have the requisite *intent* to make an agreement on specified terms. There must be a "meeting of the minds" in which both parties know what they are getting into. Contracts can be voided by courts in case of reasonable mistake or misrepresentation, or if a party was intoxicated or legally insane at the time of formation.

Each party to a contract must promise to exchange valuable *consideration*. Consideration can be anything of value (a good or service or a promise to deliver the same). It must have some value, however minimal, as when a contract is made to buy a parcel of land for £1. It cannot be something that the party is already obligated to do (e.g. to pay his taxes). Rather, consideration must be *bargained for*, which means that (1) the promisor seeks it in exchange for his promise and (2) the promisee gives it in exchange for the promise.[7]

After forming a valid contract, the parties are legally obligated to *perform* according to its terms. If one fails to perform, then the other can sue her for *breach of contract*. If the court determines that the contract is valid and the defendant in breach, then it may grant a remedy, requiring her to perform or to pay the plaintiff *damages*.

The doctrine of consideration entails that a single promise, as such, does not form a contract. On Thursday, Jack leaves his friend, Jill, a signed note, promising that he will give her his old computer on Saturday. Then he changes his mind and refuses to deliver it. Jill may be disappointed, but she has no legal claim against Jack. The signed note did not form a contract because Jill did not promise to do anything in exchange for the computer.

An important qualification to the doctrine of consideration is known as *detrimental reliance*:

Suppose Jill tells Jack on Wednesday that she plans to purchase a new Model Z computer on Friday, when the store is having a one-day sale. On Thursday, Jack leaves her a note stating that he has an extra, brand-new Model Z computer lying around, and that he promises to give it to her on Saturday as a gift, so she need not buy a new one. Then Jack changes his mind after the sale has ended. Jill is worse-off than if Jack had not made the promise because she missed the sale. Jack knew, or should have known, that Jill would rely on his promise to her detriment. In this case, they have an enforceable contract, despite the fact that Jill did not offer any consideration. Her detrimental reliance substitutes for consideration. She may be able to recover from Jack the difference between the regular price of the Model Z and the sale price (or he could just do as he promised and give her his Model Z).

There are many other nuances to contract law. Promises to do unlawful deeds, for example, are unenforceable. In the twentieth century, courts began to void some contracts as *unconscionable* (a kind of unfairness in contractual terms; see example in Chapter 1, sec. 6). And so on.

5.2 Theories of contract

The elements of contract are well established and understood, but there are several competing theories of contract, both interpretive and prescriptive. Each theory is incomplete and inadequate from the perspective of the others.

There is no immediate hope of consensus emerging. Some have argued that contract law is internally incoherent (Dalton 1985). Others deny that contracts generate a distinctive kind of obligation, separate from obligations in tort, equity, and the like.

I shall begin with an interpretive question concerning the way in which courts measure damages for breach of contract:

> Raoul learns that a thunderstorm is forecast for tomorrow. He has been trying for days to hire someone to fix a hole in his roof, but no one is available. He is about to give up when he meets Iris and explains his situation to her. She offers to fix the hole if Raoul will perform a one-hour private concert for her in the morning and then stay home in the afternoon to wait for her to return with her tools. Raoul accepts her offer and performs a private concert for her. He is a well-known singer who regularly earns $500 per hour to sing. Raoul has also been offered a two-hour singing engagement at a party that afternoon. The offer pays $1,000, but he declines in order to wait for Iris. She never shows up. The next day rain pours through the hole, causing $2,000 damage to Raoul's floor.

Iris has breached their contract. Raoul can recover damages from her. There are three possible interests that the law might protect (Fuller and Perdue 1936). First, Iris has been *unjustly enriched* by Raoul's private concert, the market rate for which is $500. Raoul has a *restitution interest* in recovering $500 from Iris.

Secondly, Raoul has relied on Iris's promise to his detriment. He could have earned $1,000 singing at the party. He has a *reliance interest* in recovering $1,000, which would put him where he would have been had he not relied on her.

Thirdly, Raoul has an *expectation interest* in the $2,000 of floor damage that he would have avoided if Iris had fixed the hole.

5.3 The puzzle of expectation damages

The law would, in fact, award Raoul $1,000 in reliance and $2,000 in expectation damages. He could probably also recover an additional $500 in restitution. Reliance damages are relatively easy to justify. In private law, damages are supposed compensate victims for wrongful losses. Raoul wrongfully lost a $1,000 opportunity, which he would have taken had it not been for Iris.

The theoretical puzzle is how to justify expectation damages, which give the plaintiff something he never really had. Raoul did not have a fixed roof when he met Iris. She did not take a fixed roof from him or damage his roof. In fact, he was unable to find anyone to fix his roof and had almost given up.

For all we know, he would not have found anyone had Iris not come along. For this reason, expectation damages do not seem to fall within corrective justice (see sec. 3.3). If Iris pays Raoul $2,000 in expectation damages for his ruined floor, then she seems to be positively benefiting him, rather than compensating him for a wrongful loss. This is a puzzling discovery because private law is supposed to impose liability for wrongful losses, not for failures to benefit someone else.

Other aspects of settled contract law raise similar puzzles. For example, courts enforce contracts even if plaintiff did not rely to her detriment on defendant's promise.

> Petra offers to pay Diego £15 million upon receipt of Monet's 1904 painting, *Londres, Le Parlement, trouée de soleil dans le brouillard*. Petra has a buyer who has offered to pay £16 million for it. Diego accepts Petra's offer but never performs. Petra is no worse-off than before she made the offer, but Diego must still sell her the Monet at the agreed price or pay her expectation damages in the amount of £1 million. Again, the law forces Diego to *improve* Petra's situation, not to compensate her for wrongful losses. What is the rationale?

Identifying a rationale for expectation damages is one of the enduring puzzles of contract theory. Theorists offer a range of answers. In some cases, expectation and reliance damages coincide, in which case courts can protect the reliance interest simply by awarding expectation damages. This is the case if plaintiff could have and would have obtained a similarly valuable substitute elsewhere, but did not do so in reliance on defendant's promise. Also, expectation damages are usually easier for courts to measure than reliance damages. So expectation damages are sometimes an acceptable proxy for reliance damages.

In many cases, however, the expectation and reliance interests diverge sharply, in which case expectation damages cannot be justified as a convenient proxy for reliance damages. An interpretive theory of contract law must look elsewhere for its justification of expectation damages.

At this point we could abandon a search for corrective justice rationales. Expectation damages could be seen as punitive, rather than corrective, although punishment is primarily the domain of criminal law (see Chapter 7). Alternatively, we could appeal to consequentialist considerations. Awarding expectation damages creates economic incentives, encouraging commerce and routing resources to those who are willing to pay the most for them. Economic theories of contract law are especially influential in the United

States. I shall examine them in section 5.5. In the next section, I shall consider nonconsequentialist theories.

5.4 Nonconsequentialist theories

5.4.1 Reductionist theories

Recall the case of the Monet. If the court awards Petra damages, then it effectively announces that Diego was not entitled to change his mind and that Petra was entitled to expect him not to change his mind. This is a surprising claim. Individuals are ordinarily free, both morally and legally, to change their minds. Of course, Petra does not want Diego to change his mind, but why should her desire take priority over his (Atiyah 1981)?

By contrast, when Iris promises to fix Raoul's roof, her promise has some definite effects. First, she induces Raoul to sing for her, unjustly enriching herself at his expense. She also induces him reasonably to rely on her promise, losing out on $1,000 that he could have earned. Inducing such detrimental reliance constitutes a tort claim independent of any contract. So Raoul has legal claims against Iris for restitution and detrimental reliance without presupposing any obligation to keep promises. But that leaves no moral basis to award him (or Petra, in her case) expectation damages.

Refusing to enforce promises in the absence of detrimental reliance or unjust enrichment might, in fact, be a good prescription for law reform. As an interpretive theory of contract law, however, any theory with these implications is problematic. Courts do, in fact, enforce mutual promises from the moment the contract is formed even if, as in the Monet case, there is no detrimental reliance or unjust enrichment. And courts often award expectation damages. Any interpretive theory that reduces contractual obligation to the restitution and reliance interests must confront these facts.

5.4.2 Deontological theories

Many commentators believe that courts should enforce "bare" mutual promises. They seek a theory that respects the fact that courts sometimes do so. These writers develop *deontological* theories based on the premise that promises, in themselves, bind the promisor.

The most prominent deontological theory of contract is the work of Charles Fried (1935–), a Justice of the Supreme Judicial Court of Massachusetts and former Solicitor General of the United States. Fried believes that we have a moral obligation to keep promises and that contract law is morally justified because it enforces that obligation (Fried 1981). Promises create new moral obligations where none existed. They do so, he claims, because there is a social convention that individuals can voluntarily commit themselves to future performance by promising. Everyone knows that promises do this, everyone knows that everyone else knows, and so on (Lewis 1969). With this convention in place, a promisor becomes morally obligated to keep his promises because, by using the convention of promising, he invites the promisee to trust him on moral grounds. The promisor invites the promisee to make himself vulnerable to the promisor. On Kantian grounds (see Chapter 3, sec. 2), Fried argues that breaking the promise disrespects and misuses the promisee, treating his welfare with contempt. Fried insists that fairness requires extracting expectation damages from the promisor, even if the promisee did not rely.

Fried's theory has been widely discussed and criticized. Some object that Fried's theory fails as an interpretation of contract case law. Fried reclassifies some standard contract cases as tort cases. He also concedes that his theory fails to vindicate the standard doctrine of consideration, but he argues that the standard doctrine is incoherent and hence cannot be explained.

Another objection to Fried proceeds from the fact that there are better and worse reasons for breaking a promise. Breaking a promise in order to humiliate the promisee, for instance, is surely disrespectful of her. But breaking a promise in order to meet a more important obligation or to take advantage of a highly profitable opportunity does not necessarily disrespect anyone. It is noteworthy that contract law does not appear to care to what *degree* a breach is disrespectful. Courts do not take such reasons into account in determining liability or damages. Would they not do so if Fried's theory were correct as an interpretation of contract law?

A different objection to Fried applies even to cases in which breaching is concededly disrespectful. A moral obligation to keep promises does not entail that it is fair for courts to coerce promisors, much less coerce them into paying expectation damages. Fried appears to assume a debatable version of legal moralism: the view that the law should enforce much of private morality (see Chapter 3, sec. 3.6).

A deontological theory must explain why the state is justified in coercing promisors. One way to deal with this problem is to abandon promise-based or "will" theories for *consent* theories, which have their origins in the works of Hugo Grotius (1583–1645) and Thomas Hobbes (1588–1679). Consent theory sees private law as a set of rules for dealing with individuals' enforceable entitlements to scarce resources. These rules establish moral boundaries between us: they define what you may do with your property without being coerced by the state. Anyone who interferes with your entitlements is subject to state coercion, himself. Property law governs acquisition of entitlements, tort law their protection and use. Contract law governs the valid transfer of entitlements from one person to another. A valid transfer relocates the enforceable moral boundaries between the parties. Consent theory understands a contract as a mechanism for such transfers. Because Diego owns the Monet, only he has the right to use, damage, or take possession of it. Diego understands that his entitlements are legally enforceable—he can invoke the power of the state against others who try to interfere with his entitlements. Only he has authority to transfer these entitlements to others. Therefore, if he intends to transfer ownership to Petra, then he understands that he is transferring to her the right to call upon the state to enforce these entitlements against others, including him. Furthermore, if Diego's behavior would reasonably lead Petra to infer that he consents to the transfer, then she is entitled to assume that she has acquired these entitlements. According to consent theory, courts are justified in enforcing contracts because the transferor himself has consented to be legally bound by the new arrangement, not because he has an individual moral obligation to keep his promises (Barnett 1986).

5.5 Economic theories

The major theoretical opposition to deontological theories of contract law comes from economic theories (see the introduction to law and economics in sec. 3.2). As explained earlier, these are consequentialist theories, although not all consequentialist theories are economic.

At the center of economic analysis is the image of two rational, informed, self-interested parties who voluntarily form a contract. Rahul has a car, but he would prefer Seema's boat. Seema would prefer Rahul's car to her boat. Rahul offers to trade Seema, with the exchange to take place tomorrow. Seema agrees. If both perform, then both get what they wanted. Economists further stipulate that one's well-being increases if one gets what one wants. Therefore, mutual performance increases the well-being of both parties. The completed transaction is Pareto superior: it makes at least one party better-off and no one worse-off (see sec. 3.2). This conclusion assumes, as always, that performance negatively affects no other than the parties: there are no negative externalities.

This reasoning fails, however, in cases of regret. After contracting, but before the exchange, Seema might discover that she needs to sell the boat in order to pay a credit card bill and avoid a huge interest charge. She regrets accepting the offer. Now the transaction makes her worse-off and is not Pareto superior, but the law still requires her to perform.

Perhaps, Rahul will use the boat to start a fishing business and will earn so much that he could pay Seema's debt and still be better-off than he was with his car. In that case the transaction is Kaldor-Hicks efficient (see sec. 3.2). If he actually compensates her, then the transaction is again Pareto superior. But the law does not require him to compensate her. And in any case, courts enforce the contract even if he could not afford to compensate her—even if the transaction is not Kaldor-Hicks efficient. So far, economic analysis does not appear to succeed as an interpretive account of contract law.

At this point, economists shift focus from the micro- to the macrolevel— from particular transactions to the social incentives generated by law. In any given transaction the law may or may not succeed in promoting efficiency. Some inefficient contracts will be formed, whatever rules are adopted. And after an inefficient contract is formed, it is often too costly—if not impossible—for the courts to identify the efficient remedy. However, economists suggest that contract law can be seen as encouraging parties to make and perform on more, rather than fewer, wealth-maximizing contracts in the aggregate.

> Dick promises to buy an heirloom from Jane for £1,000 in 30 days. Jane might now spend and borrow more than she otherwise would have during that month. This is *beneficial reliance* on Dick's promise. Of course, Dick could renege, in which case Jane's reliance would prove to have been detrimental to her. If Jane is prudent, then she will try to estimate the probability that Dick will perform. How trustworthy is Dick? How likely is it that an intervening contingency will make performance impossible or induce him to renege? How much protection does the law give Jane if Dick backs out? How much does she stand to gain from relying on Dick?

Dick has complementary calculations to make. If he is prudent, then before he promises he considers the possibility that he will come to regret it. Maybe next week he will find another heirloom that he prefers to Jane's. Maybe he will incur unexpected expenses, or suddenly have to move overseas. Dick must estimate the likelihood that he will regret the promise, consider the costs of breaching, and decide if making the promise is a good bet for him. However, as a self-interested actor, he disregards the costs to Jane. These include her detrimental reliance loss if Dick reneges and foregone beneficial reliance if she decides not to increase consumption in the intervening month because of the risk that he will renege. Of course, if Jane does not sufficiently trust Dick, then she may refuse to deal with him at all, but Dick takes that possibility into account, since he wants the exchange to take place.

However, the costs to breaching promisors and the protection afforded promisees are partly determined by the rules of contract law itself. Consider what happens if lawmakers announce in advance that courts will enforce promises with damages. Lawmakers thereby increase the expected cost of breach in Dick's mind. This increase has four interacting effects. First, Dick becomes more likely to perform if he promises. Secondly, because she understands this fact, Jane becomes more likely to accept Dick's offer. Thirdly, Jane becomes more likely to rely on his promise to her benefit. Fourthly, Dick becomes less likely to promise in the first place. Or, if he is still willing to promise, then he becomes more likely to qualify his promise with self-protective "escape clauses" that he believes courts will enforce. These clauses, in turn, make Jane less likely to accept his offer.

Economic theorists propose that contract rules should encourage Dick to make promises, but should also encourage him to take into account the costs to Jane if he breaches. The law should provide damages that encourage promisors to make promises that increase beneficial reliance overall, without encouraging them to take excessive self-protective measures. Much of contract law, economists claim, can be explained in these terms (Goetz and Scott 1980).

The difficult question, however, is what type of damages the law should provide. Limiting recovery to reliance damages, for example, encourages promisors to form more contracts than expectation damages. But expectation damages discourage more inefficient breaches than reliance damages do. Some economists conclude that there is no uniform measure of damages that encourages both efficient contract formation and efficient breaching (Polinsky 1989).

Deontologists (sec. 5.4.2) object to economic theories of contract on moral grounds. If Dick promises to buy Jane's heirloom, then deontologists conclude that Jane has a moral right to receive payment or at least some amount of damages. Yet, economic theories do not allow us to reach that conclusion so quickly. Prescriptive economic theory entails that Jane is entitled to damages only if an efficient set of rules would require such awards in Jane's circumstances. It is a complex empirical question which set of rules is efficient. Efficient rules might require damages, but they might not, so economic theory makes Jane's entitlement contingent on empirical facts. It makes no difference whether Dick's conduct was fair or reasonable. For those who believe that establishing fair and reasonable conduct rules is a purpose of contract law, economic analysis misses the point.

5.6 Default rules

Deontological theories have their own problems, however, which economic theorists eagerly point out. Deontological theories explain why promisors should keep their promises, but what do such theories say about *default rules*? These are rules that courts apply when a question arises that is not covered by specific contractual language. What is the remedy for breach? Under what conditions is performance excused? What information must the parties disclose to one another? Some contracts are drafted to cover these issues, but some are not. When an issue arises that the contract did not address, courts must invoke default rules.

Recall Rahul and Seema's car/boat trade. Six months later, Seema discovers that the car needs a new radiator. She sues Rahul for breach of contract. The contract did not specify anything about the condition of the radiator. Rahul did not warn Seema about it, but neither did she ask. How does a deontological theory, such as Fried's, tell the court to rule? Here Fried asks if the parties shared a subjectively intended meaning with respect to this issue. Suppose the contract just described the vehicle as "a Honda Accord with 200,000 kilometers." Did the parties understand that to mean "an Accord with a radiator in good condition" or just "an Accord, with or without a good radiator"? Fried answers this question by appealing to background social conventions: when reasonable people in the society buy vehicles with 200,000 kilometers, do they expect them to have good radiators? If so, then the court should award Seema expectation damages in the amount needed to replace the radiator. If not, then Seema should lose.

Economic theorists find this appeal to background social conventions unsatisfying for two reasons. First, there is not always a social convention that resolves the matter. If half the people in the community expect a good radiator when they buy a used car and the other half has no such expectation, then there is no social convention. A complete prescriptive theory of contract should offer guidance to courts, nevertheless.

Secondly, even if there is an established social convention that covers the issue, the convention itself was probably influenced by the law. If most people in Seema's community expect a good radiator in a used car, then this may simply reflect the fact that courts routinely award expectation damages to purchasers of used cars with bad radiators. That is no problem for an interpretive theory, but the question for prescriptive contract theory is how courts *should* rule in such cases. If courts are applying an inefficient rule, then economic theory advises them to announce that they no longer plan to do so, even though this change requires consumers to adjust their expectations. Deontological theories, by contrast, go silent on the question of *which* social conventions the law ought to foster for such situations.

Study questions

(1) What is the best justification that can be given for the modern law of private property? Is it based on utility, desert, virtue, liberty, or something else?
(2) Can a set of property rules be just if the initial distribution is not?
(3) How is a tort different from a crime?
(4) Is tort law best understood in consequentialist terms, as economists propose, or in nonconsequentialist terms, as corrective justice theorists claim?
(5) Is a contract a pair of reciprocal promises? Do contracts have moral significance in virtue of being promises?
(6) Should the law award expectation damages for breach of contract? Why or why not?
(7) What is the difference between causation-in-fact and proximate causation?
(8) How, if at all, should a theory of legal causation take into account facts about the spatial and temporal remoteness of cause and effect?

Recommended reading

Aristotle. 1941. *Nichomachean Ethics*. In *The Basic Works of Aristotle*. Ed. Richard McKeon. New York: Random House.

Atiyah, P. S. 1981. *Promises, Morals, and Law*. Oxford: Clarendon Press.

Coase, Ronald. 1960. "The Problem of Social Cost." *Journal of Law and Economics* 3: 1–44.

Coleman, Jules. 1992. *Risks and Wrongs*. Cambridge: Cambridge University Press.

Dalton, Clare. 1985. "An Essay in the Deconstruction of Contract Doctrine." *Yale Law Journal* 94: 997–1114.

Dworkin, Ronald. 1980. "Why Efficiency?" *Hofstra Law Review* 8: 568–70.

Epstein, Richard A. 1995. *Simple Rules for a Complex World*. Cambridge, MA: Harvard University Press.

Fletcher, George P. 1972. "Fairness and Utility in Tort Theory." *Harvard Law Review* 72: 537–73.

Fried, Charles. 1981. *Contract as Promise*. Cambridge, MA: Harvard University Press.

Hart, H. L. A., and Tony Honoré. 1959. *Causation in the Law*. Oxford: Clarendon Press.

Mackie, J. L. 1974. *The Cement of the Universe: A Study of Causation*. Oxford: Clarendon Press.

Moore, Michael S. 2009. *Causation and Responsibility*. New York: Oxford University Press.

Perry, Stephen R. 1992. "The Moral Foundations of Tort Law." *Iowa Law Review* 77: 449–514.

Polinsky, A. Mitchell. 1989. *An Introduction to Law and Economics*. 2nd edn. Boston: Little, Brown, and Co.

Posner, Richard A. 2010. *Economic Analysis of Law*. 8th edn. New York: Aspen.

Postema, Gerald J., ed. 2001. *Philosophy and the Law of Torts*. New York: Cambridge University Press.

Satz, Debra. 2010. *Why Some Things Should Not Be for Sale*. New York: Oxford University Press.

Shiffrin, Seana Valentine. 2007. "The Divergence of Contract and Promise." *Harvard Law Review* 120: 708–53.

Sunstein, Cass, ed. 2000. *Behavioral Law and Economics*. Cambridge: Cambridge University Press.

Weinrib, Ernest J. 1995. *The Idea of Private Law*. Cambridge, MA: Harvard University Press.

Wright, Richard W. 1985. "Causation in Tort Law." *California Law Review* 73: 1735–828.

6
Criminal Law

The criminal law is traditionally divided into two parts, the *special part* and the *general part*. Some, but not all, criminal acts involve causing, attempting, or risking harm to others. The special part of the criminal law concerns those harms and the associated wrongful actions. The general part concerns all other factors that are relevant to deserved punishment. I shall consider the general part in this chapter. The special part is addressed primarily in Chapter 3.

1. Elements

A criminal statute defines a crime as a set of necessary and sufficient *elements*. Under the Model Penal Code (MPC) of the American Law Institute there are three types of elements: *conduct, attendant circumstances*, and *result*. Consider the MPC definition of the crime of indecent exposure:

> A person commits a misdemeanor if, for the purpose of arousing or gratifying sexual desire of himself or of any person other than his spouse, he exposes his genitals under circumstances in which he knows his conduct is likely to cause affront or alarm.[1]

This definition illustrates all three element types: conduct (exposing one's genitals); result (arousing or gratifying sexual desire); and attendant circumstances (those in which the actor knows his conduct is likely to cause affront or alarm). I shall discuss the three element types in the next sections.

2. Conduct

All crimes have a conduct element: a voluntary act or failure to act. Most require a voluntary act: an intentional movement or attempt to move one's body by someone who is otherwise in control of his intentions. No one today is convicted for thoughts, intentions, or status without an accompanying action. It is not a crime to wish for someone's death, to form an intention to embezzle, to have sexual desires for children, or to be addicted to heroin.

There are several philosophical issues pertaining to the act requirement. I shall address two in this chapter. First, under what conditions does the law consider an act not to be voluntary? Secondly, what is the relationship between the act requirement and the general requirement of culpability? Another question is whether criminal law always requires an act, or whether failures to act—omissions—can constitute crimes as well (see Chapter 3, sec. 4).

2.1 Defeaters of voluntariness

Not all bodily movements are voluntary acts for the purposes of criminal law. Some movements are not even considered "acts." These include movements by unconscious persons, such as rolling over in your sleep, and reflexive movements, such as jumping at a thunderclap. Other movements are acts, but involuntary ones, as when the actor is in a state of altered consciousness (sleepwalking, hypnosis, etc.). One might assume that insanity also functions as a defeater of voluntariness, but this is not technically the case. The law generally treats insane actors as acting voluntarily, but allows them to assert insanity as a defense (see sec. 5.3).

A similar analysis applies to cases of *duress*. Suppose someone threatens to maim you or your son unless you commit a crime for him. If you comply, then your compliance is a voluntary action. This is not to suggest that you deserve punishment or that the law requires that you be convicted. The point is simply that you will have to assert a defense of duress at trial (see sec. 5.2).

Nonlawyers tend to call actions "voluntary" if they think the actor deserves to be convicted and "involuntary" otherwise. You should resist this tendency. Voluntary action does not entail conviction. Defendants can assert *defenses*: excuses or justifications (see secs 4, 5). You will misunderstand the legal analysis of crimes if you assume that any excuse or justification negates voluntariness.

The philosophical premise of these doctrines is that an actor is not blameworthy if his capacity for rational agency is too compromised: if he lacks sufficient control over his actions or if his mental condition prevents him from recognizing his reasons for action. In either case, his actions are not voluntary. Some theorists argue that criminal law should treat voluntary action not as a separate requirement for liability, but rather as an aspect of the culpability requirement. The factors that defeat voluntariness also defeat culpability. Most voluntary actions are not culpable.

2.2 Legality and retroactivity

Can someone be punished for an act that was not criminal under positive law at the time of commission? The Fifth Amendment of the US Constitution prohibits such *ex post facto* laws. In the United Kingdom, matters are less clear. Article 7 of the European Convention on Human Rights (ECHR) prohibits retrospective criminal laws, and the United Kingdom is a signatory to the ECHR. However, the United Kingdom also retains parliamentary sovereignty, so the ECHR probably does not forbid retrospective laws in the United Kingdom.

The prescriptive question is whether ex post facto laws are unjust. In many cases they seem to be. If you could not possibly know that an act is criminal, then it seems unfair to punish you. And if your act was not criminal at the time, then obviously you could not know otherwise. However, we might make an exception for certain acts that everyone is presumed to know are wrong, such as acts of unprovoked violence. Imagine a jurisdiction in which the law permits child abuse (e.g. causing children physical pain for one's own amusement). It might not be wrong to punish a child abuser in this jurisdiction, notwithstanding the law. In the Nuremberg trials after the Second World War, Nazi officials were convicted and punished for acts that were arguably legal under Nazi law.

3. Mens rea

Every criminal statute has a conduct element, but conduct is not usually enough to get one convicted of a crime. Some elements, including conduct elements, must be accompanied by a culpable mental state. This requirement is historically referred to as the guilty mind or *mens rea* requirement. Modern statutes specify mental states with respect to each element of the crime. The three mental states are *purpose, knowledge,* and *recklessness.* Each of these states can apply to any element of a crime. An actor has the mental state of purpose with respect to a conduct element if and only if he intends to engage in specified conduct while aware of its nature. Hector intentionally removes his pants in public. If he sincerely believes that he is wearing swim trunks underneath, then he does not purposely expose his genitals, even if he does, in fact, expose them. Whereas, if he knows that he is naked under his pants, then he purposely exposes his genitals.

3.1 Purpose and knowledge

An actor has the mental state of *purpose* with respect to a result element if and only if he has "the conscious object of causing that result."[2] The indecent exposure provision of the MPC mentions a result of sexual arousal. An actor has purpose with respect to that element if and only if it is his conscious object to cause sexual arousal. It is not enough merely to believe that sexual arousal will occur, even if he is certain that it will. That is *knowledge,* but not purpose. An actor has knowledge with respect to an element if he believes that it exists or, in the case of result elements, if he believes with "practical certainty" that it exists. An actor can have knowledge of a result element whether he is pleased, displeased, or indifferent toward it. By contrast, he can have purpose with respect to a result element even if he thinks it unlikely to occur, although he must *want* it to occur—it must be his conscious object— and he must believe that his conduct makes the intended result at least a bit more likely.

3.2 Recklessness

The indecent exposure provision of the MPC also specifies attendant circumstances: those under which the actor "knows his conduct is likely to cause affront or alarm." What sort of element is this? The MPC defines "recklessness" as disregard of a "substantial and unjustifiable risk" that the element exists or will exist. The indecent exposure provision does not specify that the risk is substantial or unjustifiable, but it otherwise reflects a recklessness standard: the actor can be guilty if he believes that his conduct is likely to cause affront or alarm, even if causing it is not his purpose and he is not certain that it will occur. Expecting to be alone, Hector plans to drop his pants and masturbate at noon on the deck of his boat. When noon arrives, he sees a family sailing nearby. He is chagrined, not wishing to alarm anyone, but he proceeds with his plan. He acts recklessly, despite lacking any purpose to alarm. Whereas, if Hector fails to notice the family and sincerely believes that he is alone, then he is not reckless, even if his exposure alarms them.

There are many questions concerning what makes an actor reckless with respect to an element. The test has both objective and subjective components. The actor must be subjectively aware of the nature and magnitude of the risk:

> Marvin mixes chlorine bleach with ammonia in his office, intending to create a refreshing smell and mistakenly believing this to be safe. In fact, he runs a 50 percent chance of creating toxic fumes that will injure his coworkers. Marvin is not reckless because he believes that he is running a risk of less than 0.0001 percent, and such a miniscule risk is not objectively substantial. Imagine, instead, that Marvin knows of the 50 percent risk of injury, but genuinely believes that such a risk is "not substantial." (This is hard to imagine, but perhaps he believes that everyone likes to live dangerously.) Despite this belief, Marvin is reckless because he believes that the risk is 50 percent, and such a risk is, objectively, substantial. Or perhaps he believes that a 50 percent chance of injury, albeit substantial, is justified by his goal of refreshing the air. Again, he is reckless. A 50 percent chance of injury is not objectively justified by his trivial goal.

Interesting philosophical questions now arise. Suppose Marvin knows that mixing chlorine and ammonia creates a 50 percent risk of injuring others, but he mistakenly uses water instead of ammonia, diluting the chlorine. Does he act recklessly? Some theorists argue that he does, but the law is not settled (Alexander and Ferzan 2009).

It is also hard to know what "substantial risk" means in practice. We do not lead our daily lives consciously quantifying the risks of our many decisions. When I drive through a red traffic light I know that I risk a crash, but I do not know if that risk is 10 percent, 1 percent, or 0.001 percent. When I serve my guests raw oysters, I believe that there is some risk that they will become ill as a result, but I cannot put a number on it. Some of my actions seem "dangerous" to me. Most do not. Rarely are my thoughts more precise than that. The law does not expect actors to have quantified probabilities in mind. However, the actor's subjective awareness of the magnitude of risk is relevant.

Finally, one might wonder whether the substantiality of a risk is fundamentally independent of its justifiability. Even a substantial risk can be justifiable in the right circumstances. A sharpshooter fires a rifle at a fleeing suspect in a crowded park, running a substantial risk of injuring a bystander. If the target is a suspected terrorist, then the substantial risk may be justifiable, but not if he is merely a suspected shoplifter. Conversely, one might wonder whether even a miniscule risk is justifiable if the actor takes it for bad reasons. Nick throws a rock at his ex-girlfriend from 100 meters. No one else is nearby. Nick hopes to hit her, but knows that his chance of success is miniscule. Has he acted recklessly? What if, miraculously, he hits her? Because running this risk is completely unjustifiable, some would argue that Nick is culpable, however small his chance of success.

3.3 Negligence

An actor who is not reckless with respect to an element might nonetheless be *negligent* with respect to it. But negligence differs from the mental states of purpose, knowledge, and recklessness. Negligence is historically classified as a mental state, but this is a misclassification. Negligence refers to the risk taken, not the actor's mental state with respect to that risk. An actor is negligent if and only if she takes a substantial and unjustifiable risk. She need not be consciously aware of the risk. You park your car on an incline without engaging the parking brake, mistakenly believing that it engages automatically. You have taken a risk that a reasonable actor in your situation would not take. You are unaware of the risk, but a reasonable actor would be aware of it. You are negligent.

Negligence plays a central role in tort law (see Chapter 5, sec. 3), but only a peripheral role in criminal law. There are, however, some crimes of pure negligence. The MPC, for example, includes several such crimes: negligent homicide, assault with a deadly weapon, and criminal mischief with dangerous means.[3] But the very idea of punishing someone for negligence strikes some observers as unjust. After all, if you are merely negligent, not reckless, then by definition you are unaware that your conduct is wrong. How can you be blameworthy or criminally liable for it? Moreover, when you are unaware of a risk you have no control over your lack of awareness. You are unaware of the risk, and you are unaware that you are unaware, and you are unaware that you are unaware that you are unaware, ad infinitum. Only if someone else informs you of your mistake will you be able to avoid it. So it seems unfair to punish you for negligence.

3.4 Strict liability

All of the objections against crimes of negligence, and then some, apply also to crimes of *strict liability*. Few crimes fall into this category in the United States, but there are examples: possession of certain illegal narcotics, statutory rape, possession of child pornography, and a few other crimes. Strict liability means that, in principle, an actor is guilty of the crime even if she is not negligent with respect to any element.

> Justin buys a box of powdered sugar which, unbeknownst to him, has been filled with powder cocaine. No reasonable person in Justin's position would suspect this. Nonetheless, if the police lawfully search Justin's bag and discover that the box contains cocaine, then Justin could be convicted of possession in the United States. He has committed the criminal act—taking possession of the cocaine. His mental state is legally irrelevant. This is not to suggest that, in the real world, Justin would inevitably be prosecuted. The prosecutor might believe Justin's story and drop the charges. But she is not legally obligated to drop them, even if she believes him. Strict liability statutes allow for conviction in such cases.

Strict liability has some advantages over more permissive standards. By eliminating defenses based on mental state, strict liability reduces prosecution costs and ensures that fewer guilty defendants are acquitted. Accordingly, it deters prospective criminals who would otherwise bet on winning acquittals by introducing reasonable doubt about their mental state. However, strict liability also generates more false positives—convictions of morally innocent defendants such as Justin. It may also encourage actors to take excessive precautions and to avoid certain socially valuable activities altogether. For these reasons, strict liability remains even more controversial than criminal negligence (Wasserstrom 1960).

3.5 Mistakes of fact and law

A knowledge element requires that the actor know that a certain fact exist (see sec. 3.1). An actor who does not know this fact has made a *mistake of fact* and is not guilty. An actor who does not know that his act is criminal, by contrast, makes a *mistake of law*. Unlike mistakes of fact, mistakes of law rarely exculpate because very few statutes specify knowledge of the law as an element of a crime. As the saying goes, "ignorance of the law is no excuse." This makes moral sense when it comes to acts that are immoral independent of their legal status, such as sexual assault and many cases of homicide and theft (known as *mala-in-se* offenses). But many criminal acts are only immoral (if they are) because they are criminalized. Consider the crime of failing to file one's income tax return. Someone who has no idea that he is required to file a tax return may still be convicted for failing to do so. Mistakes of law do not exculpate. As with strict liability, there are advantages to this principle. It would be harder to convict defendants if they could always introduce reasonable doubt as to whether they had made a mistake of law. The legal system imposes on each of us an affirmative obligation to learn the laws that apply to us. However, as with strict liability, the policy can generate unfair results. Even someone who is ignorant of the law, but not unreasonably so, may be convicted. Of course, if the state makes it too difficult to learn the laws with which one comes into contact, then the rule of law begins to suffer (see Chapter 1, sec. 10).

4. Justification

If all statutory elements of a crime are present, then the actor is guilty, unless she has a valid *justification* or *excuse*. This section (4) addresses justifications. Section 5 addresses excuses.

A justification is a kind of exception to a crime—a defense. Some criminal statutes include specific justifications, but there are also background justifications that apply to all crimes. An otherwise criminal act is justified if, under the circumstances as they actually are, the act is not objectively wrong. There is no reason, in other words, to wish that the actor had behaved differently. Fred and Wilma are walking in a remote area when Fred has a heart attack. Wilma runs to a nearby farmhouse for help, but no one is home. She breaks a window and uses the phone to call an ambulance. The elements exist for the crime of breaking and entering, but if Wilma is charged, then she can assert a "lesser evil" defense. She was justified in the circumstances and should be acquitted. (The homeowner can, however, recover tort damages from Wilma for the broken window.) Under the MPC, the burden falls on the prosecution to prove beyond a reasonable doubt that the defendant had no justification for his conduct, although the defendant must produce evidence of justification.

Justifications raise many fascinating philosophical questions. What moral principles underlie the several justifications recognized in criminal law? Under what conditions can a defendant claim a justification?

Of course, individuals can be mistaken about the presence of justifications. A defendant who sincerely and reasonably, but mistakenly, believes her conduct to be legally justified is not guilty because she lacks a necessary mental state (unless the statute provides strict liability; see sec. 3.4). A rarer, but intriguing, kind of case involves a defendant whose conduct is, unbeknownst to her, justified:

> Mrs Smith shoots and kills Mr Smith, not knowing that he was just about to shoot her. How do we judge Mrs Smith? If she had known of the imminent threat that Mr Smith posed to her, then she would have been justified in shooting him. But she did not know of the threat. Should she be convicted of murder, as she would have been had he posed no threat? Or should she be acquitted, as she would have been had she reasonably believed that he posed a threat? There is something to be said for each of these conclusions, but there is a third position: convict Mrs Smith of attempted murder. This compromise reflects the fact that she has killed someone and that her mental state was that of a cold-blooded killer, while also reflecting the fact that the killing was actually permissible under the circumstances. Notice, however, that Mr Smith could have offered the same defense had he shot first, not knowing that Mrs Smith was about to kill him. Each would have been justified in shooting the other.

Notice, also, that the law allows the defendant to make complete use of a justification as a defense at trial, provided she can persuade the fact finder that she was aware of its existence when she acted. She need not persuade anyone that she was actually *motivated* by the justification. Imagine that Mrs Smith resolves to shoot Mr Smith in cold blood, but then notices him drawing his revolver to shoot her just before she shoots him. If she was aware of the existence of this justification, then she can rely upon it at trial, even if her awareness made no difference to her decision (this is called *overdetermination*). She reveals herself to have bad character, in that she was prepared to shoot Mr Smith in cold blood, but the law does not convict her for bad character, alone. She is akin to a man who resolves to kill his enemy if the opportunity ever arises, although it never does. He has bad character which circumstances never allow him to manifest in action.

Part of the challenge of drafting criminal statutes is anticipating and including justifications that are specific to the subject matter of the statute. There are, however, a handful of general justifications recognized in the law that should be addressed.

4.1 Defense against aggression

One familiar category of justification is defense against aggression. If someone threatens you with bodily harm, for example, then the law allows you to use force, or threat of force, for the purpose of defending yourself. You may also use force or threat of force, again for the purpose of blocking a threat, against someone who threatens your property. There are several questions to ask about defensive justifications. What are their limits and qualifications? What is the normative basis for them? How should they be classified?

In general, modern law does not allow individuals other than authorized public officials to use force against one another (this is called "self-help"), even for the purpose of doing justice. Using force against someone usually compromises her freedom, self-determination, and interests, so there is a presumptive moral reason against the use of force, on any number of moral theories. A defensive justification of force is available under the law only if the aggressor threatens person or property, either the defendant's own or that of another. The threat posed by the aggressor can be death, bodily injury, theft, unauthorized use, or destruction of property, among other things.

Force may be used only for the purpose of blocking a threat. If I am sitting on you and punching you in the face, then you are permitted to punch me in the face in order to get me to stop. However, if I break your nose and walk away, then you are not permitted to follow me and break my nose for any reason, including retaliation, much as you may want to do so.

The defendant's use of force must be directed only at the aggressor himself. If you steal my motorcycle and are riding away, I may not begin vandalizing your nearby car in order to motivate you to return. If you have kidnapped my daughter, I may not injure your son in order to get you to return her to me. Likewise, the threat must originate with the aggressor. Suppose my son is dying in the street and needs an emergency blood transfusion that only you can provide. I may not hold you down and take a pint of your blood, even if doing so is necessary to save my son's life and will cause you no lasting harm. I may not do so because you do not pose the threat to my son, even though only your blood can save him. My use of force would not serve to block a threat that you initiated, so it would be unlawful.

Force may be used only as a last resort in most cases. There is a legal duty to *retreat*, particularly before using deadly force. If someone runs toward you, brandishing a switchblade knife, and you can easily ride away on your motorcycle, then you must do so, rather than dismounting and continuing the fight. One exception to the duty to retreat, recognized in some jurisdictions, is limited to residents defending their homes against invasion. In some jurisdictions a resident is not expected to retreat from his home and may use even deadly force against a home invader, rather than fleeing for safety.

Related to the duty to retreat is the *imminence* requirement. If you send me an email, credibly threatening to kill me next week, then I am not required to retreat or to notify the police. I am even permitted to track you down, but I may not use deadly force until the danger to me becomes imminent.

Even when the use of force is justified, it is limited by the *proportionality* requirement. Deadly weapons generally must not be used against unarmed assailants (although, again, some jurisdictions allow the use of deadly force against home invaders). A large, strong person must exercise some restraint if attacked by a smaller, weaker one. You may not shoot a thief in the leg as he speeds away on your scooter, even if that is the only way to stop him. Wrestling an unarmed pickpocket to the ground is fine, even if he sustains some bruises, but deliberately breaking his arm is not. Using defensive force is always risky because it is difficult to know, especially in the heat of the moment, whether one has gone too far.

There are also the fascinating cases of so-called innocent aggressors (McMahan 1994). Imagine aggressors such as the following: a five-year-old boy brandishing a loaded firearm; a mental patient hallucinating; a sleepwalker; or simply someone who, through no fault of his own, does not understand the danger he poses to others. Any of these aggressors could threaten others with death or serious bodily harm. The laws of most jurisdictions are not entirely clear about using force against innocent aggressors. Some writers suggest that defendants who use force against innocent aggressors should be held to a higher standard than those who use force against ordinary (culpable) aggressors. Others suggest that the use of force against innocent aggressors is not justified, but merely *excused*. Still others would forbid any use of force against the innocent. Distinguishing between culpable and innocent aggressors reflects the notion that the former, but not the latter, have waived some of their rights not to have force used against them. Innocent aggressors waive nothing, so how can the use of force against them ever be justified? Imagine a toddler innocently threatening you with deadly force, which you can deflect only by using deadly force against him. Why should your rights take priority over his? True, he is the aggressor and we normally give priority to the rights of victims over those of their aggressors. But that may be simply a reflection of the fact that aggressors are usually culpable and their victims innocent. If both parties are innocent, as in innocent aggressor cases, then the basis for preferring one party to the other is not obvious. An interesting comparison case is the forcible quarantine of persons with highly contagious, fatal diseases, which is lawful in most jurisdictions. Quarantines are morally justified only if the rights of the general public to avoid a heightened risk of infection trump the rights of quarantined individuals to freedom of movement.

4.1.1 Rationales

What might be said in favor of having the law permit the defensive use of force? A simple argument begins from the observation that individuals (especially men, perhaps) are strongly inclined to use force in defense of persons and property. Perhaps, the law should not resist such widespread and strong inclinations.

More principled arguments are also available. Most people believe that police officers, for example, are morally permitted (even obligated) to use force for the purpose of blocking aggression against persons and property. Most of the arguments in favor of official use of defensive force can be adapted to cover private uses of force under narrower conditions. Police officers cannot be everywhere (nor would we want them to be), so there will always be some cases in which the burden of thwarting aggression falls upon private parties, and force is necessary. This is not to say that private parties are, or should be, held to the same standards as police officers when they use force.

4.2 Lesser evils

Another general justification for otherwise criminal actions is the "lesser-evils" or "necessity" defense. An actor who commits an action that would otherwise constitute a crime can assert the lesser-evils defense if the harm he tries to avoid is greater than the harm the act would cause.[4] The defense is most clearly available when the defendant commits a property crime for the purpose of preventing serious physical injury. Imagine that Victim is bleeding from a wound and First Bystander uses Second Bystander's towel as a tourniquet, without Second Bystander's permission. If Second Bystander charges First Bystander with theft or destruction of property, then First Bystander can assert a necessity defense.

Many jurisdictions exclude homicide from the scope of the necessity defense. There are several famous cases, real and hypothetical, that raise the issue. The most famous is a British decision from 1884, *Regina v. Dudley & Stephens:*[5]

> A ship sailing from England to Australia hit a storm and began to sink. Four men ended up in a lifeboat hundreds of miles from shore with few supplies. After twelve days their food supply was exhausted and it was unlikely that anyone would live to be rescued. The captain, Thomas Dudley, and a crewman, Edward Stephens, decided to kill another crewman, Richard Parker, who was the youngest and weakest and who was by then sometimes falling unconscious. After Dudley and Stephens killed Parker, the three survivors lived by eating Parker's flesh for four days before being rescued. Dudley and Stephens were tried for murder and asserted a defense of necessity. A jury agreed that it was very unlikely that anyone would have survived had someone not been killed for food. Nevertheless, the high court of England convicted the defendants of murder. Writing for the court, Lord Coleridge rejected the necessity defense. Although he recognized that the killing in this case saved more lives than it cost, Lord Coleridge was concerned about setting a dangerous precedent. An acquittal might lead individuals in subsequent cases to make mistakes, to give free rein to malicious motives and self-interest.

There is also a famous hypothetical case about the necessity defense in Lon Fuller's (1949) article, "The Case of the Speluncean Explorers":

> Fuller tells the story of five explorers trapped in a cave. After twenty days in the cave, their provisions have run out, but they discover a radio in their possession that allows them to communicate with rescuers. They learn that help will not arrive for at least ten days. Doctors inform them that they are unlikely to survive that long without food. One of the explorers, Roger Whetmore, suggests that they roll dice in order to determine which of them should be killed and eaten so that the other four may survive. Ironically, Whetmore subsequently changes his mind and refuses to participate, but the other four roll the dice for him. He loses, whereupon the others kill and eat him. They are rescued five days later and charged with murder.

Finally, there is a real case involving conjoined twins in the United Kingdom:[6]

> Each of the twins had her own head, brain, heart, and lungs, but one twin, Jodie, was stronger than her conjoined sister, Mary. Jodie's heart and lungs provided oxygenated blood for both twins, via a shared artery. Experts concluded that Jodie's heart would not continue to support both twins. It was predicted that both would die in three to six months, or perhaps a little longer.
>
> A surgical separation of the twins was entirely feasible and was likely to make it possible for Jodie to live a life of normal length and quality. Mary, however, was certain to die immediately after separation, because her own heart and lungs were too weak

to support her. Mary also had an abnormal brain and impaired cognitive development. Interestingly, the twins' parents opposed the separation, while the doctors and hospital favored it and sought an injunction requiring the surgery against the parents' wishes. A trial court ruled in favor of the doctors and the appellate court affirmed. The twins were separated, killing Mary. Jodie survived.

Is the necessity defense more applicable in the conjoined twins case than in the other two cases? One of the judges in the twins case, Lord Justice Brooke, thought so. Lord Brooke distinguished *Dudley & Stephens* by observing that the sailors made a decision about who would live or die, whereas Mary's survival was impossible: only Jodie, at most, could survive. But this reasoning is puzzling. After all, the surgery ended Mary's life, and probably did so a few months earlier than it would otherwise have ended. Under the law, depriving someone of even a minute of remaining life is a homicide. Why is it relevant to a necessity defense how much time Mary had left? True, the separation gave Jodie many years of extra life and cost Mary only a few months. But Richard Parker would have died soon, too, had Dudley and Stephens not killed him. So would Whetmore, had the other explorers not killed him. Distinguishing the conjoined twins case from the other two is not so simple.

5. Excuse

Lawyers traditionally distinguish between justifications and excuses. The distinction is not always clear (Greenawalt 1984), but the basic idea is simple. Justifications are impersonal: recall the case of Wilma, who breaks a window in order to call an ambulance for someone who is suffering a heart attack (sec. 4). Anyone in Wilma's circumstances—helping a heart-attack victim— would be justified in breaking the window. Excuses are more personal. An actor is excused if her rational agency is somehow compromised so that she is not morally responsible for her actions, or if her beliefs about her reasons, although mistaken, are ones that a reasonable person would take to justify her actions. Stuart plays a prank on Neve, donning a disguise and threatening her with a realistic toy revolver. Neve is terrified, pulls a real gun from her purse, and shoots Stuart. Shooting him is not *justified* because he posed no actual threat to her. But she has an *excuse* because she reasonably believed herself to be in imminent danger.

We might say that, if everyone were fully rational and fully informed, then the criminal law would not need to provide excuses. Justifications, by contrast, would still be needed unless we were able to draft criminal statutes that incorporated exceptions to cover every possible case in which morality permits a criminal act. In such cases, defendants should have legal justifications available to them.

A defendant who asserts an excuse is claiming that he is less morally culpable than he would otherwise be for his actions, perhaps not culpable at all. He must claim either that he is not a rational actor, and hence not morally responsible, or else that avoiding the criminal act was unusually difficult for him, and hence that he is less responsible for it than he would otherwise be. Common excuses at law are *infancy*, *intoxication*, *insanity*, and *duress*.

5.1 Infancy

"Infancy" is a technical term, referring not just to babies but to all children below a certain age, such as seven. Before that magical age, children are understood to be less morally responsible for their actions. Young children have committed terrible crimes, but we do not hold them to the same moral standard as adults. In some cases, they do not even understand that their action is wrong. In other cases, they do not understand the importance of morality. And children have poor impulse control and little power: a six-year-old boy may shoplift a candy bar simply because he wants it badly. We cannot judge him as harshly as we judge a sixteen-year-old shoplifter, much less a thirty-year-old.

No one denies that the law should recognize infancy as an excuse. But there is much room for debate about the details. Should there be a sharp cutoff between infancy and legal adulthood? How many age categories should the law recognize? Two? Three (infancy, adolescence, and adulthood)? More? What year(s) should the law specify as the cutoff(s)? Seven? Twelve? Sixteen? Should legal infancy be defined uniformly for all crimes, or should different crimes get different definitions? These are difficult questions for lawmakers.

5.2 Duress

We can usefully contrast the excuse of *duress* with the lesser-evils justification. A defendant has a lesser-evils defense if he causes harm in order to prevent harm that is, impartially considered, of greater magnitude (e.g. breaking a window in order to protect someone from serious physical injury). The excuse of duress, by contrast, can be used even when the harm prevented is *not* of greater magnitude than the harm caused. The underlying idea is that individuals are expected to give extra weight to their own safety and that of their loved ones and are not blameworthy for doing so. Consider a man who seriously injures two children in order to spare himself or his own child a similar injury. He may be excused on grounds of duress, even though he chooses a greater over a lesser evil. Even homicide can be excused by duress: picture a military officer tortured by a terrorist who wants him to enter the launch codes for a nuclear attack. The duress excuse is well suited to situations in which someone uses a substantial threat to coerce a defendant into a criminal act. The magnitude of the threat, however, must be considered relative to the magnitude of the harm done. If someone threatens to expose embarrassing secrets about a security guard unless he gives her unauthorized access to the building, then the guard may be able to assert an excuse of duress. But what if the blackmailer orders the guard to break someone's legs? If he complies, he probably will not be able to win acquittal merely by claiming duress. The gap between the harm done and the harm avoided is here too large.

5.3 Insanity

The most widely debated excuse in modern times is the *insanity defense*. The basic idea is that a defendant's insanity at the time of a criminal action can be relevant to his legal responsibility. The main argument in favor of the insanity defense is that someone who commits a crime as a result of a mental disorder is less morally responsible than someone without a disorder. There are also consequentialist arguments for and against the defense. It may be impossible to deter an insane individual, so a practice of punishing the insane causes suffering without any compensating benefit to society. On the other hand, providing the insanity defense may weaken the deterrent effect of the criminal law in general, if crime-prone individuals who would otherwise be deterred by the threat of punishment come to believe (truly or falsely) that they can successfully plead insanity. Consequentialists also recognize that successful insanity pleas in highly publicized trials often lead to public outrage and loss of respect for the law, which are negative effects.

The insanity defense has been formulated in several different ways over the past two centuries. The most famous formulation is the *M'Naghten Rule*, named after the 1843 case of Daniel M'Naghten:

> Mr M'Naghten believed (on no basis whatsoever) that the Prime Minister of England was plotting against him. He formed a plan to assassinate the Minister, firing a bullet into the official's carriage and killing an innocent passenger. M'Naghten performed a criminal action with the intention of causing a death, and he caused one. Ordinarily, he would be guilty of murder (despite having missed his intended target), but the House of Lords acquitted him on grounds of insanity. Instead of going to prison, he spent the rest of his life in a mental institution.

The Lords stated their criteria as follows:

> [T]o establish a defence on the ground of insanity, it must be clearly proved that, at the time of the committing of the act, the party accused was labouring under such a defect of reason, from disease of the mind, as not to know the nature and quality of the act he was doing; or, if he did know it, that he did not know he was doing what was wrong.[7]

The M'Naghten Rule has many elements. First, it concerns itself exclusively with insanity at the time of action. A prior history of insanity might be probative, but ultimately what matters is the defendant's mental condition at the time of the crime. Notice, also, that having gone insane after the fact is not relevant to one's legal responsibility for the action, although it is relevant to one's competence to stand trial—a separate matter.

The Rule requires one of two forms of ignorance. Either the defendant did not know the "nature and quality of the act" or, if he knew the nature and quality of the act, then he did not know that it was wrong. What is it not to know the "nature and quality" of one's act? Picture a nanny who drowns a baby in the sink, all the while believing herself to be washing a potato. This is a pronounced form of insanity, but such persons exist. Should this nanny really be convicted of a crime? Many would say not.

Of course, we cannot read the nanny's mind, so there is always room for doubt as to what she was thinking. It is natural to worry that the insanity defense provides an easy cover for individuals who are not insane and who want to commit crimes. If we accept the nanny's insanity plea, what is to prevent sane killers from falsely claiming insanity?

The answer is twofold. First, the nanny cannot simply assert insanity. She must produce evidence of it. This will typically include expert testimony by mental health professionals who have examined her. If professionals find no evidence of mental defect, then her defense is unlikely to persuade a fact finder.

Secondly, the circumstances of the crime itself may suggest insanity to the fact finder. Although prosecutors are not required to prove "motive," the absence of motive can suggest insanity. If the nanny makes no effort to conceal her crime and had no apparent reason to want the infant dead, or even to be angry with the infant, then it becomes plausible that she did not understand what she was doing at the time. Most sane felons, by contrast, commit crimes for reasons that are quite apparent to the fact finder. They are motivated by power, profit, revenge, jealousy, entertainment, or the desire to conceal other crimes.

The second form of ignorance that qualifies as insanity under the M'Naghten Rule is failure to know that one's action is wrong. (The Lords did not specify whether the wrongness in question is legal or moral wrongness, a distinction that I shall ignore.) Imagine a different nanny, Abraham, who sincerely believes that obeying God is never wrong and that God has commanded him to drown the baby, Isaac. Abraham understands the nature and quality of his act to be homicidal, but he sincerely believes it not to be wrong. He has the second form of exculpatory ignorance mentioned in the Rule. Of course, Abraham will have to produce evidence that his belief was sincere, and the prosecution will do its best to discredit his evidence.

Ignorance is necessary for one to be excused under the M'Naghten Rule, but it is not sufficient. Only ignorance "from disease of the mind" is exculpatory under the Rule. Some writers wonder why the source of the ignorance should matter. If the defendant did not know the "nature and quality" of the act or that it was wrong, then it would seem that she has lower culpability—or none—for that reason alone, regardless of whether her ignorance results from a mental disease. Many crimes already require knowledge of one or more elements. Consider a host who picks lethal wild mushrooms in the forest and serves them to his guests, having no idea that there is even a risk that they are poisonous. If a guest dies, then the host could be charged with involuntary manslaughter, but a conviction would require proof that he knew about, and consciously disregarded, a substantial and unjustifiable risk of harm (see sec. 3.2). If he did not know about the risk, then he did not know that serving the mushrooms was wrong. If the fact finder has reasonable doubts as to whether he knew of the risk, then he will be acquitted. He need not attribute his ignorance to any mental disease. So why does anyone need the insanity defense? It would seem that someone who sincerely fails to understand important facts about her actions will have a defense to serious criminal charges, whether or not she suffers from a mental disease.

The M'Naghten Rule does not let defendants off the hook for just any sort of ignorance. I have no defense if I attack you because my mental illness leads me to believe, mistakenly, that you are someone whom I detest. The Lords in the *M'Naghten* case stated that the defendant

> must be considered in the same situation as to responsibility as if the facts with respect to which the delusion exists were real. For example, if under the influence of his delusion he supposes another man to be in the act of attempting to take away his life, and he kills that man, as he supposes, in self-defence, he would be exempt from punishment. If his delusion was that the deceased had inflicted a serious injury to his character and fortune, and he killed him in revenge for such supposed injury, he would be liable to punishment.[8]

The killer in the latter hypothetical is still guilty, despite his delusion, because his action—vengeance killing—would have been criminal even if the facts had been as he believed them to be.

The M'Naghten Rule remains the law in the United Kingdom and some reformers in the United States favor a return to it. Its main shortcoming is that it is a strictly *cognitive* test: it excuses only behavior that results from ignorance. But insanity does not always work in a cognitive way. It can also interfere with *volition*, also known as the *will*. In some cases, a defendant knows what he is doing and knows it to be wrong, but cannot help himself. This is known as an *irresistible impulse*. Some pyromaniacs, for example, feel an "irresistible" impulse to light dangerous fires. They understand what they are doing and that it is wrong, but they light the fires anyway. They cannot help themselves.

The idea of an irresistible impulse raises deep philosophical questions about the insanity defense. After all, most criminal defendants understand what they are doing and that it is wrong, but they do it anyway. If the law provides an insanity defense based on irresistible impulse, then it presupposes that some of these defendants (who know what they are doing and that it is wrong) can help themselves and should be convicted, while others cannot help themselves and should be acquitted. What does it mean to say that one defendant "could have" done otherwise, while another defendant, who did the same thing, "could not" have done otherwise? To draw this distinction is to assume that most of us, most of the time, have free will and that our free will can be compromised by mental disorders. These are controversial claims in philosophy (see Fischer et al. 2007). Some philosophers, known as *hard determinists*, deny that anyone has free will. They argue that human beings are subject to the same physical laws that govern everything else in the universe, and that there is no room in the physical world for genuine freedom. According to hard determinists, it cannot be true that a defendant could have done otherwise, given everything that happened prior to his decision. Given the prior state of the world, the defendant's decision was inevitable—determined. Hard determinism entails that no one ever "freely" chooses to commit a crime. Some hard determinists conclude, on this basis, that no one ever deserves punishment. Therefore, they see no difference between what sane and insane defendants deserve.

Other philosophers, known as *libertarians*,[9] believe that human beings— at least some of us, some of the time—have free will and are not governed by the same physical laws as everything else. Libertarians can easily hold that a defendant deserves to be punished if she knew what she was doing and knew it to be wrong. They can support an insanity defense for defendants who did not know what they were doing or that it was wrong. It is difficult, however, for libertarians to support a volitional insanity defense. The insanity defense presupposes that certain mental disorders deprive actors of the capacity to choose freely. Libertarians believe that human choice is not subject to the physical laws that govern everything else. So they bear a burden of explaining how a mental disorder can deprive actors of the capacity to choose, if not by way of physical causation. Otherwise, libertarians cannot maintain that an insane defendant is ever less responsible for his actions than a sane one.

Is any position on free will compatible with the claim that sane defendants are responsible for their actions, and insane defendants less responsible? Maybe so. A third group of philosophers—*compatibilists*—try to reconcile free will with the premise that the same physical laws apply to human beings as to everything else. For compatibilists, to say that a decision was made freely is not to say that it had no physical cause, but that it had a certain kind of physical cause. Compatibilists believe that to say that a particular decision is made under conditions of free will is to say that it is made by someone whose brain is in a certain physical state. Compatibilism, therefore, leaves open the possibility of brain states that are incompatible with free will. Mental disorders could be just such states.

If compatibilism is true, then there is at least conceptual space for a volitional insanity defense. Various legal tests developed since M'Naghten incorporate a volitional prong that recognizes irresistible impulses. One such test excuses a criminal act if the defendant was "impelled to do the act by an irresistible impulse" because "his reasoning powers were so dethroned by his diseased mental condition as to deprive him of the will power to resist the insane impulse to perpetrate the deed."[10] A less florid formulation is found in the MPC:

> A person is not responsible for criminal conduct if at the time of such conduct as a result of mental disease or defect he lacks substantial capacity to appreciate the criminality [wrongfulness] of his conduct or to conform his conduct to the requirements of law.[11]

The MPC formulation requires that the mental disease be a cause of either a cognitive or a volitional incapacity in the defendant. But the fact finder still has the job of determining whether the defendant lacked the capacity to obey the law. What evidence should she consider in assessing an asserted defense of insanity? I have already mentioned the absence of motive, which is not a formal element of a crime, but which lends credibility to an insanity defense. Someone who embezzles funds, spends them on luxuries, and tries to conceal his crime cannot assert a credible insanity defense because there is an obvious explanation for his conduct that does not involve any mental disorder. More controversial are cases such as that of John Hinckley, Jr:

> Hinckley attempted to assassinate US President Ronald Reagan in 1981. Hinckley's lawyers presented psychiatric testimony that their client suffered from psychosis that drove him to attempt the assassination and that substantially impaired his capacity to obey the law. Prosecution witnesses countered that, leading up to the shooting, Hinckley engaged in sophisticated planning, displayed great self-control, and made decisions to delay the crime until the time was right. Such behavior, the prosecutors argued, demonstrated that a mental disorder had not substantially impaired Hinckley's capacity to obey the law. Hinckley's plan was foolish, of course, but he had the capacity to abandon it and chose not to do so, argued the prosecution.

After Hinckley was acquitted on his insanity defense, public outcry led to substantial limiting of the defense in the United States. Some states abolished the volitional prong. Several reduced the burden of proof on insanity from "beyond a reasonable doubt" to "clear and convincing evidence." Others restricted the scope of expert testimony on insanity. A few abolished the defense altogether.

5.4 Intoxication

Intoxication is an excuse only in limited circumstances. The first is the rare case of involuntary intoxication: someone drugs you without your knowledge or consent and you subsequently commit a crime as a result. You are not, in that case, criminally responsible.

The much more common case of voluntary intoxication is a different matter. Consider a defendant who drinks to excess and then commits a crime as a result of being inebriated. Under the MPC, he has no defense unless two conditions hold: (1) the crime requires a mental state of purpose or knowledge with respect to a particular element; and (2) due to his intoxication he fails to achieve that mental state. Suppose our voluntarily drunken man fires a gun into a crowd and kills someone. If, as a result of his intoxication, he did not form the intention to kill someone, then he lacks the mens rea for murder— purpose—and cannot be convicted of that crime. Intoxication has, effectively, served as a defense. However, he has no defense to a manslaughter charge, even if his voluntary intoxication caused him to be unaware that his action exposed others to a substantial and unjustifiable risk. By contrast, a sober person who was unaware of the risk would not be convicted of manslaughter. In this way, voluntary intoxication subjects one to a higher standard of liability, rather than exculpating one.

6. Inchoate offenses

Thus far I have discussed so-called complete offenses, in which every element of the crime exists. But many crimes have corresponding *inchoate offenses*, which constitute incomplete parts of complete offenses. The most familiar inchoate offense is *attempt*, which I shall address at length. The others, which I shall not discuss, are *solicitation* (encouraging someone else to commit a crime)[12] and *conspiracy* (forming an agreement with another person or persons to commit a crime).[13]

6.1 Attempt

An unsuccessful attempt to commit certain crimes constitutes a crime in its own right for which one can be convicted and sentenced. An actor engages in a *completed attempt* if

> he acts with the purpose of achieving a forbidden result, engaging in conduct that he believes will suffice to make the result more likely to occur; or
>
> he acts with the belief that the forbidden result is almost certain to result from his conduct; or
>
> he believes himself to be engaged in forbidden conduct.[14]

A completed attempt is unsuccessful if things do not happen as the actor expected. Wally booby-traps Jonah's house, hoping to kill Jonah. The booby-trap malfunctions, so Wally is guilty of attempted murder, not murder. Attempted murder is one of the most serious felonies, with a maximum sentence of life in prison in some jurisdictions.

An actor makes an *incomplete attempt* if he intends to commit a crime that requires multiple actions in sequence and he takes some of the necessary actions, but not all of them. Merely preparing to commit a crime does not ordinarily constitute an attempt unless it takes one of several specified forms. The MPC lists several of these *substantial steps*, including the following:

> (a) lying in wait, searching for or following the contemplated victim of the crime;
>
>   . . .
>
> (d) unlawful entry of a structure, vehicle or enclosure in which it is contemplated that the crime will be committed;
>
> (e) possession of materials to be employed in the commission of the crime, which are specially designed for such unlawful use or which can serve no lawful purpose of the actor under the circumstances.[15]

> If Bruno follows Norman, intending to assault him, then Bruno has committed an incomplete attempted assault, even if Bruno abandons his plan before catching up to Norman. This is a crime under the MPC, but scholars disagree about whether it should be. One can imagine a consequentialist argument for criminalizing Bruno's conduct. There is no social value to Bruno's conduct and it provides some evidence that Bruno is a dangerous character and probably worth detaining for the sake of protecting others. If we convict Bruno, then perhaps he and other like-minded individuals will be less inclined to act on their violent tendencies in the future. We punish Bruno not because of any harm done, but because we send the right message by doing so.

Some retributivists would also favor punishing incomplete attempts such as Bruno's. Bruno has revealed himself to have bad character, although perhaps not as bad as if he had completed his attempt. He deserves *some* punishment for his character, as revealed by his actions (see Chapter 7, sec. 6 on retributivism).

Other retributivists, however, oppose punishing incomplete attempts. Some of them believe that punishment should be proportional to harm done, in which case they must oppose punishment for unsuccessful attempts in general, whether complete or incomplete. More interesting are retributivists who favor punishing complete attempts, but not incomplete ones. They suggest that actors are not culpable for incomplete attempts. By definition, the actor has not yet done everything necessary to complete the crime. He might change his mind. His intention to commit the crime might be contingent on some conditions that are, in fact, unlikely to obtain. So we cannot really say that the actor has yet exposed anyone to an increased risk of harm until he completes the last act necessary for the crime (Alexander and Ferzan 2009).

6.2 Unsuccessful completed attempts

One important debate, dating back to Plato, concerns whether offenders who cause harm are more culpable than inchoate offenders—those who attempt or culpably risk harm, but cause none. Picture two hired assassins: Jack and Jill. Each fires a rifle at an innocent target, attempting to kill him. Jill hits her target. Jack narrowly misses his, despite his best effort. Is Jill more culpable than Jack? Or consider Bert and Ernie, each of whom recklessly speeds through a red light. Bert's car strikes a pedestrian. Ernie's narrowly misses one. The view that Jill and Bert are more culpable than Jack and Ernie, respectively, is *differential culpability*. Many criminal codes do, in fact, assign lesser penalties to inchoate offenses. Defendants who cause harm are punished more severely than those who merely attempt, or culpably risk, causing harm. This is *differential punishment* (Enoch and Marmor 2007). Criminal law scholars are evenly divided on differential culpability and punishment (Moore 1997).

Jill is a *harm-causer* and Jack is a *failed attempter*. If we take for granted that both are culpable and should be punished, then how might we justify greater punishment for the harm-causer, when the two actors had the same mental state and performed the same basic actions (e.g. firing a rifle at an innocent target with intent to kill)? One argument for differential punishment is as follows:

> (1) If an action, *x*, causes more harm than another action, *y*, then *x* is morally worse than *y*, all things being equal.
> (2) If A's action is morally worse than B's action and A is culpable, then A is more culpable than B, all things being equal.
> (3) The state has a pro tanto moral reason to maintain a criminal code that imposes heavier sentences on more culpable convicts.
> (4) Therefore, the state has a pro tanto moral reason to maintain a criminal code that imposes heavier sentences on culpable convicts who cause more harm.

Premise 1 is quite plausible. If I try to cut off your finger and cut off your whole arm by mistake, then my action is morally worse than if I had cut off only your finger. If I unintentionally, but recklessly, cut off your whole arm, then my action is morally worse than if I had unintentionally cut off only your finger. Cutting off an arm is objectively "more wrong" than cutting off a finger.

Thus, there is a central sense in which causing harm is more wrong than unsuccessfully attempting to cause it. Taken together, premises 1 and 2 entail differential culpability.

One argument against differential culpability is the *control argument*:

> (1) Moral blameworthiness is unfair unless it attaches only to things that we control.
> (2) Actors are not in control of the results of their actions.
> (3) Therefore, there is no (added) moral responsibility for the results of our actions.

Michael Moore (2009) rejects the control argument as equivocating on two different senses of "control." The first premise uses a compatibilist sense of "control," while the second premise uses an incompatibilist sense of "control." The argument is valid only if both premises use the same sense of control. In the incompatibilist sense, however, no one controls anything, so no one is responsible for anything. That cannot be correct. In the compatibilist sense, by contrast, actors *do* control results. Moore asks us to imagine the situation where some defendant D intends to kill victim V, and where D carefully loads his gun, checking all bullets to be sure none are duds; tests the firing mechanism of the pistol; isolates V from all possible help or medical attention; screens off all birds or other objects that could interfere; puts the gun at

V's head, pulls the trigger, and kills him. In this situation, Moore concludes, "D controlled V's death," even though D did not control every possible factor that might have prevented or disrupted V's death.

Study questions

(1) Do crimes always involve a voluntary action?

(2) What is the difference between the mental states of purpose and knowledge? Can you think of cases in which the law should distinguish between them?

(3) Is someone who acts with a negligent state of mind any more culpable than someone who acts nonnegligently? Should the criminal law punish negligence? Should there be any crimes of strict liability?

(4) How does a legal justification differ from a legal excuse?

(5) How should the law treat the use of defensive force against innocent attackers?

(6) Is the necessity defense ever available in a homicide case? Should it be?

(7) What implications do various theories of free will have for the justifiability of the insanity defense?

(8) Does the law currently punish successful attempts more severely than unsuccessful complete attempts? What is the best rational for the current state of the law?

Recommended reading

Alexander, Larry, and Kimberly Kessler Ferzan. 2009. *Crime and Culpability: A Theory of Criminal Law*. Cambridge: Cambridge University Press.

Deigh, John, and David Dolinko, eds. 2011. *Oxford Handbook of Philosophy of Criminal Law*. Oxford: Oxford University Press.

Dressler, Joshua. 2009. *Understanding Criminal Law*. 5th edn. Newark, NJ: LexisNexis Matthew Bender.

Fischer, John Martin, Robert H. Kane, Derk Pereboom, and Manuel Vargas. 2007. *Four Views on Free Will*. Malden, MA: Blackwell.

Fuller, Lon L. 1949. "The Case of the Speluncean Explorers." *Harvard Law Review* 62: 616–45.

Greenawalt, Kent. 1984. "The Perplexing Borders of Justification and Excuse." *Columbia Law Review* 84: 1897–927.

Husak, Douglas N. 1987. *Philosophy of Criminal Law*. Totowa, NJ: Rowman & Littlefield.

Katz, Leo. 2000. "Why the Successful Assassin Is More Wicked Than the Unsuccessful One." *California Law Review* 88: 791–812.

Moore, Michael S. 1997. "The Independent Moral Significance of Wrongdoing." In *Placing Blame*. Oxford: Oxford University Press.

—. 2009. *Causation and Responsibility*. New York: Oxford University Press.

Wasserstrom, Richard A. 1960. "Strict Liability in the Criminal Law." *Stanford Law Review* 12: 731–45.

7

Sentencing and Punishment

Chapter Outline

1. Sentencing

In addition to defining crimes, lawmakers must also specify how the state will deal with convicted criminals. They must create *sentencing schedules* that assign to each type of crime a particular sentence or range of sentences. After conviction, convicts are sentenced by *sentencing authorities* (usually courts), within the bounds of the sentencing schedule. *Sentences*, as I shall use the term, usually include *punishments*, but they can take other forms, such as involuntary commitment to a treatment facility, which is not technically a punishment. Many questions arise about sentencing and punishment. Some of these are as follows:

(1) What is punishment? Which sentences constitute punishments?
(2) A descriptive question: on what basis do lawmakers in actual legal systems design sentencing schedules (i.e. why do they assign to each particular type of crime a particular sentence or range of sentences)?

(3) A prescriptive question: on what basis should lawmakers design sentencing schedules? What reasons should they take into account?

(4) How much latitude should lawmakers grant to sentencing authorities?

(5) On what basis do sentencing authorities in actual legal systems sentence convicts?

(6) On what basis should sentencing authorities sentence convicts? What reasons should they take into account?

(7) Which sentences do convicts in various legal systems actually receive?

(8) Which forms of punishment, if any, is the state morally permitted to impose?

This chapter addresses questions 1, 3, 6, and 8.

2. Defining punishment

What is punishment? In this book, we are interested in punishment under law, although punishment takes place not just in legal systems, but in families, private associations, schools, churches, workplaces, and so on. For our purposes we can understand the "central case" of punishment in terms of these five elements:

(1) It involves pain or other consequences normally considered unpleasant.

(2) It is imposed because of a legal offense.

(3) It is imposed upon an actual or supposed offender because of his offense.

(4) It is intentionally administered by human beings other than the offender.

(5) It is imposed and administered by agents of the legal system against which the offense was committed.[1]

Consider each of these elements in turn. Regarding the first element: suppose I force you to listen to a Bach concerto. This does not ordinarily constitute a punishment, even if you happen to loathe Bach. However, if I know that you detest Bach, and the other elements are present, then perhaps this would constitute a punishment, albeit an unusual one. States do not normally tailor punishments to the convict's idiosyncratic dislikes.

Regarding the second element, suppose a police officer amuses himself by twisting your arm. Painful as this is, he has not punished you, as he did not do it because of a legal offense.

The third element—limiting punishment to the offender himself—is a relatively modern idea. In past centuries, states would sometimes punish family members of an offender, or even complete strangers as *scapegoats*. At common law, the punishment for committing suicide was forfeiture of the man's estate to the crown, which severely burdened his family. Today, however, states do not openly punish one person for the crimes of another. If a state were to do so, we might continue to claim that the individual was "punished," but we would call it unjust. Note, however, that various forms of vicarious liability survive in modern legal systems. If two or more people conspire in a criminal enterprise, then each can be punished for offenses of the other. A principal (e.g. an employer) is punished for crimes that he directs an agent (e.g. an employee) to commit. Some jurisdictions punish parents for crimes committed by their minor children. Parents are often liable for children's torts. Employers are liable for civil wrongs committed by employees. The two latter cases are not punishments, however.

Regarding the fourth element, some people do, in fact, "punish themselves." In the Italian town of Guardia Sanframondi, on the "Day of Blood," hundreds of Christian men voluntarily atone for their sins by beating their chests and striking their backs with spiked metal instruments. This is not, of course, punishment under law.

Finally, as to the fifth element, imagine a Frenchman who commits a crime under French law on French soil. He flees to Japan, where a Japanese court convicts and sentences him to prison for his French crime. Perhaps, we should say that Japan "punishes" him, but without legal authority. Philosophers of law are primarily interested in legally authorized punishment, so we can ignore such cases. (Offenses under international law are a different matter; see Chapter 10.)

In the English-speaking world, punishment is the province of the criminal law, with one major qualification: "punitive" damages are awarded in certain civil lawsuits. Although civil damages serve a primarily compensatory purpose, punitive damages are understood to serve an additional, punitive purpose within civil proceedings.

Some writers draw further distinctions. For example, Joel Feinberg (1970) insists that the state only punishes if it expresses moral disapproval. Otherwise, he claims, it merely exacts a *penalty*. Fines for parking violations and minor regulatory infractions, for example, are mere penalties, not punishments, on Feinberg's view. There may be differences in the justifications that can be given for penalties, as opposed to punishments.

3. Types of sentence

Human beings have concocted a wide range of punishments over the centuries. These include banishment, execution, and myriad corporal punishments.

Modern states still banish foreign nationals as punishment, although few banish their own citizens. Corporal punishment is still used in a few developed nations, such as Singapore, and in some developing nations. Over two-thirds of nations have abolished capital punishment, but it is still used in the United States, Japan, China, Saudi Arabia, Iran, and others.

In the modern world, the most familiar punishment is incarceration. Most philosophical work on punishment assumes, implicitly, that incarceration is the standard punishment for serious crimes. Modern states also impose criminal fines and withdraw legal privileges such as one's license to drive a car or to practice a profession. Almost any punishment involves a measure of public humiliation and a few modern penalties aim precisely at such humiliation. Many convicts receive probation as part of their sentence. Probation should probably be seen as a conditional punishment or heightened threat of punishment.

Sentences are not limited to punishments, but may include various forms of rehabilitation, such as medical or psychiatric treatment, treatment for substance abuse, or educational programs. Writers often refer to "rehabilitation" as a reason for punishment. Some such statements reflect the idea that traditional incarceration itself can serve rehabilitative purposes, in which case the writer sees the sentence as a punishment with a rehabilitative purpose. More often, however, proponents of rehabilitation believe that convicts should receive treatment and/or educational programs instead of incarceration or in conjunction with it, in which case rehabilitation is best seen not as a goal of punishment, but as an alternative or supplement to it.

In what follows, I shall distinguish between lawmakers who establish sentencing schedules (legislators and executives), sentencing authorities who sentence convicts (judges or juries), and other authorities who actually carry out sentences (e.g. corrections and parole officers). Philosophical attention overwhelmingly concentrates on lawmakers and sentencing authorities, as I will.

4. Reasons to sentence

In Chapter 3, I discussed theories of criminalization. Let us suppose that the law has defined a set of crimes, specifying forbidden acts, relevant mental states, defenses, and so on. Take the crime of theft, defined in the United Kingdom as follows: "A person is guilty of theft, if he dishonestly appropriates property belonging to another with the intention of permanently depriving the other of it."[2]

Now the lawmakers' job is to design a sentencing schedule for theft. Several philosophical questions arise. First, what moral constraints apply to lawmakers as they design sentencing schedules? Secondly, subject to those constraints, what reasons do lawmakers have to establish sentences for theft? In other words, what is the *justifying aim* of a sentencing scheme for theft? Third, what sentence range should lawmakers establish for theft?

4.1 Incapacitation

One reason for establishing and using a sentencing scheme is simple: *incapacitation*. Incarcerated thieves cannot offend against anyone on the outside for the duration of their imprisonment.[3] If incapacitation prevents a convict from harming someone, then that is a reason to incapacitate him.

The fact that someone has committed a crime is, in many cases, a predictor of future criminal activity. Someone who steals a car for profit is likely to do so again. But evidence of criminality can take other forms. A psychotherapist may predict that her patient, who has committed no crimes to date, is likely to commit crimes in the future. Social scientists may predict that a member of certain social classes, family backgrounds, races, or religions is more likely to offend than others, even before a first offense. Lawmakers who see incapacitation as an important value might propose to preemptively and involuntarily incapacitate such "probable offenders." This could involve making an exception to the act requirement of criminal law (see Chapter 6, sec. 2) for specified classes of probable offenders. Alternatively, lawmakers could handle probable offenders outside the criminal justice system.

Modern Western legal systems largely abstain from preemptive, involuntary incapacitation. Most commentators strenuously object to it. The simplest objection is that any such policy will yield too many false positives: we cannot identify probable offenders with sufficient accuracy. In response, a defender of preemptive incarceration might observe that all criminal justice systems mistakenly incarcerate a certain number of innocents. How, she might ask, does her critic define "too many" false positives (Laudan 2011)? But most writers believe that our technologies for identifying probable offenders are too imperfect to support even the most limited policy of preemptive incarceration.

Today's technological limitations do not, however, foreclose philosophical questions. What if, in the future, we are able to predict criminality with greater confidence than we can today? This is the subject of Steven Spielberg's film, *Minority Report*.[4] Consider a future lawmaker who sees incapacitation as the only value relevant to sentencing. If she had sufficient confidence in the ability of experts to identify probable offenders, then she would see no reason, in principle, not to institute preemptive incarceration. Many writers, however, oppose preemptive incapacitation in principle. They deny, in other words, that incapacitation is the only value relevant to sentencing. They accept, as an independent moral constraint on sentencing, the

Legal Guilt Requirement
The state must not sentence anyone who has committed no crime.

Lawmakers could circumvent this requirement by defining as a crime the mere condition of being psychologically disposed, in the future, to commit a crime, but this would violate the more fundamental requirement that a crime involve either an act or a failure to act (see Chapter 6, sec. 2).

4.2 Deterrence

The Legal Guilt Requirement plays a large role in punishment theory, especially in connection with another reason for sentencing: *deterrence*. As is incapacitation, deterrence is a means of crime control. The idea is that lawmakers can deter prospective criminals by threatening to punish them. Of course, the threats are effective only if prospective criminals find them credible, and the threats are credible only if actual offenders are, in fact, punished. So lawmakers undertake to punish actual offenders in order to deter prospective offenders.

Deterrence raises several important questions. First, are prospective criminals actually deterred by threatened sanctions? Secondly, which sanctions, if any, are sufficiently effective to be justified as deterrents? Third, is deterrence a morally permissible reason to punish?

The first question is empirical. A sentencing scheme only deters if the sentences are sufficiently unpleasant and prospective offenders are sufficiently rational, informed, and self-interested. One who actually attempts a crime was, by definition, not deterred by whatever sanctions the state threatened. Perhaps, more severe sanctions would have deterred her, but crimes are attempted even when the known penalty is torture unto death. No punishment scheme can eliminate crime. Punishment does, however, reduce crime. If the sentence for shoplifting were reduced to a one-penny fine, then shoplifting would increase dramatically. The interesting empirical question is: what is the marginal deterrent effect of a unit of punishment for a particular crime in a particular society?

The second and third questions have both empirical and moral components. A sanction is unjustified as a deterrent if it has bad effects that are too great relative to its deterrent effect. A five-year prison term for public indecency might virtually eliminate this offense, but the public benefit would not justify the suffering of the occasional drunken offender languishing in prison.

Writers often treat deterrence and incapacitation as the main social benefits of punishment, but there are others. Punishment can give pleasure to crime victims and their affiliates (friends and family members). It can relieve their emotional distress. It can reduce vigilantism, reinforce societal bonds, and confirm the legitimacy of the state. These social benefits of punishment have something in common: they represent relatively *external* reasons for punishment. They have a relatively remote connection to the criminal herself and the nature of her crime, in contrast to relatively *internal* punishment values, which are more closely connected to the criminal and her crime. In the eighteenth and early nineteenth centuries, philosophers of punishment such as Immanuel Kant and G. W. F. Hegel emphasized internal values. In the nineteenth century, British philosophers such as Jeremy Bentham and John Stuart Mill emphasized external values. Over the course of the twentieth century, however, Anglophone philosophers increasingly reintroduced internal values. Many concluded that external reasons are not the only punishment values—that the state is morally constrained by internal values in its punishment policies. Some even concluded that it is morally impermissible to punish for external reasons. Here is a basic argument for internal punishment values:

(1) If a state acts only on external reasons, then it will sometimes punish innocent people.
(2) Punishing innocent people is unjust.
(3) Therefore, it is unjust for states to act only on external reasons.

The following thought experiment depicts a state that acts only on external reasons and punishes innocents as a result:

> A recent murder has attracted great attention from the city's criminal underground. They regard it as a test case of the criminal justice system. If the murderer is not brought to justice, then criminals in the city will conclude that law enforcement is incompetent. More murders will result. Victor has been charged with the murder. However, the prosecutor has just discovered evidence that exculpates Victor. The prosecutor can easily destroy the evidence without fear of discovery and win a conviction of Victor with a life sentence. Because the prosecutor considers deterrence to be the only punishment value, he does so.

Similar scenarios can be constructed using any external reason for punishment, such as preventing vigilantism or giving people pleasure. The point is that, if the state considers only external reasons, then the innocent might be punished. This violates the Legal Guilt Requirement.

Philosophers disagree about the proper lesson to draw from these hypothetical scenarios. Some consequentialists (see Chapter 3, sec. 2) abandon the Legal Guilt Requirement (Smart 1990), but most take a different path. Some observe that the scenario is unrealistic and insist that there could never really be conclusive external reasons to punish innocents. Their critics respond that the hypothetical need not be realistic in order to discredit externalist theories of punishment. The fact that these theories could, in principle, conflict with the Legal Guilt Requirement is enough to refute them, according to the critics. This is itself a controversial claim.

5. Hybrid theory

One way to retain the Legal Guilt Requirement is to assign different principles to the legislative, executive, and judicial stages of the sentencing process. Consider the following position:

Hybrid Theory 1
(1) It is permissible for legislators to draft laws for external reasons.
(2) The Legal Guilt Requirement applies to police officers, prosecutors, and judges.

This position, a type of *hybrid theory*, allows legislators to aim at maximizing social welfare, using deterrence and/or incapacitation. The Legal Guilt Requirement protects everyone from framing.

Because the hybrid theory combines two different principles, one might wonder whether the two have a common moral foundation, and whether the two are even compatible. Some theorists argue that both principles can, in fact, be supported by a version of consequentialism—*indirect consequentialism* (see Chapter 3, sec. 2.2.4). Consider the following principle:

> An act is wrong if and only if it is forbidden by the code of rules whose internalization by the overwhelming majority of everyone everywhere in each new generation has maximum expected value in terms of well-being. (Hooker 2000: 32)

Some indirect consequentialists argue that it maximizes social welfare to include the Legal Guilt Requirement in our code of rules for police officers, prosecutors, and judges. Consider a rule that permits police officers to frame suspects whenever they believe that doing so will increase social welfare. What would happen if most police officers followed such a rule? One effect might be a reduction in deterrence. Punishing people does not work as a deterrent unless would-be criminals believe that committing a crime increases one's chance of being punished. If would-be criminals come to suspect (correctly or not) that the convicts in prison are just unlucky victims, not actual offenders, then the deterrent effect of punishment is lost.

In addition, if police officers frequently framed people, it might provoke widespread anxiety. Each citizen would worry that he would be the next victim. In addition to suffering from emotional distress, people might waste time and effort avoiding contact with police. Citizens might also lose respect for the criminal justice system. For all these reasons, following the framing rule would probably not maximize social welfare. If it would not, then indirect consequentialism would support hybrid theory.

Although it forbids framing, the hybrid theory does not preclude other injustices. Hybrid theory sets no limits on the severity of sentences. If legislators conclude that executing reckless drivers maximizes social welfare, then the theory allows such a law to be enacted and enforced. The Legal Guilt Requirement requires only that individuals be convicted of a crime before being punished. The punishment need not fit the crime.

The prospect of sentences that are grossly disproportionate to what the convict deserves is not as disturbing as the prospect of framing someone who is completely innocent, but it is still disturbing. In order to rule out such disproportions, we need a principle that applies to legislators:

Minimal Retributivism
The state must not punish anyone in excess of what he deserves as a result of his individual conduct and character.

Minimal retributivism forbids legislators to assign disproportionate penalties to crimes. A common argument for minimal retributivism as a nonderivative principle appeals to our moral intuitions about particular cases. When a European hears about men in Iran being sentenced to whipping for drinking alcohol, he is inclined to condemn the sentence as excessive. Combining our principles yields:

Hybrid Theory 2
(1) It is permissible for legislators to draft laws for external reasons, subject to minimal retributivism.
(2) The Legal Guilt Requirement applies to police officers, prosecutors, and judges.

These principles jointly preclude disproportionate punishment, including framing, but they do not require punishment at all. They allow a prosecutor to drop charges against a defendant who has committed a serious crime and deserves to be punished, if the prosecutor believes that prosecution would do more harm than good. American prosecutors do this when they offer plea bargains, but some observers question the justice of this practice (Lippke 2008).

One might also wonder whether minimal retributivism can be derived from indirect consequentialism. An indirect consequentialist might argue that enacting disproportionate penalty schedules does not, in fact, maximize social welfare. It might undermine respect for the legal system, but this is less plausible than the claim that a widespread practice of framing would have such effects. In any case, there is a more basic point to be made. Regardless of whether disproportionate penalties maximize social welfare in the real world, many people have a strong conviction that disproportionate penalties are wrong, and would be wrong even in a hypothetical world in which they maximized social welfare. This leads them to characterize minimal retributivism as fundamentally backward-looking, rather than forward-looking. Minimal retributivism is either derived from a more basic backward-looking principle or it simply stands on its own as a principle that is both nonderivative and backward-looking (Moore 1987). Both positions are represented in the literature.

Hybrid Theory 2 condemns all disproportionate punishment, including any punishment of innocents. But some theorists remain dissatisfied with it for two main reasons. First, the theory allows the state to punish convicts according to sentencing schedules that lawmakers drafted for extrinsic reasons, such as deterrence and incapacitation. Some theorists, following Kant (see Chapter 3, sec. 2.2), object that punishing someone for extrinsic reasons is wrong, even if you punish her no more severely than she deserves. Here is the basic Kantian argument:

(1) Everyone (including the state) is morally required to treat every rational agent as an *end-in-himself*, never merely as a means.
(2) Punishing a rational agent for the sake of deterring others from criminal activity, or for the sake of incapacitating him, treats him merely as a means, not as an end-in-himself.
(3) Therefore, the state is morally forbidden to punish a rational agent for the sake of deterring others from criminal activity, or for the sake of incapacitating him.

The conclusion of this argument leads right to the second reason for dissatisfaction with Hybrid Theory 2. If, as the argument concludes, the state is morally forbidden to punish for extrinsic reasons, then we have two options. One option is to conclude that the state must not punish at all. A few writers have, in fact, defended abolishing penal institutions altogether (Boonin 2008; Golash 2005; Barnett 1977). But most wish to defend state punishment, so they need to find a different rationale if they accept the Kantian argument.

Kant himself believed that the state was morally permitted to punish criminals, provided that it did so exclusively for the purpose of giving the criminal his just deserts. This rationale is known as *retribution*.

6. Retribution

Both incapacitation and deterrence are *instrumental* or forward-looking reasons for punishment. The time has come to discuss a noninstrumental, backward-looking reason for punishment: retribution. Someone who believes that retribution constitutes a reason to punish is a *retributivist*. Retributivists, by definition, believe that penalties must be a function of what the convict deserves as a moral matter: more deserving convicts should receive more severe penalties; less deserving convicts, less severe penalties; innocent individuals, no penalty at all.

Retributivism is both easily understood and easily misunderstood. Before examining what it is, it helps to discuss what it is not. People often identify retributivism with the familiar Old Testament principle, "an eye for an eye," also known as *lex talionis* (Exodus 21.24). *Lex talionis* suggests a retributive principle, but it is a particular crude one that retributivists today reject. I shall discuss the flaws of *lex talionis* below.

Retributivists today are quick to emphasize that retribution is not the same as vengeance. The title character in Euripides' play, *Madea*, takes vengeance on her husband for abandoning her by killing his new fiancée. She is motivated by anger and retaliates without regard to proportionality or desert. By contrast, retributivists understand retribution as a form of justice, to be meted out by an impartial third party. Retributivists do not justify punishment as a means of satisfying the victim's desires or anyone else's. Nor do they justify it as a bulwark against acts of vigilantism. They justify punishment simply as a way of giving the guilty what they deserve, no more and no less.

However, retributivists disagree with one another about how to measure desert. Historically, they hold that desert is a function of three and only three variables. The first is the actor's actions: how did she move her body (or not move it) and under what circumstances? Did she pour arsenic into someone's teacup, sign someone else's name on a check, or enter someone's hotel room without his permission?

The second variable concerns the consequences of the actions: did anyone suffer harm to person or property as a result? Some theorists believe that wrongdoers whose acts cause harm deserve to suffer because of those results and deserve more suffering if they succeed in their attempt than if they fail (see Chapter 6, sec. 6.2).

The third variable is the actor's mental state. Did she know that the liquid might be arsenic, rather than vanilla syrup, when she poured it into the teacup? Did she intend harm? Did she act under duress? Was she mentally competent at the time?

6.1 Lex talionis and harm

There are many philosophical issues surrounding each of these three variables. In this section, I shall examine a controversy concerning the second variable—harm. Early retributivists endorsed *lex talionis*. In biblical times, *lex talionis* was understood merely as a limitation on retribution. The message was: if someone injures you, then you may retaliate, but do not harm him more than he harmed you. Over the centuries, however, *lex talionis* came to be understood not merely as a limitation on private retribution, but as a general principle of retributive justice, applicable to rules of law and to particular sentences.

There are various ways of understanding *lex talionis*. On one reading, the principle merely expresses retributivism in a colorful way. It suggests that punishments may properly be proportioned to the wrongdoer's desert and must not be disproportionate. Of greater interest to us, however, is *lex talionis* understood as theory of desert itself. It would be uncharitable to read it literally, as applying only to lost eyeballs. At least we should read it as applying to all physical attacks. If I pull your hair, then I deserve to have my hair pulled; if I break your arm, then I deserve to have my arm broken; if I kill you, then I deserve to be killed.

Lex talionis stands for the principle that desert is, at least in part, a function of harm done: the more harm you cause, the more punishment you deserve. There are different ways of understanding this idea, too. One could, for example, hold that harm to an identifiable victim is necessary for desert, in which case no one could deserve punishment for actions without identifiable victims. Alternatively, one could deny that harm is necessary for desert and hold that harm, when present, simply increases deserved punishment.

However one understands *lex talionis*, two observations are appropriate. First, if we wish to base laws on *lex talionis*, then we need a *prelegal* theory of harm. We cannot, for example, claim that lawbreaking itself is the relevant harm for the purpose of applying the principle. Instead, we must define harm in terms of a theory of the good, referencing human welfare or interests (see Chapter 3, sec. 2.1).

Another question is whether the punishment should actually mimic the harm done. Some states execute murderers, although none executes everyone convicted of criminal homicide. No jurisdiction sentences rapists to be raped, although this could be arranged. The man who deliberately splashed sulfuric acid in Katie Piper's face in 2008 could be sentenced to have acid splashed in his face. Few retributivists today support such punishments, although some outliers argue that criminals who inflict physical pain or injury should be sentenced to comparably severe pain or injury (i.e. torture; see Kershnar 2011). But how should we punish someone who kidnaps a child and confines her (humanely) for two months? Confining the kidnapper for two months hardly seems adequate.

A complementary question about *lex talionis* concerns its implications for crimes that cause little or no harm. Should someone who steals a $500 necklace be punished with a mere fine of $500 (after returning the necklace)? And what about inchoate offenses such as attempt, solicitation, and conspiracy (see Chapter 6, sec. 6)? No retributivist today believes that those who unsuccessfully attempt to commit serious crimes should avoid punishment altogether. A retributivist who accepts *lex talionis* must therefore read it as not entailing that harm is necessary for deserved punishment. Her position might be that a guilty mind alone suffices for desert and that harm adds to it. But state of mind and severity of harm are difficult factors to quantify. Losing an arm is worse than losing a finger, but how much worse? Someone who drives over your cat intentionally deserves more punishment than one who does so recklessly, but how much more? Some theorists doubt that we can quantify these factors precisely enough to design usable penalty schedules.

6.2 Unfair advantage

For the reasons just examined, some retributivists completely abandon *lex talionis*, denying that harm is even relevant to desert and proposing alternative desert bases. A prominent nonharm-based version of retributivism is grounded upon the principle of *fair play* (Morris 1976; Hart 1955). Begin with the observation that my life would be easier and more rewarding if I, alone, could commit crimes without consequences. I would possess an awesome power. I could take and use the property of others at will. People would obey me and cater to my needs. I could eliminate competitors and retaliate against anyone whom I disliked. Each of us would benefit greatly from being able to commit crimes without consequences while others obeyed the law. However, the law asks us to obey—to bear the "burdens of self-restraint"—and it gives us reasonable assurance that others will do likewise. And we do so: law-abiding individuals bear the burdens of self-restraint. Therefore, the criminal law can be viewed as establishing a cooperative system encompassing everyone in its jurisdiction. Law-abiding individuals are cooperators. When someone commits a crime, she partially renounces the burdens of self-restraint. She makes an unjustified exception of herself, taking advantage of the rest of us who obey the law, thereby violating the fair-play principle. If she goes unpunished, then she will have gotten away with doing less than others have done. She will have benefited at our expense (see Chapter 4, sec. 1.3).

The purpose of criminal punishment, on this theory, is to effectively "take back" the advantage over the rest of us that the criminal unfairly gains when she renounces the burdens of self-restraint. This suggests a theory of desert very different from *lex talionis*. Instead of proportioning punishment to the degree of harm caused, unfair-advantage theories proportion it to the benefit gained by the criminal. It is also important to note that the relevant benefit never takes physical or pecuniary form. A shoplifter might acquire a blouse, but the blouse is not the relevant benefit for the purpose of this theory. If it were, then unfair-advantage theory would recommend that the state punish her simply by taking back the blouse. Of course, the shoplifter is legally required to return the blouse (or compensate the merchant). But this is no punishment at all. The benefit to the shoplifter is the intangible value of having gotten to break a rule that the rest of us obey.

So unfair-advantage theories do not proportion punishment either to harm caused or to tangible benefits received by the criminal. This feature nicely accommodates existing criminal law. Many felonies cause no harm. Many do not benefit the criminal in any tangible way. Consider an unsuccessful attempted murder. It harms no one and does not benefit the criminal, but it is a serious felony. Other inchoate offenses—solicitation and conspiracy—are likewise harmless (see Chapter 6, sec. 6). They do not benefit the criminal, either, absent a successfully completed crime. Traditional versions of retributivism have difficulty justifying punishment for such crimes. Therefore, retributivists who support the current policy of punishing inchoate offenses should consider unfair-advantage theories a promising alternative to *lex talionis*.

The most ambitious unfair-advantage theorists argue that their theory can help to justify specific penalty schedules. This requires that we first rank different types of crime based on the degree of unfair advantage associated with each. Suppose we conclude that committing manslaughter gives one a greater unfair advantage than vandalism does. In that case, the theory would recommend a heavier penalty for manslaughter than for vandalism. But how might we estimate relative degrees of unfair advantage? Michael Davis (1992) proposes a thought experiment designed to extract this information. He asks readers to imagine a set of licenses, each of which authorizes its owner to commit a specific crime once without consequences. There are murder licenses, shoplifting licenses, reckless driving licenses, and so on. The value of such a license would depend on what it licensed one to do. A murder license, for example, would give its owner the fearsome power of life and death. People would strive to stay in your good graces if they knew that you could murder them with impunity. A shoplifting license has much less value, by contrast, although it has some. In other words, murder takes more unfair advantage of the public at large than shoplifting does. Again, the point is not that criminals take advantage of their victims. They do so, but that is not the point for unfair-advantage theory. The point, rather, is that they take advantage of the rest of us who would like to break the law but instead obey. Unfair-advantage theorists recommend ranking crimes from most to least severe, based on the price that we imagine the corresponding licenses would command in an efficient market. The crime type with the most expensive license should be assigned the most severe penalty that we are prepared to inflict (death, perhaps, or life in prison without parole). The next most expensive license gets the next most severe penalty, and so on until we arrive at the cheapest license and the lightest penalty that is worth the bother (a small fine, perhaps).

Unfair-advantage theory boasts an impressive elegance and generality. It promises to justify punishing the many crimes that cause no harm and/or garner no tangible benefit for the criminal. It accommodates a wider range of crimes than earlier versions of retributivism. There are, however, serious challenges that the theory must overcome. One objection is that it depends on a reliable rank-ordering of crimes. How are we supposed to determine which licenses would command the highest prices? Davis recommends a license auction, but he envisions this as a thought experiment. It seems likely that different thinkers will arrive at different rankings when they run the experiment in their minds.

6.3 Communicative theories

Recent years have seen theories of punishment emerge that cannot be neatly classified as either consequentialist or retributivist. We have already examined hybrid theories that combine these elements. *Communicative* theories of punishment do so as well. The leading defender of communicative theories is an English philosopher, Antony Duff. In Duff's words:

> Criminal punishment should communicate to offenders the censure they deserve for their crimes and should aim through that communicative process to persuade them to repent those crimes, to try to reform themselves, and thus to reconcile themselves with those whom they wronged. (2001: xvii)

Duff's theory is based on a liberal-communitarian political philosophy. He aims to justify criminal punishment in terms of the values of a liberal political community, including freedom, autonomy, privacy, pluralism, and mutual regard. Punishment is problematic for liberals because it involves forcible exclusion of individuals from the community (at least when incarceration is used). It divides us into law-abiding citizens and criminals. Duff argues that a liberal community cannot justly incarcerate convicts purely for the purposes of incapacitation or deterrence. To this extent, Duff endorses minimal retributivism, and then some. Convicts, he believes, should be punished in proportion to their desert.

The just purpose of incarceration, according to Duff, is to address convicts as rational agents—to persuade them. The criminal law must speak to each criminal as a member of the normative community, aiming to persuade her to do what is right because she sees it to be right. Communication necessarily involves expression, but communicative theories are distinct from expressive theories (Feinberg 1970). On expressive theories, the state simply expresses our collective disapproval of the convict's behavior, without any intention of communicating with him. On communicative theories, by contrast, "reaching" the convict is the whole point.

Critics might wonder how communicative theories, which aim at goals such as repentance, reform, and reconciliation, avoid being consequentialist. The answer is that communicative theories are not consequentialist because they do not support imposing sentences as "contingently efficient means to the independently identifiable end of crime-prevention" (Duff 2001: 80). Whereas consequentialist theories punish criminals for instrumental reasons, communication serves aims to which it is internally, not instrumentally, related.

What methods of punishment do communicative theories permit and recommend? Critics object that communicative theories cannot accept the major method of punishment used in the civilized world today: incarceration. If the purpose of punishment is, indeed, communication, then it would seem that the state should use purely verbal or symbolic methods. For example, the state could require (or perhaps just request) that convicts listen to a lecture presenting all the reasons not to commit crimes. This is a far cry from how real states punish criminals. Duff argues that it is, indeed, permissible and often necessary for the state to subject the convict to "harsh treatment." Harsh treatment makes the convict's apology to the community more likely and his repentance more genuine. Penalties must not exceed desert and must be humane, but this is compatible with harsh treatment, at least in principle. Duff admits, however, that punishment as practiced in modern penal systems is difficult to justify in communicative terms and may require extensive reform for the sake of justice. He supports sentences that involve mediation between criminals and their victims and that aim to keep convicts in their communities.

A challenge for communicative theories is the case of an offender who repeatedly commits violent crimes over many years. At some point, should the state not conclude that its communicative efforts have failed? Is it unjust for the state to incapacitate the incorrigible repeat offender at that point? These are difficult questions for communicative theorists to answer. It remains to be seen if their position has the resources to do so.

7. Defensive theories

Another recent development in punishment theory is the rise of *defensive* or *threat-based* theories (Montague 1995; Farrell 1990; Quinn 1985). Their premise is that individuals have a moral right (probably a natural right) to use force or threats of force against unjustified aggressors for the purpose of defending themselves or others. Defensive theorists argue that, if individuals have this right to threaten aggressors, then groups of individuals—communities—have a collective right to threaten anyone who threatens a community member. The next step in the argument is that the right to threaten entails a right to follow through on the threat. Otherwise, threats would be ineffective. Therefore, if a society has a moral right to threaten would-be aggressors, then it has a right to carry out the threat. The state makes and carries outs the threat on behalf of the community.

Defensive theories, like communicative theories, cannot be neatly classified as either consequentialist or retributivist, but incorporate elements of each. As does retributivism, defensive theories forbid the punishment of innocents. As does consequentialism, defensive theories justify punishment in terms of the value of protecting the innocent from criminal aggression. But defensive theories try to avoid objections to both consequentialism and retributivism. They incorporate these elements in a natural way, rather than awkwardly combining them in a hybrid theory.

Consequentialists justify punishment in terms of deterrence and incapacitation, but we have already seen the moral objections that arise. Defensive theories avoid such objections. Whereas a consequentialist justifies after-the-fact punishment in terms of our need to discourage *future* offenders, which is morally suspect, a defensive theorist justifies it as an exercise of our right to defend ourselves against the very crime that was committed.

A consequentialist might object that punishing someone after he has committed a crime serves no purpose if not to prevent future crimes. Punishment cannot change the past and undo the crime. So why bother to spend the money and inflict the unpleasantness? The defensive theorist responds that, if there is a societal right to threaten someone with incarceration for acting on an intention to violate the rights of others, then society has the right to incarcerate him after he acts on that intention by attempting (successfully or not) to violate rights.

Someone might object that the use of force as punishment differs in a basic way from defensive uses of force. The defensive use of force is justified only if the unjustified aggression has not yet occurred. Punishment, by contrast, always takes place after the crime. It is morally permissible for Lara to threaten Randy with a rifle if she has no other realistic way to prevent Randy from breaking Moe's arm. If Randy ignores her threat, then she is morally permitted to shoot him in the chest so as to prevent him from breaking Moe's arm. But what if Randy ignores her threat, breaks Moe's arm, and runs away, whereupon Randy falls into a deep hole from which he cannot escape. With Randy thus incapacitated, Lara is not now permitted to shoot him so as to follow through on her earlier threat. Likewise, it would seem that the state is not permitted to punish convicts once they pose no threat to the original victim. To rebut this objection, defensive theorists argue that state actors are not engaged in piecemeal defensive acts. Rather, the state maintains a system of punishment that defines roles with certain moral prerogatives. Following through on threats is necessary for the sake of maintaining a credible system of threats, insists the defensive theorist. But this makes defensive theory sound like a consequentialist theory, after all.

Retributivist critics of defensive theories also express concerns about proportionality. Defensive theories seem to set no limit on the severity of punishment. As long as the state warns everyone that shoplifters will be executed, for example, defensive theories seem to approve of such sentences. The state is said to have the right to threaten and the right to follow through on its threats. Defensive theorists must either accept the execution of shoplifters, or provide an independent principle for limiting punishment. If the limiting principle is, itself, retributivist, then defensive theories become hybrid theories.

A final question for defensive theories is whether they can justify criminalizing much of what modern systems criminalize. Defensive theories require both harm and fault for punishment. As noted (sec. 6), many serious crimes do not even threaten anyone with harm. Some regulations aim at maintaining fairness or preventing intrinsically immoral conduct. Could a defensive theorist justify punishing violators of such laws?

8. Capital punishment

Although the death penalty has been abolished in most of the world, it is vigorously debated in the United States. It raises all of the philosophical issues of punishment in general, and then some. For many centuries, capital punishment was used for a wide range of crimes, but in this century its use has been narrowly restricted to the most serious crimes, such as the rape of children, treason, and certain murders. The central philosophical question is whether, given current institutions and social conditions, a death sentence is ever morally permissible for premeditated murder. *Retentionists* believe that it is. *Abolitionists* disagree.

8.1 Retributivist arguments for retention

I have already discussed the flaws in *lex talionis* (sec. 6), but capital punishment is one case in which the principle has some plausibility. It seems just to kill someone who has killed. Retributivist retentionists argue that someone who does not respect the lives of others has waived his own right to life and deserves to die. Executing him is, at least, morally permissible. Some retributivists make the stronger claim that nothing short of execution suffices to give killers what they deserve.

One objection to the use of *lex talionis* by retentionists is that their use of the principle is inconsistent. They do not favor punishing crimes other than homicide in accordance with *lex talionis*: maiming those who maim; stealing from those who steal; raping those who rape; to say nothing of "attempting to kill" those who attempt to kill, which is just silly. Retentionists can respond that *lex talionis* is only appropriate to crimes that cause harm, as homicide does.

They then face two other objections. First, all homicides cause death, but some are not criminal at all. Even within criminal homicides, some are more culpable than others. No one favors executing everyone who commits criminal homicide. That would include a mother who recklessly and inadvertently drives over her own child, killing him. She is guilty of vehicular manslaughter, but no one thinks she should be executed. Retentionists must qualify *lex talionis* to cover, perhaps, only murders, not all criminal homicides.

Most retributivist retentionists today reject *lex talionis*. They argue, instead, that execution is a proportionate punishment for the worst murders. Some emphasize the expressive function of punishment and suggest that execution uniquely expresses to the convict and the public at large the condemnation we feel for murderers.

8.2 Consequentialist arguments for retention

A consequentialist supports capital punishment only if she believes that it has more good effects than bad. There are reasons for retention that almost all consequentialists accept. Knowing that murderers have been and will be executed makes some people happy. Some feel safer knowing that their state has capital punishment. But knowing that their state executes murderers makes other people unhappy, so these considerations do not amount to a solid consequentialist argument for either position.

One reason for retention that all consequentialists accept is incapacitation. Execution completely incapacitates the convict: he can commit no more crimes. Even a convict who is imprisoned for life can commit crimes against his fellow inmates and prison employees. Executing murderers might be the only way to prevent them from committing more crimes in prison.

The threat of death might also be the most effective way to *deter* inmates from killing, although there is no evidence that the threat of execution actually deters them. However, general deterrence of violent crime—inside prisons as well as outside—is the most important consequentialist argument for retention. The question is whether maintaining capital punishment as a policy deters more effectively than would the next most severe penalty available—typically assumed to be life in prison without the possibility of parole. This is a *marginal deterrent effect*. Consequentialist retentionists argue that capital punishment has such an effect. Consequentialists who deny marginal deterrence usually favor abolition because execution has some very bad effects (on the convict and any loved ones) and they believe that nothing less than protecting others from violence can outweigh such bad effects.

Whether capital punishment deters violent crime turns out to be an extremely difficult question to answer. It is not a philosophical question, but an empirical one, although careful reflection is required to evaluate various empirical answers that researchers offer. It is sometimes observed that inmates on death row overwhelmingly try to avoid execution, which strongly suggests that they prefer life in prison to death. Does this fact suggest marginal deterrence? Not necessarily. The question is whether anyone who commits a capital crime, when the threatened punishment is life in prison without parole, would have abstained had the death penalty been in place. Many abolitionists argue that this is unlikely because life in prison without parole is already a terrible punishment. Anyone who would risk life in prison to commit murder, they claim, would probably risk the death penalty as well, so there is no marginal deterrence.

Social scientists have extensively studied the deterrent effect of capital punishment, but have not reached consensus. Some studies compare the murder rate in a state without capital punishment to the rate in an otherwise similar state that has capital punishment. There is no consistent pattern of lower murder rates in states with the death penalty. Other studies look for correlations over time between fluctuations in the murder rate and the execution rate. Others look at the murder rate in death penalty states during the period 1972–6, when states stopped performing executions as a result of a decision by the US Supreme Court.[5] The murder rate rose over those four years in states that had previously executed murderers, but it also rose in other states and it continued to rise after states reinstituted the death penalty. Some argue that executions actually encourage at least some individuals to kill, perhaps by conveying a general disregard for the sanctity of human life, or perhaps by some other mechanism. This is known as the *brutalization* effect. If the effect exists, then it could account for the inconclusiveness of the empirical research: perhaps executions deter some murders while encouraging others, with the brutalization and deterrence effects counteracting each other in complicated ways (Shepherd 2005).

The most sophisticated empirical studies of capital punishment use data at the level of individual counties. These studies look for statistical correlations over time between executions in a particular county and murders committed there in subsequent months. A complex statistical technique, *multiple regression analysis*, is used to rule out variables that could account for apparent correlations in order to estimate the likelihood that executions have a causal impact on the murder rate. Some prominent recent studies conclude that, statistically speaking, a single execution deters many murders, perhaps as many as 18 (Shepherd 2005; Dezhbakhsh et al. 2003).

These studies have been criticized on methodological grounds, which I cannot examine here (Donohue and Wolfers 2005). But we may someday have conclusive research on deterrence. If the research reveals no marginal deterrent effect, then the deterrence argument for capital punishment collapses. But what if the research reveals substantial deterrence? In that case, consistent consequentialists will no longer be able to claim that the death penalty is morally objectionable. In fact, some scholars argue that, in the face of convincing evidence for deterrence, the state would be morally obligated to institute the death penalty (Sunstein and Vermeule 2005). Their argument is simple: if the death penalty minimizes the number of innocent lives lost, and the state has a moral duty to minimize the loss of innocent life, then the state has a moral duty to use the death penalty.

Critics of this argument reason as follows. True, the state has a moral duty to minimize the loss of innocent life. But it also has a moral duty not to kill someone who poses no imminent threat to others (and who does not consent to be killed). A convicted murderer poses no imminent threat. The state therefore has a moral duty not to kill him. This duty is much stronger than its moral duty to deter murder. If the state abolishes the death penalty, and murders occur as a result, then the state has knowingly allowed murderers to take innocent lives, which is unfortunate, of course. But if the state executes a murderer, then it has, itself, intentionally killed a helpless person. The abolitionist argues that intentionally killing a helpless person (even a convicted murderer) is morally worse than knowingly allowing 20 or 30 helpless persons to be murdered (Steiker 2005). Retentionists challenge this claim, as do most consequentialists (Sunstein and Vermeule 2006). (For more discussion of the philosophical issues see Chapter 3, sec. 2.2.)

8.3 Arguments for abolition

In addition to consequentialist arguments premised on the denial of marginal deterrence, there are many moral arguments for abolition.

8.3.1 Absolutism

One such argument proceeds from an absolute moral prohibition on homicide. In the *King James Bible* the Ten Commandments state "Thou shalt not kill." This could be read, uncharitably, as an absolute prohibition. In fact, no major world religion or legal system accepts an absolute prohibition on homicide. It is widely seen as permissible to kill someone who poses an imminent threat of death or serious bodily harm to someone else. Many believe that killing in a just war is also permissible. Some accept mercy killing (euthanasia). Nevertheless, someone who accepts an absolute moral prohibition on homicide must, and can consistently, favor abolition.

8.3.2 Inconsistency

A popular, but fallacious, argument holds that executing murderers is inconsistent or "hypocritical" because it amounts to killing someone in order to demonstrate that killing is wrong. There are two flaws in this argument. First, states do not assert that all homicides are wrong. *Unjustified* homicides are wrong, but some homicides are justified, as noted earlier. Retentionists believe that executing a convicted murderer who received a fair trial is, at least sometimes, also a justified homicide. Abolitionists disagree, of course, but they cannot make their case simply by observing that execution is a homicide.

The second problem with the argument from inconsistency is that it fails to recognize the moral difference between the state and a private individual. The state does many things to us that we must not do to each other. The state forces us to give up our money when it taxes us. Private citizens who do so commit theft and other crimes. The state confines prison inmates against their will. Private citizens who do so are kidnappers. The point is that there are types of action that are impermissible when a private citizen performs them, but permissible when the state does so. The state's position is not hypocritical.

A more carefully stated abolitionist premise is that it is wrong to kill someone who poses no imminent threat to anyone else. This might be true. If so, then the abolitionist can consistently make her claim. But retentionists suggest a qualification: it is wrong to kill *an innocent person* who poses no imminent threat. Murderers are not innocent, so retentionism is an equally consistent position, on this premise.

8.3.3 Humanity and civilization

Some abolitionists accept the retentionist qualification and the claim that murderers deserve, morally speaking, to die. They claim that, nonetheless, the state should not execute murderers because doing so is *inhumane*. Executing someone, they contend, is just too terrible. An inmate on death row suffers great emotional distress as his execution date approaches. It is inhumane to inflict such distress, even on those who deserve it.

A slightly different abolitionist argument assumes that the state, as such, operates under special moral restrictions. It is uncivilized, abolitionists suggest, for the state to kill someone who poses no imminent threat. Part of the meaning of civilization is that the state limits its use of violence to protective purposes. Civilized states do not use violence just because someone deserves it. This is why civilized states do not use corporal punishment or torture. Surely such punishments are sometimes deserved, but civilized states do not stoop so low. Police are legally permitted to injure suspects for defensive and subduing purposes, but not for punitive purposes. Prison inmates often sustain injuries, but the law does not authorize the state to injure them, and actually requires the state to provide them with medical care. Most of the civilized world has abolished capital punishment. Death is the only remaining punishment in the United States in which the state deliberately inflicts physical damage on the convict's body as a form of punishment. This unique attribute is enough to convince many abolitionists that capital punishment is uncivilized, akin to torture (Sarat 2001; Reiman 1985).

8.3.4 Mistake and irrevocability

No criminal justice system can eliminate the possibility of wrongful convictions. In recent years, DNA evidence has exonerated convicted criminals in widely publicized cases. Some abolitionists argue that capital punishment should be abolished because we cannot eliminate the possibility of executing an innocent convict (Sarat and Ogletree 2009).

This argument must be made carefully. After all, wrongful convictions are, if anything, less common in capital cases than in others. Abolitionists do not favor abolishing other punishments just because mistakes are inevitable. So they need a reason to single out capital punishment. They could point out that some punishments are necessary for crime control purposes, whereas capital punishment is unnecessary. This is really a consequentialist argument.

Instead, abolitionists emphasize that execution is *irrevocable*. Dead people cannot be brought back. We should abolish the death penalty so the state never makes the mistake of executing an innocent person. An innocent convict at least has a chance for exoneration while he lives.

The problem with this argument is that incarcerating an innocent person is also a terrible mistake—more terrible the longer his sentence. True, incarcerating an innocent person is not *as* terrible as executing him and an inmate can work to prove his innocence. But incarcerating an innocent person is still terribly unjust. Even if he is ultimately exonerated and released, he will never receive full compensation for his period of lost freedom. Yet, abolitionists do not favor eliminating incarceration altogether just because innocent convicts languish in prison today. Again, the abolitionist can argue that eliminating incarceration would have disastrous social consequences, whereas eliminating the death penalty would not. But again, this is a consequentialist argument, not an argument from mistake.

8.3.5 Caprice

The only argument against the death penalty that has ever been accepted by a majority of the US Supreme Court is the argument from caprice.[6] In the United States, murder defendants have a constitutional right to a jury trial, which they almost always request. If the prosecution seeks the death penalty, then the jury, in addition to determining whether the facts of the case warrant conviction, is charged with deciding whether to sentence the convict to death. Prosecutors in death penalty states prosecute thousands of cases of first-degree murder every year, but they seek the death penalty in only a tiny fraction of those cases. Juries in capital cases render thousands of convictions for first-degree murder every year, but they sentence only a tiny fraction of those convicts to death. Abolitionists argue that this unlucky fraction is selected for death on a morally arbitrary basis—virtually at random. No one has been able to demonstrate that the murderers who are executed are, on average, more deserving of death than those who are allowed to live. Brutal, sadistic murderers go to prison while much less culpable murderers in the same state are executed. This is not to say that the executed murderers do not deserve to die—that would be a different argument. The objection here is based on *comparative justice* (see Chapter 3, sec. 2.5): morally similar cases should be treated similarly. It is especially unfair when a less culpable convict is treated more harshly than someone more culpable. Add to this the fact that one of the two is actually being executed, rather than incarcerated—a difference of kind, not just degree.

The caprice argument is not an argument against capital punishment, as such. It is an argument against the imperfect administration of capital punishment in actual legal systems such as the United States, in which a small, unlucky subset of those who deserve death are actually executed, for reasons unrelated to their relative desert.

Critics of the argument from caprice make several points. Some deny that it is unjust to execute a murderer who deserves to die just because another murderer, who is equally or more deserving of death, escapes execution. The only question of justice, they claim, is whether the murderer, himself, deserves to die. If he does, then executing him is not unjust. How others are treated is irrelevant. Critics also note that caprice pervades the criminal justice system, not just the death penalty system: a wide range of random factors determine who is arrested, charged, prosecuted, convicted, and sentenced for crimes. Many prison inmates are much less deserving of punishment than individuals still roaming the streets. We should not release these inmates for the sake of comparative justice, nor should we abolish the death penalty.

The defender of the caprice argument counters that the injustice is more pronounced in the case of the death penalty because the penalty is more severe. Also, the state should take whatever reasonable steps it can to minimize comparative injustice, even if it cannot eradicate such injustice. Eliminating caprice by abolishing capital punishment has fewer social costs than eliminating other sources of comparative injustice.

8.3.6 Bias

Finally, an important version of the caprice argument concludes that the death penalty in the United States is presently unjust because *racial factors* influence the behavior of prosecutors and juries (and, perhaps, that of judges and police officers). There is substantial empirical evidence that, holding constant a wide range of other variables that influence sentencing decisions, convicted black murder suspects in the United States are more likely to be executed than convicted white murder suspects. Blacks convicted of murdering whites are also more likely to be executed than blacks convicted of murdering blacks, whites convicted of murdering whites, or whites convicted of murdering blacks (Baldus et al. 2007, 1998). These correlations are statistically significant and consistent with the nation's history of racist criminal justice. The documented effects derive partly from the decisions of prosecutors to seek the death penalty and partly from the sentencing verdicts of juries. No one has been able to explain the statistical correlation between racial variables and executions without adopting the hypothesis that race plays a role. This does not prove that any juror or prosecutor is consciously acting from racist motives, but it suggests that, at least subconsciously, many are treating defendants differently because of race.

On the basis of this empirical evidence, many abolitionists contend that justice requires a moratorium on the death penalty in the United States until the states can offer reasonable assurances that racial factors will no longer influence capital sentencing (Nathanson 2001). Because no one currently has a feasible method for neutralizing the influence of race in capital sentencing, such a moratorium would be in place for many years to come.

Some retentionists contest the empirical evidence, but others accept it while denying that it makes a good case for a moratorium. Some argue that the current death penalty system in the United States is not unjust because, assuming that all capital murder convicts deserve to be executed, the state never knowingly gives anyone a harsher sentence than he deserves, despite the fact that white murderers (and blacks who murder blacks) are more likely to get *less* punishment than they deserve.

This argument has surprising implications. Imagine a *facially racist* statute that authorizes juries to impose death sentences only on blacks, not on whites, who are convicted of capital murder. Assuming, again, that all capital murder convicts deserve to be executed, this statute gives no one anything worse than he deserves. Nevertheless, few retentionists would support the facially racist statute, so they cannot consistently defend the current death penalty system by appealing to the fact that it gives no one a harsher sentence than he deserves. Rather, retentionists who accept the empirical studies about race and execution should concede that injustice plagues the current system. They should distinguish the facially racist statute from the current system by arguing that, whereas the state is entirely responsible for the facially racist statute, it is not morally responsible for the racial injustice of the current system. Instead, the responsibility falls entirely on racially biased prosecutors and jurors. Justice does not require the state to institute a moratorium on the death penalty just because some actors within the system are racially biased. This is the position taken by the US Supreme Court in the 1987 case of *McCleskey v. Kemp*:

In this case, a black man convicted of murdering a white man presented statistical evidence of racial bias in capital sentencing.[7] The Court held that a black defendant cannot get his death sentence overturned simply by proving that black defendants are more likely to be executed than similarly situated white defendants in his state. Rather, a black defendant must carry the much greater burden of proving that racial factors adversely influenced actors in his specific case (e.g. his prosecutor, his jury). Such evidence is almost never available, so *McCleskey* made the death penalty almost impossible to challenge in court on grounds of racial bias (Kennedy 1988).

Study questions

(1) Should the state punish all convicts, or should some be sentenced to treatment or other nonpunitive measures?

(2) Does the story of Victor, who is framed for murder, persuade you that promoting good consequences, such as deterring crime, is not the only value relevant to punishment?

(3) Should sentences take into account the amount of harm done by a convict? Should convicts who cause no harm be punished at all?

(4) Does the state have the right to use coercion for the purpose of getting convicts to apologize for their crimes?

(5) Is it unjust for the state to sentence a convict to life in prison for a minor offense, such as marijuana possession, if he was forewarned of the sentence before he chose to commit the crime?

(6) Which do you see as the strongest arguments for and against capital punishment?

Recommended reading

Barnett, Randy E. 1977. "Restitution: A New Paradigm of Criminal Justice." *Ethics* 87: 279–301.

Boonin, David. 2008. *The Problem of Punishment*. Cambridge: Cambridge University Press.

Davis, Michael. 1992. *To Make the Punishment Fit the Crime*. Boulder: Westview Press.

Duff, R. A. 2001. *Punishment, Communication, and Community*. Oxford: Oxford University Press.

Feinberg, Joel. 1970. "The Expressive Function of Punishment." In *Doing and Deserving*. Princeton: Princeton University Press.

Golash, Deirdre. 2005. *The Case against Punishment*. New York: NYU Press.

Kant, Immanuel. 1797. *The Metaphysics of Morals*. Trans. Mary J. Gregor. Cambridge: Cambridge University Press, 1996.

Kershnar, Stephen. 2011. *For Torture: A Rights-Based Defense*. Lanham, MD: Lexington Books.

Laudan, Larry. 2011. "The Rules of Trial, Political Morality and the Costs of Error: Or, Is Proof Beyond a Reasonable Doubt Doing More Harm than Good?" In *Oxford Studies in Philosophy of Law*, ed. Leslie Green and Brian Leiter. Oxford: Oxford University Press.

Montague, Philip. 1995. *Punishment as Societal-Defense*. Lanham, MD: Rowman & Littlefield.

Moore, Michael S. 1987. "The Moral Worth of Retribution." In *Responsibility, Character, and the Emotions: New Essays in Moral Psychology*, ed. Ferdinand Schoeman. Cambridge: Cambridge University Press. 179–219.

Morris, Herbert. 1976. *On Guilt and Innocence: Essays in Legal Philosophy and Moral Psychology*. Berkeley: University of California Press.

Nathanson, Stephen. 2001. *An Eye for an Eye: The Immorality of Punishing by Death*. 2nd edn. Lanham, MD: Rowman & Littlefield.

Sarat, Austin D. 2001. *When the State Kills: Capital Punishment and the American Condition.* Princeton: Princeton University Press.

Steiker, Carol S. 2005. "No, Capital Punishment Is Not Morally Required: Deterrence, Deontology, and the Death Penalty." *Stanford Law Review* 58: 751–89.

Sunstein, Cass R., and Adrian Vermeule. 2005. "Is Capital Punishment Morally Required?" *Stanford Law Review* 58: 703–50.

—. 2006. "Deterring Murder: A Reply." *Stanford Law Review* 58: 847–57.

8
Statutes

1. Statutory interpretation

Most of the law in modern legal systems is made by legislatures and codified in *statutes*. A statute can be as short as a single sentence or as long as a novel (the No Child Left Behind Act in the United States approaches 275,000 words). Examples of statutes include:

- Acts of Parliament in the United Kingdom
- Acts of the Legislative Assembly of Ontario
- Laws passed by the New York State Assembly
- Ordinances of the City of Los Angeles

Parts of statutes are referred to as *provisions*. Lawyers addressing a lengthy statute with many components sometimes refer to the *statutory scheme*. Legislatures sometimes authorize an administrative agency (e.g. the Medicines and Healthcare products Regulatory Agency in the United Kingdom; the Food and Drug Administration in the United States) to develop *regulations* for the purpose of implementing provisions of a statute that have been left general or vague. Such regulations are similar to statutes.

Statutes are the main source of our legal rights and duties in the modern world. The process by which one understands a statute and applies it to particular circumstances is *statutory interpretation* (more obscurely: *statutory construction*). Judges and executive branch officials routinely engage in statutory interpretation. So do lawyers and, occasionally, private citizens.

It is sometimes observed that judges lack a sophisticated theory of statutory interpretation (O'Connor 2003/04). In many cases, statutes are easy to interpret, but in interesting cases it can be difficult and leaves much room for philosophical debate. Some of the debate concerns a prescriptive question: how should public officials interpret statutes in a given legal system? The corresponding descriptive question is: how do public officials interpret statutes? I shall focus mainly on statutory interpretation by courts, although similar things could be said about interpretation by members of the executive branch and lawyers.

A statutory provision might run only a dozen words, but courts do not generally interpret provisions in a vacuum. Rather, they consider a provision in relation to other provisions of the same statute and related statutes, as well as related common-law doctrines and applicable constitutional provisions.

In common-law countries, when a court interprets a statute that interpretation binds lower courts and (to a lesser extent) those at the same level under the doctrine of stare decisis (see Chapter 2, sec. 9). Reported court opinions interpreting statutes become, to this extent, part of the law as well, whether or not the interpretations make reference to the original legislators.

Statutory interpretation raises three basic philosophical issues:

(1) Should statutes be interpreted in strict accordance with their written terms, or more loosely, perhaps in light of broader social purposes?
(2) Is the true meaning of a statute given by how readers would understand it, or by the intentions of the legislature?
(3) Is the meaning of a statute permanently fixed when it is enacted, or can its meaning change over time?

Each of these questions could be asked prescriptively (how should courts interpret?) or descriptively (how do courts interpret?).

2. Intent versus understanding

There is a complex relationship between *legislator's intent* and *reader's understanding*. Legislators draft legislation in light of how they expect readers, including courts, to understand it. Readers understand legislation in light of what they believe legislators intended to convey. If readers correctly understand legislative intent, then the legislature succeeds in communicating. But readers sometimes misunderstand legislative intent. What should we say about such misunderstandings? If reader's understanding and legislative intent diverge, which reflects the true meaning of the legislation? The following are three possible answers:

(1) The true meaning of the statute is given by the reader's understanding.
(2) The true meaning of the statute is given by legislative intent.
(3) The statute has no true meaning.

The first answer raises several questions. To which reader does it refer? One could say that the true meaning of a statute is whatever meaning a particular reader assigns. But this position has several problems. First, it gives no guidance to the reader herself. It simply tells her that the statute means whatever she thinks it means. Secondly, this position entails that misreading a statute is impossible, which is counterintuitive. Thirdly, this position entails that two readers who disagree about the meaning of a statute are both correct, which entails, paradoxically, that they never really disagreed in the first place.

Because of such absurdities, defenders of the position that statutory meaning is given by reader's understanding do not claim that just any reader will do. Rather, the reader must be a *reasonable* individual (Lawson and Seidman 2006). So the claim is actually:

2R. The true meaning of the statute is given by a reasonable reader's understanding.

The main argument for 2R concerns fair notice (see Chapter 1, sec. 10). The state threatens lawbreakers with force, so individuals are entitled to know in advance which actions are unlawful. It would be unfair for the state to use force against someone under a statute if a reasonable reader would not have concluded that her actions were unlawful under it. The fact that the legislature intended to outlaw her actions should not matter if she could not be expected to understand this fact.

But who is a reasonable reader? Can two reasonable readers disagree? What does the statute mean if they do? The identity of the reasonable reader varies with the type of legislation. For laws that affect ordinary residents on a daily basis, the reasonable reader is an ordinary, mentally competent adult speaker of the local language with no specialized knowledge. One interesting question is whether courts should judge defendants by different standards depending on their level of fluency in the language. It seems unfair to hold someone liable for violating a law that was never translated into a language that she understands. On the other hand, many would argue that visitors to a jurisdiction are responsible for learning the local laws in advance, via translation if necessary.

Another question is: what level of intelligence should courts ascribe to the reasonable reader? Assuming a high level of intelligence seems unfair to average citizens who do not understand statutes as well. But assuming a low level of intelligence could unduly restrict legislatures to simple statutes that cannot meet the needs of modern societies.

In the modern world, many statutes address specialized topics, such as patents, environmental regulations, corporate taxation, and telecommunications. Such statutes are difficult or impossible for nonexperts—even highly intelligent ones—to understand. The reasonable reader of such a statute is an expert in the relevant subject matter.

One question about the reasonable reader that receives special attention concerns the reader's presumptive location in time and space. *Originalists* ask us to think of the reader as a reasonable individual who belonged to the legal system for which the statute was enacted at its time of enactment. Originalists hold that a statute means what reasonable people at that time would have understood it to mean. *Nonoriginalists* also see the reader as a reasonable individual who belongs to the local legal system, but they would not confine her to the time of enactment. Rather, the reader could be someone from a later time, typically the present.

Instead of asking what the enacting legislature intended, or how reasonable readers at that time would have understood the statute, nonoriginalists ask, first, whether a contemporary legislature would pass the statute. If not, then the nonoriginalist does not apply it at all. If so, then the nonoriginalist asks how a contemporary legislature would intend for such a statute to be interpreted upon its passage (Eskridge 1994).

3. Originalism

Originalists offer several arguments for their position, preeminently the following:

> (1) Courts should not change the meaning of statutes.
> (2) Only originalism forbids courts from changing the meaning of statutes.
> (3) Therefore, only originalism forbids courts from doing what they should not do.

The first premise is plausible. Originalists emphasize that, in a system with separation of powers, changing statutes is the job of the legislature, not the judiciary. Legislators repeal, revise, correct, and update statutes all the time. It is neither necessary nor appropriate for courts to usurp this function by disregarding the original meaning of statutes.

4. Nonoriginalism

Nonoriginalists counter with several arguments. One is that the original understanding of a statute enacted long ago can be impossible to identify. In order to know how reasonable people at the time of enactment would have understood a statute, we would have to know how they thought. Yet, the lives of people in 1900—to say nothing of 1800 or 1700—were very different from ours. How can we read with their eyes?

Originalists have some answers. They admit that it is sometimes difficult to know what reasonable people from centuries past would have thought. But courts can appeal to historical documents: old dictionaries, letters, diaries, newspapers, and books. Nonoriginalists object that this process takes more time and historical training than most real judges have.

Maybe so in some cases, retorts the originalist. But if legislators believe that courts have misread a statute, they can always repeal it and replace it with a new one. According to originalism, the new statute should, indeed, be interpreted in terms of contemporary understandings. This is a straightforward and proper way for statutes to be updated. Legislators are more democratically accountable than courts, so they are more likely to accurately represent contemporary popular judgments.

Nonoriginalists object that this method is too inefficient. Legislators at any given moment are aware of only a miniscule fraction of the court cases being heard in their system. They have no time to consider every statute that the courts read in an outdated way. Only courts themselves are in a position to keep the law up to date when the legislature fails to take notice.

Nonoriginalists (also known as "dynamic theorists" or "evolutionists") observe that large hierarchical organizations, such as legal systems, corporations, and the military, operate most effectively when subordinates have the authority to adapt to changing circumstances without constantly consulting their superiors. Such systems require flexibility. Courts should have the authority to interpret statutory meaning as changing over time without awaiting the blessing of the legislature.

Even if we could determine how readers long ago would have understood a statute, why should courts today interpret statutes in accordance with older understanding? Societies change in many ways over time. These changes are demographic, economic, religious, cultural, linguistic, and technological. A good policy in 1850 might be a bad policy under modern conditions. Some policies of 1850, moreover, were bad even at the time (e.g. men were legally permitted to rape their wives in many jurisdictions). Our collective knowledge has vastly increased over the decades in the fields of history, social and natural science, and engineering. We are also arguably more enlightened about morality and justice. Why should we read a statute as it would have been understood by people long ago who were so much less informed?

Originalists respond again that it is the job of the legislature to repeal bad laws, including laws that have become obsolete and those that we now believe to have been misguided all along. But nonoriginalists argue that some degree of dynamic statutory interpretation is inevitable.

5. Originalism and the evolution of meaning

Originalists disagree with nonoriginalists about the conditions under which statutory meaning changes. But originalists should not be caricatured as denying that meaning ever changes. They recognize that statutory meaning can change in various ways. For example, originalists recognize that the *extensions* of statutory terms—the set of entities actually designated—fluctuate over time. The set of "minor children," for example, changes every day as new babies are born and children become legal adults (or die in childhood). Originalists do not believe that statutory references to "minor children" refer only to individuals who were children on the date of enactment.

Originalists also recognize that some statutory provisions explicitly invite readers to interpret them in accordance with contemporary understandings, rather than the understandings of the time of enactment. I shall call these *prospective provisions*. Consider a statute banning the sale of materials considered "offensive under contemporary community standards" or a statute empowering an agency to "promote public health." Which books are considered offensive will change over time. So will our knowledge of what promotes public health. One can imagine a reader at the time of enactment distinguishing between two ideas. The first is what he, himself, considers to be offensive. Secondly, there is how he believes a future court should go about deciding what to ban. He might well say to himself, "Although I am offended by the word 'crap,' I recognize that future generations might not be. Future courts should interpret this statute in terms of the standards of their time, not mine, because the statute refers to *contemporary* community standards." Having these thoughts requires the reader to imaginatively detach himself from his own beliefs, but the resulting position is not incoherent. Originalists agree that courts interpreting prospective provisions should consult the current state of knowledge and opinion because this is what reasonable readers at the time of enactment would understand the provision itself to require. This is another qualification of the caricature of originalists as claiming that statutory meaning never changes.

Most originalists in common-law systems also believe that judges should give some weight to precedent (see Chapter 2, sec. 9). Such precedents could include a binding ruling by a previous court that interpreted a statute in a way that departs from the original understanding. Some originalists might still deny that the true meaning of the statute has changed, but they accept that judges should nevertheless rule as though the meaning had changed.

Originalists also appreciate that it could be unfair to base a criminal conviction upon the original understanding of a statute. It might be unreasonable to expect the defendant to have known that the original understanding would be used and that his actions constituted a crime under it.

For all these reasons, we should reject the caricature of originalists as believing that statutory meaning never changes. Originalists accept that meaning changes, or at least that judges should sometimes decide cases as though meaning had changed. So what is the actual dispute between originalists and nonoriginalists? Here is one way to appreciate the difference: originalists believe that statutory meaning changes only for the reasons mentioned above, whereas nonoriginalists believe that meaning changes for these reasons and others as well. In order to illustrate this point, recall the previous discussion of prospective provisions—those that invite readers to use contemporary understandings of statutory terms. Originalists and nonoriginalists agree that the meaning of a prospective provision can change over time. But they often disagree about which provisions are, in fact, prospective. Nonoriginalists tend to regard more provisions as prospective than do originalists. Imagine a statute, first enacted in the Victorian Era and never revisited by lawmakers, authorizing a public official to terminate the employment of anyone who engages in "lascivious conduct." Notice that this provision does not make reference to "contemporary standards." It simply references "lascivious conduct." An originalist would be more likely to read this provision nonprospectively, taking it to cover all conduct that would have been seen as lascivious in the Victorian Era. He might, therefore, uphold the termination of an employee for private fornication, which was then regarded as lascivious. A nonoriginalist, by contrast, might ask whether reasonable people today regard private fornication as lascivious and, upon concluding that they do not, reinstate the terminated employee.

Originalists object to this reasoning. The aforementioned judge seems to have substituted his own opinions for the original legislature's opinions about what conduct is lascivious. What evidence do we have that the legislature granted the judge this authority? Nonoriginalists reply that this grant of authority is implicit in the law, or that it should be inferred because it makes for a more just or more practical method of adjudication.

Originalists are even more alarmed by judges who disregard provisions that they believe to be obsolete, or who "read into" a statute language that does not actually appear on the page.

6. Legislative intent

I shall now turn to the second answer to my earlier question, which is that courts should defer to legislative intent over reader's understanding. Now the question becomes: how might courts go about ascertaining legislative intent? What evidence might they use? The main evidence of intent is, of course, the language of the statute itself. But statutory language is available to all readers.

Readers infer from it what the legislature intended to convey. There is no reason for a court to infer that the legislature intended to convey anything other than what a reasonable reader would understand by the statutory language. The legislator chooses words that she believes will lead the reasonable reader to understand what she (the legislator) means. There is no reason for a court to conclude that legislative intent diverges from reader's understanding.

Philosophers emphasize that statutory language is meaningful to the court only because the court also has a body of general background knowledge. But this knowledge is available to ordinary readers, as well. Again, there is no reason for the court to conclude that legislative intent diverges from reader's understanding.

The point is that, in many cases, the court has no *external* evidence of legislative intent—evidence that anyone who reads the statute does not also possess. In other cases, however, a court has evidence that cannot be obtained just by reading the statute. This external evidence usually takes the form of *legislative history*—documentation of legislative debates, committee reports, records of revisions made to bills prior to passage, and other materials that suggest why legislators enacted a statute, what aims they sought to achieve, what they anticipated its effects would be, and the like.

Courts do, in fact, consult, cite, and rely upon legislative history in their opinions. Often they treat it as evidence of legislative intent, although it may also be consulted as evidence of how a reasonable reader would understand a statute. The basic normative question is whether courts *ought* to consult legislative history when they interpret statutes.

Some writers doubt that legislative intent is a useful concept. The concern is that legislatures consist of many individuals, often hundreds, each of whom has his own intentions. If these intentions conflict with one another, then how do we determine legislative intent? In some cases, legislative intent is difficult or impossible to determine.

7. Obsolete statutes

Thus far in this chapter, I have discussed statutory *interpretation*, but related questions arise concerning the treatment of obsolete statutes, when the question is not how to interpret a statute, but whether to interpret it at all, rather than ignoring it. American legislatures, for example, pass laws today more frequently than ever, increasingly tailoring them to address present-day problems. As societal values and technologies change, these statutes become obsolete. Some are accordingly repealed, but many are not. How should a judge handle a statute that she believes to be obsolete? Courts today take various approaches:

(1) Courts sometimes twist the meaning of an ostensibly obsolete statute so as to avoid its implications, or else they pretend that its meaning is less clear than it is.
(2) Courts in the United States sometimes pretend to find a constitutional problem with a statute where no such problem actually exists (an obsolete statute is not necessarily an unconstitutional one).
(3) Courts sometimes simply apply the obsolete statute and try to bring its obsolescence to the attention of the legislature.

The conventional wisdom is that courts should enforce obsolete statutes as usual because only legislatures have the authority to change statutes. But scholars such as Guido Calabresi (1932–) have made some unconventional prescriptions. Calabresi, a federal judge and former Dean of Yale Law School, observes that statutes today are drafted in order to solve specific problems of the moment. Many are therefore destined for rapid obsolescence. He advises courts to take it upon themselves to identify obsolete statutes and decline to enforce them. An obsolete statute is one that would not receive public support if it were proposed today. Courts, he suggests, should ask whether the statute fits in with the overall "fabric" of the current legal system as a way of determining if the public still supports it. Is the statute out of place, relative to the values and priorities that inform the current body of law? Has the statute been relatively unenforced for many years? If the statute does not fit with the current legal fabric, then the court should alter or nullify it, or at least threaten to do so, thereby pressuring the legislature to place the statute on its agenda. Then the legislature can take a second look at the statute and determine if constituents still favor it (Calabresi 1982).

Calabresi's critics object that he would have courts usurp the legislature's role (Hutchinson and Morgan 1982). What constitutional authority do courts have to review statutes for obsolescence? One might also doubt that judges are actually competent to identify obsolete statutes. But Calabresi emphasizes that the legislature still has the power to reenact a statute after a court nullifies it. If the statute was not, in fact, obsolete, then legislators can be counted upon to reenact it.

8. Textualism or purposivism?

Statutes also fail to cover everything (see Chapter 2, sec. 4). Language is open-textured, so there are always peripheral cases—those in which the proper application of the statute is not obvious. A functioning, twenty-two-caliber pistol is obviously a "weapon." A popsicle is obviously not a "weapon." A pair of sewing scissors is a harder case. It is not obvious either that they are a weapon or that they are *not* a weapon. Is it correct to say that in hard cases the statute has no true meaning? The problem of open texture confronts both intentionalist theories and those that focus on the reader's understanding. It may be unclear whether the legislators intended "weapon" to include scissors and also unclear whether a reasonable reader would understand "weapon" to include scissors.

In some cases, a statutory provision contradicts itself or another provision within the statutory scheme. How are we to interpret a statute that specifies a sentence of "at least five, but no more than three, years in prison"? Read literally, the statute provides for no sentences whatsoever because no number is at least five, but no more than three. We could read it that way, but then what was the point of the words? It seems more reasonable, in this case, to assume that the drafters inadvertently swapped "three" and "five," and to interpret the statute accordingly. This is a case in which we might infer that legislators mistakenly drafted language that fails to reflect their own intent. That is probably also how a reasonable reader would interpret the text.

In other cases, drafters make false factual assumptions. Imagine the following statute: "No flammable gases, including helium, shall be transported by railroad." Helium is not, in fact, a flammable gas, but the statute implies otherwise. Should we read it as banning helium, which is specifically mentioned, in addition to gasses that are actually flammable? Or should we read it as banning only flammable gasses and therefore not helium? The former reading is supported by this argument:

Textualist Argument

(1) Statutes should be interpreted in accordance with their specific terms.
(2) The statute specifically mentions helium as banned for transport.
(3) Therefore, the statute should be interpreted as banning helium transport.

The latter reading—which does not ban helium transport—is supported by this argument:

Purposivist Argument

(1) Statutes should be interpreted consistently with the legislature's intended general purposes.

(2) The legislature's intended general purpose for this statute is to promote safety.

(3) Helium poses no safety hazard.

(4) Therefore, the statute should not be interpreted as banning helium transport.

Notice that premise 2 of the Purposivist Argument makes an assumption about legislative intent—that the intended general purpose is to promote safety. The textualist, by contrast, has no interest in discerning legislative intent. The statute mentions helium, therefore helium transport is banned. The textualist does not care that the language implies that the legislators banned helium only because they believed it to be flammable.

Two famous cases decided by the US Supreme Court further illustrate the textualist/purposivist debate:

> At issue in *Church of the Holy Trinity v. United States*[1] was a federal statute that forbid anyone to facilitate "the importation or migration or any alien . . . into the United States, . . . under contract or agreement . . . to perform labor or service of any kind in the United States." The statute also contained many specific exceptions, including actors, artists, lecturers, singers, and domestic servants. The church had contracted with an English citizen to serve as its pastor. The Court admitted that hiring this pastor fell within the letter of the statute: a pastor certainly performs "labor or service" and does not fall within any of the statutory exceptions. Nevertheless, the Court concluded that Congress could not have intended to forbid contracts such as this one, and ruled in favor of the church.

Unlike the (fictional) helium statute, the statute in *Holy Trinity* contains no false factual assertions. It does not, for example, deny that pastors perform a "service." The Court's decision does not attempt to correct a factual error by the legislature. Rather, it aims to rectify a perceived legislative oversight. The Court concludes that Congress simply failed to include pastors in the exceptions and would have included them had they thought to do so. The Court's decision exemplifies purposivism.

The Court's assumption is quite plausible. There was no evidence, for example, that Congress specifically considered and rejected a proposal to include an exception for pastors. And it is implausible that nineteenth-century lawmakers would really have wanted to exclude foreign pastors while admitting foreign actors and lecturers. Textualists, however, see these facts as irrelevant. The pastor was an alien. The church brought him into the United States under contract to perform a service. The statute contains no exception for pastors. Therefore, the church violated the statute. This result is entailed by the statute Congress passed. If Congress disapproves of the Court's decision, then Congress can amend the statute to include pastors, even retroactively acquitting the church.

Textualists and purposivists both appeal to the text, but for different reasons. Textualists ask how a reader would understand the text if she were relatively indifferent to legislative intent, but otherwise reasonable. Purposivists, by contrast, use the text as evidence of legislative intent, in conjunction with their knowledge of their society and its values. Some purposivists also use legislative history as evidence of intent.

Within the purposivist camp there is a distinction between those who use *actual intent* and those who use *constructive intent*. Some purposivists want to know what legislators actually intended. Legislative history is obviously relevant to this inquiry. For example, if a purposivist discovered a debate in which a Senate committee considered and rejected an amendment that would have included pastors, then this is evidence that at least some senators intended not to include pastors. If legislators did not consider a particular case, then we cannot say what they intended for it. Other purposivists try to imagine how the legislators would have intended for the case to be resolved, had they thought about it. Again, legislative history could be informative.

A textualist might, in fact, have firmly held beliefs about legislative intent, both actual and constructive. She might even seek out evidence of intent. For a textualist, however, legislative intent is relevant only insofar as a reasonable reader would take it into account in her own reading of the statute. A textualist ignores evidence of legislative intent that a reasonable reader would not take into account.

Textualists argue against intentionalists that much legislation constitutes a compromise between competing factions. The legislature as a whole has no unified intention, so it is futile to search for the legislative intent behind such statutes. There is no coherent "spirit" animating them.

Courts often claim to have identified the "plain meaning" of a statutory provision. But claiming it does not make it so. In some instances, a court articulates the allegedly plain meaning of a provision despite the fact that other informed readers consider its plain meaning to be quite different from what the court claims it to be, or consider its plain meaning to be far from obvious. A judge who claims to be a textualist may, in fact, be deciding on the basis of something other than plain meaning, such as her own values.

Textualists can respond to this objection by admitting that some judges are dishonest textualists. But dishonesty is possible no matter what method of statutory interpretation one adopts. The questions we should ask are two. First, which method, if followed honestly, would be best? Secondly, which method is more likely to foster honest application? These questions are difficult to answer. Critics of textualism point to cases in which avowed textualists appear to depart from their theory in the service of policy goals. Textualists respond that judges who appeal to legislative intent do this more often, such that textualism retains a comparative advantage.

9. Illustration

A widely discussed case that illustrates some of the puzzles of statutory interpretation is *U.S. Steelworkers v. Weber*:

Weber concerns an alleged conflict between a federal antidiscrimination statute and an affirmative action program voluntarily adopted by a steel company and union—a training program that gave priority to black steelworkers. Brian Weber was a steelworker excluded from the program because he was white. He sued his employer and union under Title VII of the Civil Rights Act of 1964. Section 703(d) of Title VII forbids employers to "discriminate against any individual because of his race" in an apprenticeship or training program. Section 703(a)(2) prohibits classifying employees "in any way which would deprive . . . any individual of employment opportunities or otherwise adversely affect his status as an employee, because of such individual's race." Weber argued that Title VII prohibited employers from giving any priority whatsoever to black employees. His argument found support in both legislative history and the plain meaning of the text. The statute contains no exceptions for affirmative action programs—it simply forbids discrimination "because of race." The legislative history tells a similar story: prior to passage of the Act, senators asserted that it would not require, or even permit, employers to "prefer Negroes" over whites. Both the text and legislative history appear to support a ruling for Weber. However, a majority of the Court ruled against him, upholding the affirmative action program.

A textualist sympathetic to this result could argue that disfavoring whites does not actually constitute "discrimination." But would a reasonable reader understand the statute in this way? Why would she interpret a provision prohibiting discrimination "because of race" as really prohibiting only discrimination against blacks?

Writing for a majority of the Court, Justice William Brennan takes a different approach. He suggests that the underlying legislative purpose of Title VII is to rectify the inferior employment status of blacks as perpetuated by racial discrimination against them. This is also the purpose of the voluntary affirmative action program under review. Perhaps, the legislators who enacted Title VII failed to foresee the importance of private efforts to advance this same goal via affirmative action programs. They may have also failed to anticipate that the statutory language would be used to challenge such programs. Given a choice between the basic purpose of Title VII (to improve the employment status of blacks) and the particular means by which the statute appears to advance that goal (requiring employers to be color-blind), Brennan defers to the basic purpose. Legislators in 1979 understand the importance of private affirmative action. If they were to enact Title VII in 1979, rather than 1964, then they would not intend for it to be interpreted as requiring color-blindness. Brennan decides to read Title VII accordingly, despite the fact that it was actually enacted in 1964. His opinion thus exemplifies reasoning that is both purposivist and nonoriginalist. The dissent by Justice William Rehnquist exemplifies textualist, originalist reasoning.

Regardless of her preferred theory of statutory interpretation, every judge must deal with precedents that depart from her preferred theory and that many other legal actors have relied upon. The judge must decide how much weight to give to precedents that she considers mistaken (see Chapter 2, sec. 9 on precedent).

10. Canons of construction

For centuries, courts have recognized that statutes can be interpreted in different ways. They have developed rules or guidelines for statutory interpretation, known as *canons of construction*, some of which have intimidating Latin names. Some well-known canons are as follows:

- "The expression of one thing is the exclusion of another." *Expressio unius est exclusio alterius*
- "The meaning of a word may be ascertained by reference to the meaning of words associated with it." *Noscitur a sociis*
- "When words of a particular or specific meaning are followed by general words, the general words are construed to apply only to persons or conditions of the same kind as those specifically mentioned." *Ejusdem generis*

- "Remedial statutes should be liberally construed."
- "Statutes that alter the common law should be strictly construed."

Picture a court interpreting a statute that reads "No one shall bring a dog of the pit bull breed into city playgrounds." The relevant canon is the first one mentioned above: "The expression of one thing is the exclusion of another." Because pit bulls are specifically mentioned, the implication is that dogs of other breeds are permitted in city parks. Notice that the statute does not logically entail that other dogs are permitted. For all we know, another section of the code might ban various other breeds. The implication is a pragmatic one: it would be misleading for the legislature to mention pit bulls, when it could easily mention dogs in general, unless it meant to ban only pit bulls.

An American legal realist, Karl Llewellyn (1893–1962), argued that the canons give less guidance than they appear to give because for any canon there is another canon that courts can use to reach remains an opposing result (Lewellyn 1950; see Chapter 2, sec. 2 on realism). The usefulness of the canons remains a topic of controversy (Scalia 1997; Sunstein 1997).

Study questions

(1) Can you imagine a case in which a reasonable reader's understanding of a statute would diverge sharply from legislative intent? After you have imagined such a case, explain how you would handle it if you were the judge.
(2) How might an originalist argue that her method does not trap us in the past, but makes room for social and technological progress in a rapidly changing world?
(3) If you were a judge, would you consult legislative history? Why or why not?
(4) Does Guido Calabresi put too much faith in judges to recognize genuinely "obsolete" statutes? Is this even a judge's job?
(5) Read *Church of the Holy Trinity* and write your own opinion for the case.
(6) Does the proper interpretation of Title VII depend on whether Congress intended it to require that employers be "color-blind"?

Recommended reading

Calabresi, Guido. 1982. *A Common Law for the Age of Statutes*. Cambridge, MA: Harvard University Press.

Eskridge, William N., Jr. 1994. *Dynamic Statutory Interpretation*. Cambridge, MA: Harvard University Press.

Lawson, Gary, and Guy Seidman. 2006. "Originalism as a Legal Enterprise." *Constitutional Commentary* 23: 47–80.

Lewellyn, Karl. 1950. "Remarks on the Theory of Appellate Decision and the Rules or Canons About How Statutes Are to be Construed." *Vanderbilt Law Review* 3: 395–406.

Scalia, Antonin. 1997. *A Matter of Interpretation: Federal Courts and the Law.* Princeton: Princeton University Press.

9
Constitutions

1. Constitutions and judicial review

In legal systems without constitutions, statutes are the supreme source of law. Other systems have written constitutions that are superior to statutes. As new governments are formed around the world, many are adopting written constitutions. Constitutions are like statutes in some respects. Both are *codified* sources of law, unlike doctrines of the common law, the authoritative statements of which are found in published court opinions (see Chapter 5). The text of a constitution contains a definite set of rules and principles. Constitutions are organized into articles and amendments, which in turn consist of provisions and clauses.

The main difference between constitutions and statutes is that constitutions are *higher-order* sources of law—legally superior to statutes. This is a defining feature of a constitution. Constitutions establish branches of government and lawmaking procedures. They also set limits on government, including limits on the content of law. Section 117 of the Australian Constitution provides:

> A subject of the Queen, resident in any State, shall not be subject in any other State to any disability or discrimination which would not be equally applicable to him if he were a subject of the Queen resident in such other State.

Imagine that an Australian state were to enact a statute excluding attorneys who reside in other states from admission to the bar of that state.[1] This statute appears to conflict with Section 117 of the Constitution. In cases of conflict, constitutional supremacy entails that the statute must yield. It is unconstitutional and should not be enforced. Section 117 would have no point if public officials could enforce statutes incompatible with it.

This essential difference between statutes and constitutions should not obscure the many commonalities. Constitutions must be interpreted and applied, just as statutes must. Public officials in every branch of government can be called upon to interpret constitutions, although most literature discusses judicial interpretation. Every problem faced by interpreters of statutes is also faced by interpreters of constitutions, and then some. The same questions we asked about statutes in Chapter 8 can be asked about constitutions. As before, each of these questions could be asked prescriptively or descriptively:

(1) Should constitutions be interpreted in strict accordance with their written terms, or more loosely (perhaps in light of broader social purposes)?
(2) Is the true meaning of a constitution given by how readers would understand it, or by the intentions of the framers (i.e. drafters or ratifiers)?
(3) Is the meaning of a constitution permanently fixed when it is ratified, or can its meaning change over time?

Because constitutional interpretation has so much in common with statutory interpretation, understanding the latter is important to understanding the former. Unfortunately, undergraduates in the United States often study constitutional law with no background in statutory interpretation. In this chapter, I shall concentrate on issues that are distinctive to constitutional interpretation, using the US Constitution to illustrate. Some of the issues discussed are unique to the United States. I shall address the federal constitution, although each of the United States has its own constitution to which many of the same issues apply.

The US Constitution ("the Constitution") differs from ordinary legislation in three ways. The first difference is content. Some of its most famous provisions are much broader and vaguer than typical legislation. Consider the following:

- The Congress shall have Power to make all Laws which shall be necessary and proper for carrying into Execution the foregoing Powers, and all other Powers vested by this Constitution in the Government of the United States. (Art. I, sec. 8)

- The Citizens of each State shall be entitled to all Privileges and Immunities of Citizens in the several States. (Art. IV, sec. 2)
- Congress shall make no law . . . abridging the freedom of speech. (Amend. I)
- No person shall be . . . deprived of life, liberty, or property, without due process of law. (Amend. V)
- No State shall . . . deny to any person within its jurisdiction the equal protection of the laws. (Amend. XIV, sec. 1)

These provisions contain essential terms that the Constitution leaves undefined. Which laws are "necessary and proper"? Which are the "privileges and immunities of citizens"? What is a law that "abridges the freedom of speech"? What constitutes "due process of law" and "equal protection"? The most interesting debates in constitutional law try to answer such questions because the constitutional text does not answer them. Scholars focus on vague provisions precisely because they are more controversial, not because they are representative of the Constitution as a whole, which they are not. Most provisions of the Constitution are more precise than those listed above. Many provisions are procedural or structural:

- The Senate of the United States shall be composed of two Senators from each State, chosen by the Legislature thereof. (Art. I, sec. 3)
- No Person except a Natural born Citizen . . . shall be eligible to the Office of the President. (Art. II, sec. 1)
- The right of citizens of the United States to vote shall not be denied or abridged by the United States or by any State on account of race. (Amend. XV, sec. 1)

A few provisions resemble ordinary legislation:

- No Soldier shall, in time of peace be quartered in any house, without the consent of the Owner. (Amend. III)

The second difference between the Constitution and ordinary legislation is that the Constitution is more difficult to change. Revising or repealing federal law requires merely a majority vote in both houses of Congress and the signature of the President. Revising or repealing a constitutional provision requires an affirmative vote by two-thirds of the members of both houses of Congress (or conventions called by two-thirds of the state legislatures), plus ratification by three-fourths of the state legislatures (or state conventions). Because of these *supermajority* requirements, amendments to the

Constitution are difficult to achieve and rare. The Equal Rights Amendment, which prohibits denying or abridging equality of rights on account of sex, was ratified by 35 of the 50 states as of 1979, but fell 3 states short of passing by the prescribed deadline.

The third difference between the Constitution and ordinary legislation may be an effect of the second difference: most provisions of the Constitution are much older than most legislation. Most informed citizens and lawmakers can name at least one provision of the Constitution that they consider obsolete, but they cannot do anything about it, even if a majority of them agree on a particular reform. A minority—just 13 of 50 state legislatures—can block amendments.

2. The judicial review controversy

These three special features of the Constitution (content, resistance to change, and age) account for interpretive controversies that do not arise regarding ordinary legislation. The first question is: whose prerogative is it to enforce the Constitution? One reply is that all public officials share this prerogative. A senator voting on a bill should decide if the bill violates the Constitution (in consultation with a constitutional lawyer, if necessary). If he concludes that it does, then he is entitled (and perhaps required) to vote against it. Likewise, the President can and should veto a bill that she believes to be unconstitutional. This much is understood. The real question is who should have the *supreme* authority to enforce the Constitution. In the United States, this authority is held by the judiciary, with the Supreme Court of the United States as the final court of appeal. Courts can and do engage in a process known as *judicial review*—they evaluate state and federal legislation (along with executive orders and other decisions of government officials) for constitutionality. If a court declares a law unconstitutional, then lower courts and the other branches of government must not apply it.

Judicial review is a settled part of American law, but it has always had critics. Some eminent theorists continue to challenge it. The text of the Constitution does not specifically authorize courts to engage in judicial review. Article III vests "the judicial Power of the United States" (sec. 1) in a supreme court and extends that power to cases "arising under this Constitution" (sec. 2), but it stops short of granting the Court final authority to invalidate legislation. However, the Court itself ruled that it has the power to invalidate federal statutes on constitutional grounds in the famous 1803 case of *Marbury v. Madison*.[2] The power of the Court to invalidate state laws and to reverse the decisions of state courts on matters of federal law is even more established.

A lawyerly question is whether cases such as *Marbury*, announcing the power of judicial review, were decided correctly under the law. The more philosophical questions are (1) is judicial review politically legitimate? (2) even if legitimate, is it a good policy to maintain? The first question is the one most often posed, but many of the answers given are actually answers to the second.

Judicial review by federal courts is not an especially democratic institution for several reasons. Federal judges do not stand for popular election. They are nominated by the President and confirmed by the Senate. Once appointed to the bench they are entitled to serve for life, absent misconduct, and their compensation cannot be reduced (Art. III, sec. 1). This gives them great power. In constitutional cases their power is especially great because of the aforementioned difficulty of amending the Constitution. Justices of the Supreme Court have the greatest power of all in constitutional cases because no higher court reviews them.

These facts about the Supreme Court (and, to a lesser extent, lower federal courts) generate a basic concern about the political legitimacy of judicial review. When the Supreme Court invalidates state legislation, it prevents a majority (sometimes a supermajority) of the state from enforcing a favored policy. When federal legislation is invalidated, a national majority has its will thwarted. The least representative branch of government (the judiciary) overrides the most representative (the legislature). The concern that this fact threatens the legitimacy of judicial review is known as the *countermajoritarian difficulty* (Bickel 1962).

Any system in which unelected judges invalidate legislation would raise the countermajoritarian difficulty. In the United States, the worry is especially acute for several reasons. First, the Constitution is difficult to amend, so mistakes by the Court are difficult to correct. Secondly, the document contains many vaguely worded provisions, so citizens often lack confidence that courts have interpreted it correctly. Thirdly, many provisions are two centuries old, drafted by men who are long dead. Why should their decisions control the present? This is known as the *dead hand of the past* argument (McConnell 1998). The time lag also makes the language difficult to interpret. It is also noted that the drafters were exclusively property-owning, white,

Christian, male, and (publicly, at least) heterosexual: hardly a representative demographic of the United States today (MacKinnon 1997).

The countermajoritarian difficulty is less acute in countries with constitutions that were ratified more recently and by more representative processes. But the defenders of judicial review in the United States have several responses to the difficulty, as well. The first is that judicial review is an essential part of the American system of "checks and balances." This is less an argument than a restatement of the problem. The courts do, indeed, "check" the political branches when they evaluate laws for constitutionality. But opponents of judicial review deny that this particular checking function is legitimate. The Director of the Federal Bureau of Investigation could likewise "check" the Congress by refusing to investigate violations of laws that he believes to be unconstitutional. Characterizing his refusal as a "check" would not render it politically legitimate.

Defenders of judicial review could respond that some form of checking is necessary. Otherwise, legislators will pass unconstitutional laws. But there are other checks on legislators. The chief executive (the President or the Governor of a state) can veto unconstitutional laws and citizens can vote against elected officials who pass them.

These checks are insufficient, respond the defenders. Here they mention specific laws that are now widely regarded as unjust, at least by their expected readers. Laws that disadvantage unpopular minorities are especially unlikely to be vetoed or repealed, so the courts are the only hope for justice. Some states maintained racially segregated public schools until the courts intervened. Others criminalized consensual oral sex between adults. Judicial review is justified as a means to achieving more justice. This is an instrumental argument for judicial review.

Instrumental arguments, although popular, have problems. They are contingent on moral judgments and future predictions. They infer from the premise that judicial review has done more justice than injustice in the past to the conclusion that it will do more justice than injustice in the future. Some readers will reject the premise and/or the inference (Rosenberg 1993).

The best arguments for judicial review would presuppose fewer moral judgments and fewer predictions. One such argument begins with the premise that human beings are prone to certain kinds of irrationality under certain conditions. In the abstract, American lawmakers have long believed in religious toleration. That is why the First Amendment forbids laws that prohibit the free exercise of religion. Faced with an unpopular religious minority, however, some lawmakers will irrationally try to pass such laws. Judicial review prevents them from being enforced during these temporary periods of widespread irrationality. Therefore, the argument concludes, judicial review is legitimate (Freeman 1990/1).

The argument from temporary irrationality has some force, but it reflects only a tiny fraction of what judicial review involves. Perhaps, a few of the laws that have been invalidated are ones that most reasonable people would reject. But reasonable people can and do disagree about the merits of most of the laws that courts invalidate. When a court invalidates such a law, it cannot plausibly claim to be protecting us from the temporary irrationality of our representatives. Rather, the court is taking sides on a controversial matter of public policy (Waldron 1999).

There is a more basic flaw in all instrumental arguments for judicial review. They answer the question: should a society adopt judicial review (assuming that this would be politically legitimate)? They do not answer the question: is judicial review in a given society politically legitimate? This is not to deny that a nation could establish judicial review in a legitimate way. If, for example, a supermajority of legislatures in the several United States ratified a constitutional amendment that explicitly provided for judicial review, then there would be a good case for its legitimacy. In the United States, however, judicial review does not enjoy such an impressive pedigree. At most, its defenders can emphasize that virtually all informed citizens, including lawyers, do not protest it. Perhaps such acquiescence goes to its legitimacy, after all, and perhaps citizens acquiesce because they believe that judicial review promotes justice in the long run. But it is their acquiescence that legitimizes judicial review, in that case, not its ostensible tendency to promote justice.

3. Constitutional interpretation

Whatever we decide about the legitimacy of judicial review, someone has to interpret the Constitution. In the United States today, judicial interpretations of the Constitution have final authority. But people disagree about interpretive method. An interpretive method specifies a set of considerations for interpreters to take into account and how much weight those considerations should receive. Some common considerations include the following:

(1) Framer's intent
(2) Reader's understanding
(3) Structure

(4) Values
(5) Prudence
(6) Precedent

This list is hardly exhaustive. Each of these considerations can be understood in different ways. I shall now examine some of them in more detail.

3.1 Framer's intent

Many theorists hold that constitutional interpreters should consider the intentions of the Framers. But who are the Framers? Obviously, different amendments were drafted and ratified in different centuries by different individuals. One must also decide whether the Framers are those who drafted the provision, those who ratified it, or a combination thereof. Framer's intent can be difficult to identify because the Framers did not always share intentions with one another. Questions about intention arise even if we limit ourselves to a single Framer. On a *subjective* account of intention, the interpretation of the original Constitution could be affected by evidence of Alexander Hamilton's private thoughts (found in his diary, perhaps). On an *objective* account, such private thoughts are irrelevant. Only Hamilton's public statements—including the text of the Constitution he ratified—are valid evidence of his intentions. Many of the arguments for and against using Framer's intent in constitutional interpretation parallel those discussed in connection with statutory interpretation (see Chapter 8).

Ronald Dworkin draws an important distinction between *semantic intention* and *expectation intention* (1996: 291–2). "Semantic intention" refers to what a speaker intends to say. "Expectation intention" refers to the effect that she expects her words to have. In many cases, these intentions converge, but they can diverge in cases of incomplete knowledge. Marlo orders her employee to tow all the illegally parked cars, not realizing that her husband's car is parked illegally. Marlo does not have the expectation intention to tow her husband's car. However, her semantic intention is to tow all illegally parked cars, which happens to include her husband's. The employee does not misunderstand Marlo when he tows her husband's car.

We can likewise distinguish between a Framer's semantic intention and his expectation intention. The Eighth Amendment states that "excessive bail shall not be required." The Framers may have expected that this language would always forbid requiring bail as high as $1 million. (The net worth of the US government was only $44 million in 1791.) But their language simply refers to "excessive" bail. Their semantic intention, Dworkin would say, was to ban bail that is, in fact, excessive. $1 million today is not excessive bail for the most serious crimes, so it does not contradict the Framers' semantic intention.

3.2 Reader's understanding

Another interpretive consideration is how a reader would understand the text. Who is the reader? It is generally accepted that the reader should be understood as a reasonable person. The main question is when the interpreter should imagine the reasonable reader to be living. Originalists ask how the text would be understood by a reasonable reader at the time of drafting or ratification. Nonoriginalists use a reader from a later time, typically the present. The arguments from our discussion of originalism in statutory interpretation are relevant again (Chapter 8, secs 3–5).

3.3 Structure

Many constitutional interpreters read the document in light of the governmental structures that it establishes. The main structural features are federalism and separation of powers. Some provisions of the Constitution, especially the original document, are naturally read as preserving the jurisdiction of states and as preventing one branch of government from encroaching on the others.

3.4 Values

Some constitutional arguments proceed from value premises that have no obvious source in intent, text, structure, or any of the other considerations. A proponent of marijuana legalization might begin from the premise that adults have a moral right to ingest anything they wish, if doing poses minimal risk to others (see Chapter 3, sec. 3 on the Harm Principle). The argument is value-based if it moves directly from that premise to a constitutional right to smoke marijuana, without invoking other considerations.

Another kind of value argument is an argument from prudence, which prevents a reading of the Constitution that would have especially bad effects. Imagine a judge who sincerely believes that arguments of intent, text, and structure strongly support the conclusion that banning fully automatic weapons violates the Second Amendment. He might nevertheless uphold the ban based on his prudential judgment that striking it down would result in many senseless deaths.

3.5 Methods of constitutional interpretation

A method of constitutional interpretation can be classified in terms of the particular combination of considerations that it takes into account.

3.5.1 Originalism

Until the 1980s, many constitutional originalists gave great weight to Framer's intent. Since then, many originalists have moved in the direction of Justice Antonin Scalia, for whom the ultimate guide is a reasonable reader's understanding of the provision at the time of ratification. Framer's intent is, at most, evidence of how readers would have understood the language (Scalia 1997).

A common objection to originalism is that it is impossible to determine what readers from another century would have thought about the modern world. Would someone in 1791 have considered email to be covered by the Free Speech or Free Press Clauses of the First Amendment? Critics of originalism contend that there is no answer to this question because email did not exist in 1791.

One originalist reply to this objection is that we must use our imagination. True, email did not exist in 1791, but our question is not "did people in 1791 think email constituted speech, for constitutional purposes?" The question is *"would* people in 1791 have thought that email constituted speech, had they understood email?" We can imagine traveling back in time to 1791, explaining email to a reasonable person who knows about the First Amendment, and asking her if she believes that email would constitute speech for constitutional purposes.

This proposal sounds silly to the nonoriginalist. What if we have no confidence in our imagination? What if we cannot decide what our imaginary friend in 1791 would have thought?

The originalist responds that, if a court cannot determine with confidence what the original understanding of a provision would have entailed, then the court must simply uphold the challenged legislation. This is a sensible default rule.

Originalism and nonoriginalism are best understood as mutually exclusive positions: any position can be classified as one or the other. Nonoriginalists give less weight than originalists give to the original meaning of the

Constitution, whether that is understood in terms of Framer's intent or an original reader's understanding. An extreme nonoriginalist gives original meaning no weight at all.

3.5.2 Living constitutionalism

In the 1970s and 1980s, nonoriginalists sometimes identified themselves as proponents of a "Living Constitution." It can be understood in different ways. No one denies that the text of the Constitution changes: Article V provides for amendment and the document has been amended 27 times over the years. Of course, the meaning of the Constitution changes when its text changes. But Living Constitutionalism entails that the meaning of the Constitution can also change in between formal amendments.

How are we to identify changes in meaning that occur without changes in the text? Many Living Constitutionalists advocate interpreting the Constitution as a reasonable reader today would interpret it, not as a reader would have when it was ratified. In some cases, this method yields an answer. Suppose, plausibly, that most Americans in 1791 (when the Eighth Amendment was ratified) believed that horsewhipping a shoplifter did not constitute a "cruel punishment." Suppose also that 90 percent of Americans today believe otherwise. A Living Constitutionalist might claim that a provision means x today (even if it once meant not-x) if 90 percent of contemporary readers agree that it means x. Thus, the meaning of "cruel" has changed such that horsewhipping a shoplifter was not cruel in 1791, but is cruel today.

Some Living Constitutionalists take a stronger position. They claim, for instance, that it is cruel to execute someone convicted of aggravated first-degree murder. They say so despite the fact that there is no contemporary consensus to that effect, and there certainly was no such consensus in 1791. Some Living Constitutionalists claim that the Constitution protects a woman's right to have an abortion, despite the fact that there has never been a societal consensus to that effect.

Living Constitutionalists who take such positions are using value-based arguments. They believe that the Constitution should be understood as reflecting the values of the American people, even values that are not explicit in the text. Not every value is important enough for constitutional status, but the most important ones are. This version of Living Constitutionalism is sometimes called the *fundamental values* approach (Ely 1980; Bork 1971).

The fundamental values approach requires courts to identify the fundamental values of the American people. One objection is that there is no reliable way to do this in the absence of consensus. Americans disagree about whether women have a fundamental moral right to obtain an elective, early abortion. Given that disagreement, what could justify the assertion that our fundamental values entail such a right? Critics suggest that nonoriginalists who make such assertions mistake their own values for national values.

Such objections have led most nonoriginalists in the past two decades to drop the "Living Constitution" terminology and to stop claiming that the meaning of the Constitution actually changes without its text changing (although President Barack Obama used the phrase approvingly during his presidency). A more recent version of nonoriginalism admits that the meaning of every provision is fixed by the text, but insists that our *understanding* of its meaning changes and gains accuracy over time. On this view, whether executing murderers is cruel is a moral question with a timeless, objective answer. If the practice is, in fact, cruel, then it was cruel even in 1791, when few Americans thought so. The interpreter should not try to determine what Americans considered cruel in 1791. Rather, she should consult the best available philosophical arguments for and against the claim that executing murderers is cruel and read the Punishments Clause in that light. This prescription recalls Dworkin's emphasis on semantic intention. Adapting his terminology, we can distinguish between *semantic understanding* and *expectation understanding*. A reasonable reader in 1791 might make the following statement:

> I believe that some punishments are, in fact cruel, and that others are not. I also believe that hanging murderers is not cruel. But I recognize that my opinion could be mistaken. I believe that the Punishments Clause applies to punishments that are, in fact, cruel, notwithstanding my current opinions.

This reader's expectation understanding of "cruel" diverges from his semantic understanding. Nonoriginalists argue that many provisions of the Constitution should be read semantically. The Punishments Clause does not refer to "punishments that we, in 1791, consider to be cruel." It simply refers to "cruel . . . punishments."

Some nonoriginalists are dissatisfied with this approach for several reasons (Farber and Sherry 2002). First, it presupposes that there are objective answers to difficult normative questions, such as which punishments are cruel (Harman and Thomson 1996). Secondly, it places great faith in the ability of courts to find those answers. Judges are not trained as moral philosophers, and even moral philosophers disagree about such questions (Ely 1980).

Is there any reason to believe that judges engage in better moral reasoning than the legislative and executive branches?

Yes, claim some nonoriginalists. Judges are generally well educated and thoughtful, especially at the federal appellate level. Federal judges are also largely insulated from political pressure and can vote their consciences without fear of reprisal. So their moral judgments are likely to be superior to those of elected officials.

Nevertheless, many nonoriginalists remain uncomfortable with the idea of judges using unrestricted moral reasoning to resolve constitutional cases. They seek guidelines for judges to follow.

3.5.3 Reinforcing representation

One of the most influential nonoriginalist theories was developed by the American law professor, John Hart Ely (1938–2003). Ely rejects both the fundamental values approach and originalism in favor of a "participation-oriented, representation-reinforcing approach" (1980: 87). Ely believes that American democracy, when it functions properly, can be trusted to protect most of the values that advocates of the fundamental values approach defend. Our best defense against unjust laws is our ability to vote against politicians who support them. The courts need not challenge these laws directly. Most citizens can prevent the enactment of legislation that unjustly disadvantages them by forming majority coalitions with other citizens to defeat the legislation. However, there is still a crucial role for judicial review because democracy does not always function properly. Ely found inspiration in one of the most famous passages in American constitutional law, footnote four of *United States v. Carolene Products Co.*:

> It is unnecessary to consider now whether legislation which restricts those political processes which can ordinarily be expected to bring about repeal of undesirable legislation, is to be subjected to more exacting judicial scrutiny under the general prohibitions of the Fourteenth Amendment than are most other types of legislation. . . . Nor need we enquire whether similar considerations enter into the review of statutes directed at particular religious, . . . national, . . . or racial minorities . . .; whether prejudice against discrete and insular minorities may be a special condition, which tends seriously to curtail the operation of those political processes ordinarily to be relied upon to protect minorities, and which may call for a correspondingly more searching judicial inquiry.[3]

The footnote identifies two basic problems that Ely thinks courts should address. First, elected officials often try to pass laws that make it difficult for voters to remove them from office, thereby "choking the channels of political change." Secondly, certain minorities who are unjustly disadvantaged by legislation find it too difficult to form majority coalitions with others because they are "discrete and insular," as religious, ethnic, and racial minorities sometimes are. The prejudice of others can prevent such groups from forming coalitions to oppose unjust legislation. Ely argues that the primary function of judicial review is to monitor the political process for these defects and to try to rectify them when possible. Rectifying these defects should be the guide when the courts read the more open-ended provisions of the Constitution, such as the Equal Protection Clause, the Privileges and Immunities Clause, and the Ninth Amendment. Ely argues that many of the liberal decisions of the midtwentieth century can be rationalized as attempts to facilitate the representation of minorities and clear the channels of political change, rather than as attempts to vindicate fundamental substantive values. Interestingly, however, Ely denies that the case of *Roe v. Wade*, which announced a constitutional right to abortion, can be justified in terms of his theory. He argues that women who might want abortions do not constitute a discrete and insular minority, and did not constitute one when modern abortion statutes were enacted. This is not to say that abortion bans are substantively just, merely that the proper role of the courts does not extend to overturning them (Ely 1973).

3.5.4 Multigenerational synthesis

A leading nonoriginalist theory to emerge since Ely's is the brainchild of Bruce Ackerman (1943–), a professor of law and political science at Yale University. Ackerman and Ely share the common desire to reconcile judicial review with the basic features of democracy: to solve the countermajoritarian difficulty. For Ackerman, the challenge is to justify celebrated twentieth-century Supreme Court decisions that offered interpretations of the Constitution that differed dramatically from those found in previous cases, despite the fact that no relevant provision of the Constitution had been amended in the interim. For example, in *Brown v. Board of Education* the Court held that racially segregated public schools violated the Equal Protection Clause of the Fourteenth Amendment, despite a previous case upholding segregated public facilities. Ackerman's elaborate (2000, 1991) theory holds that the meaning of the Constitution can, in fact, change without changes in the text. It changes after what he calls "constitutional moments"—occasions of extraordinary public engagement on matters of constitutional principle. Ackerman identifies only three such moments in American history: the Founding, Reconstruction, and the New Deal. When a constitutional moment succeeds, its results are institutionalized, either in formal changes to the Constitution, as in the Founding and Reconstruction, or in transformative Supreme Court opinions, as in the New Deal. The job of the courts, Ackerman contends, is to make sense of the Constitution in light of all three time periods. During the New Deal, Ackerman argues, Americans collectively approved a new understanding of the constitutional limits of governmental authority. In *Brown*, he argues, the Court synthesized the nineteenth-century concern with equal protection with the twentieth-century validation of activist government. The Court recognized that equal protection after the New Deal meant something more than it had meant in 1897, when a previous case had held that "separate but equal" public facilities for the races were permissible.[4]

4. Case study: Religious liberty

Cases involving religious liberty highlight some of the challenges of constitutional interpretation and often invite philosophical reflection. Most written constitutions in the developed world explicitly protect religious beliefs and practices.[5] Courts in the United States have been struggling with religious controversies for generations, so we can learn something by focusing on decisions of the US Supreme Court. The First Amendment of the US Constitution begins with the two Religion Clauses: "Congress shall make no law respecting an establishment of religion, or prohibiting the free exercise thereof." The Establishment Clause forbids the government from adopting an official religion or giving official preference to some religions over others. The Free Exercise Clause forbids the government from interfering with the religious practices of an individual or group. This sounds simple, but in practice it becomes exceedingly complicated. This section addresses a leading free exercise case of the past 30 years.

The case involved Alfred Smith, a drug rehabilitation counselor in Oregon. Smith was a member of the Native American Church—a common indigenous religion in which the sacramental ingestion of peyote (a psychoactive plant) plays a central role. During a Church ceremony Smith ingested peyote, as prescribed by his faith. When the private corporation that employed Smith learned about his peyote use, he was fired. No one doubted that his consumption of peyote was part of an authentic religious ritual, but peyote is a controlled substance in Oregon and its possession is criminal. Oregon's law makes no exception for sacramental use of drugs.

Smith applied to the state for unemployment compensation, but the state employment agency denied his application because the law states that employees who are fired for work-related misconduct cannot receive benefits. Smith was discharged for work-related misconduct: criminal drug possession. Smith sued the state for the benefits, arguing that Oregon violated his constitutional rights under the Free Exercise Clause by criminalizing even religious uses of peyote. He did not argue that Oregon should decriminalize peyote in general, but that it must make an exception for sacramental use. His religious use of peyote could not be constitutionally criminalized, he argued, so he was entitled to unemployment benefits, just as though he had been fired for reasons other than misconduct. The Oregon Supreme Court eventually agreed with Smith, but Oregon appealed to the US Supreme Court, which reversed in favor of the state in 1990.

In a majority opinion by Justice Antonin Scalia, the Court held that the Free Exercise Clause does not require Oregon to make an exception to its general ban on peyote in order to accommodate sacramental ingestion. The statute is a general criminal prohibition on the possession of controlled substances that happens to include peyote. The statute does not mention any religion, nor does it single out substances that have religious significance in the Native American Church or in any particular faith. Peyote falls within the statute as one of myriad drugs that are banned for their hallucinogenic properties. Therefore, the statute is *religion-neutral*. However, Scalia does not deny that the statute has a disproportionate impact on Smith's exercise of his religion, as compared to religious practices that do not involve controlled substances. Therefore, Oregon bears some burden to justify the law, but the burden is a light one: Oregon only has to show a *rational basis* for its choice not to make an exception for sacramental use of peyote. That is easy enough. Oregon asserts that it would be too difficult to police the possession of peyote in general if the law made an exception for religious uses: anyone who wanted to use peyote for unprotected, recreational purposes could claim that he intended to use it for religious purposes. It would be difficult for the state to rebut such claims. Therefore, the state chooses not to make an exception for sacramental peyote.

Was *Smith* correctly decided? Different interpretive methods suggest different paths to a decision. An originalist might begin by imagining a reasonable reader in 1791 who knows the relevant facts: peyote ingestion is an important part of Native American Church rituals; Oregon has a general ban on drug possession that happens to include peyote. Would the reader consider such a law to violate the Free Exercise Clause?[6]

One might wonder whether readers in 1791 would even have considered the Native American Church to be a religion, for constitutional purposes. Most readers would have been Protestant Christians. A nonoriginalist would say that this is irrelevant: what matters is whether the Church is, in fact, a religion. Experts on the nature of religion in 1990 would classify the Church as a religion, and courts should defer to them, according to nonoriginalism. But the answer is less obvious for an originalist.

Let us assume, however, that the Church qualifies as a religion. The next question for an originalist is whether an eighteenth-century reader would think that the Free Exercise Clause requires states to provide exemptions from general criminal laws that disproportionately burden the practices of certain religions. Only real historical research can shed light on this question. Fortunately, excellent scholars have conducted some of this research. Unfortunately, they have not reached a consensus regarding what either the framers or reasonable readers would have thought about such exemptions (Hamburger 1992; McConnell 1990).

The job of the Court is not just to choose a winner, but to shape doctrine for future courts to follow. Many legal philosophers see the crafting of doctrine as a limited lawmaking role for courts (see Chapter 1, sec. 7). Framer's intent, reader's understanding, and structural considerations offer some guidance, but philosophy also has a large role to play. Crafting doctrine for the *Smith* case requires the Court to do two things. First, it must specify in more detail what the right to free exercise of religion really means. Secondly, it must specify, at least approximately, the conditions under which the state may infringe that right (see Chapter 3, sec. 2.2 on the difference between infringement and violation).

What does free exercise really mean? This much is understood: the Free Exercise Clause gives you a right against any law if the state enacts it for the *purpose* of burdening your religion. This right has very great weight. However, Oregon did not infringe this right of Mr Smith's.

Consider, instead, the following claim: the Free Exercise Clause gives you a right against any law that burdens the exercise of your religion more than it burdens the exercise of other religions. This is the right of Mr Smith's that Oregon infringes. The disputed question is: under what conditions may the state infringe this right? Prior to *Smith*, the leading case on the subject was *Sherbert v. Verner*,[7] which held that the state could infringe this right only if it had a compelling interest in doing so. In other words, states had to provide religious exemptions in the absence of a compelling interest. The dissenting justices in *Smith* took this position, as well. But the *Smith* majority holds that the state needs only a rational basis for such laws.

How should courts choose between the *Sherbert* test and the *Smith* test? Some defenders of the *Smith* test argue as follows. If courts require the state to have more than a rational basis for enforcing neutral laws that disproportionately impact certain religious practices, then courts effectively afford greater protection to religiously motivated individuals than to those whose motives are not religious. Defenders of the *Smith* test argue that this doctrine unjustly favors religious citizens over the nonreligious.

Defenders of the *Sherbert* test counter that religiously motivated conduct does, indeed, merit more protection than other conduct. Religion is central to the lives of many individuals and religious minorities were persecuted for centuries (and still are in many nations). Therefore, religiously motivated practices should receive extra constitutional protection.

Defenders of the *Smith* test agree that protecting religious minorities from persecution is paramount, but they suggest that courts can do so without requiring the state to assert a compelling interest. Lawyers for individuals such as Mr Smith should proceed as follows. First, scrutinize the reasons that Oregon offers for making no exemption for sacramental peyote. Next, examine the other laws of Oregon and find cases in which Oregon has chosen to create religious exemptions from general laws. See if the state actually had reasons *not* to create these exemptions that were at least as compelling as the reasons it now offers as justifications for *not* exempting sacramental peyote. If the state had such reasons, but decided that free exercise rights overrode them in other cases, then Mr Smith can argue that Oregon violates his constitutional rights if it refuses to override comparable reasons in his case (see Chapter 3, sec. 2.5 on comparative justice). The *Smith* test is consistent with a free exercise doctrine that would support such a contention by Mr Smith.

Defenders of the *Sherbert* test agree that the Free Exercise Clause should, at a minimum, guarantee that minority religions receive the same consideration from the state as other religions. But some will argue that free exercise also has a *noncomparative* component. Imagine that Oregon decided to criminalize possession of alcoholic beverages, making no exception for the sacramental wine used in many Christian church services. Oregon could argue that creating a "loophole" for sacramental wine would unduly impede enforcement of the statute against possessors of nonsacramental wine. The doctrine described above would allow Oregon to ban both wine and peyote without religious exemptions in either case. This is unjust, even though religious minorities are not being singled out. It is unjust because sacramental wine is important to Christians, just as sacramental peyote is important to members of the Native American Church, and Oregon has no sufficiently good reason for interfering with their religious practices. That is why the compelling state interest test from *Sherbert* is needed.

Defenders of *Smith* might reply that the hypothetical ban on wine, without religious exemptions, is unrealistic. Legislatures in the overwhelmingly Christian United States can be trusted always to make exceptions for Christian practices—exceptions that are large enough to accommodate the practices of minority religions, as well (Ely 1980). The members of minority faiths might worry, however, that this view protects their free exercise rights only insofar as their cherished practices happen to resemble those of majority faiths.

Study questions

(1) How are constitutions, charters, and other basic laws different from statutes? How do these differences affect proper interpretation?

(2) Is the US Constitution too difficult to amend? Why or why not?

(3) Is judicial review a politically legitimate institution? Is it fundamentally less democratic than other aspects of American government?

(4) Is Ronald Dworkin's distinction between semantic intention and expectation intention useful for thinking about Framer's intent? Can you give an example of a situation outside of the law in which someone would want to have their semantic intention followed?

(5) Should religious convictions receive greater constitutional protection in the United States than other convictions? From which laws, if any, would you exempt citizens on religious grounds? Can you explain your position in terms of a consistent method of constitutional interpretation?

Recommended reading

Ackerman, Bruce. 1991. *We the People: Foundations*. Cambridge, MA: Belknap.

Berman, Mitchell N. 2009. "Originalism is Bunk." *N.Y.U. Law Review* 84: 1–96.

Bickel, Alexander. 1962. *The Least Dangerous Branch*. New Haven: Yale University Press.

Bork, Robert. 1971. "Neutral Principles and Some First Amendment Problems." *Indiana Law Journal* 47: 1–35.

Dworkin, Ronald. 1996. *Freedom's Law: The Moral Reading of the American Constitution*. Cambridge, MA: Harvard University Press.

Ely, John Hart. 1980. *Democracy and Distrust: A Theory of Judicial Review*. Cambridge, MA: Harvard University Press.

Farber, Daniel, and Suzanna Sherry. 2002. *Desperately Seeking Certainty: The Misguided Quest for Constitutional Foundations*. Chicago: University of Chicago Press.

Freeman, Samuel. 1990/1. "Constitutional Democracy and the Legitimacy of Judicial Review." *Law and Philosophy* 9: 327–70.

Kramer, Larry D. 2004. *The People Themselves: Popular Constitutionalism and Judicial Review*. Oxford: Oxford University Press.

McConnell, Michael W. 1998. "Textualism and the Dead Hand of the Past." *George Washington Law Review* 66: 1127–40.

Rosenberg, Gerald N. 1993. *The Hollow Hope: Can Courts Bring About Social Change?* 2nd edn. Chicago: University of Chicago Press.

Scalia, Antonin. 1997. *A Matter of Interpretation: Federal Courts and the Law.* Princeton: Princeton University Press.

Tushnet, Mark. 1999. *Taking the Constitution Away from the Courts.* Princeton: Princeton University Press.

Waldron, Jeremy. 1999. *Law and Disagreement.* Oxford: Oxford University Press.

10
International Law

Philosophy of law overwhelmingly addresses domestic legal systems. As the process of globalization continues, this parochialism becomes less defensible year by year. Fortunately, legal philosophers have started to give international law more attention. This chapter briefly identifies some philosophical issues in international law. The discussion is split into analytical issues and normative issues.

1. Analytical issues

Some questions about international law fall within analytical jurisprudence, preeminently the question: is international law really law (Murphy 2006)? On John Austin's theory of law, there can be no legal system without a sovereign who issues commands—orders backed by threatened sanctions (Chapter 1, sec. 1). Because there is no such international sovereign, Austin concludes that there is no international legal system. What we call "international law" is not law, Austin believes, but merely "morality" (1995/1832: 164–7). The view that international law is not law (or, put more dramatically, that there is no such thing as international law) is known as *legal nihilism*.

H. L. A. Hart mentions three reasons that are often given for doubting that international law is law:

(1) International law lacks a legislature.
(2) There is no centrally organized effective system of sanctions.
(3) States cannot be brought before international courts without their prior consent. (1994/1961: 3)

Hart challenges Austin's theory of domestic law, noting that many laws are not created by a sovereign; many laws are not commands; and laws can bind lawmakers. So none of the three reasons just given entails that international law is not law. International treaties are not created by a legislature, are not commands from a superior to a subordinate, and apply to the signatories.

There are, moreover, sanctions in international law. The United Nations Security Council imposes sanctions, as does the European Union. The World Trade Organization authorizes trade retaliation.

Hart's own theory of law does not require sanctions. However, a rule cannot exist without some form of social pressure to comply, whether that pressure comes from formal sanctions or not. International actors do, in fact, feel pressure from other international actors, including states and nongovernmental organizations, to comply with international law. Hart mentions international laws restricting the use of force (*jus ad bellum*). Actors guide their behavior in accordance with these rules. They object when others violate the rules and demand responses on the basis of the rules. Actors who violate the rules sometimes deny, or try to conceal, the violation.

Hart's theory of law does not require a sovereign, so the lack of an international sovereign does not entail that international law is not law. However, Hart requires secondary rules, including a rule of recognition that is accepted by public officials from the internal point of view (see Chapter 1, sec. 4). Therefore, Hart retains a distinction between international and domestic law. At the international level, there is no legislature, judiciary, or executive. There are few, if any, secondary rules and no rule of recognition. To this extent, international law is analogous to a primitive, prelegal system that includes mostly primary rules.

This is not to suggest that international law is simple. On the contrary, its rules are more complex than some parts of domestic law. International lawyers use many of the same techniques and mechanisms as domestic lawyers do (Hart 1994/1961: 222). So the analogy with primitive systems is imperfect, but it holds insofar as neither primitive systems nor the international system have as many secondary rules as domestic systems have. Curiously, Hart classifies international law as law despite his belief that there is no international rule of recognition, which would seem to entail, on his own theory, that there is no international law (1994/1961: 228–9; for a critique of Hart on international law see Waldron 2008).

It could be argued that various international rules of recognition have emerged since Hart wrote in 1961. In 1980, the Vienna Convention on the Law of Treaties became effective. In 2001, the International Law Commission promulgated Articles on State Responsibility. Scholars argue that these documents created international rules of recognition: they specify how to create primary rules, what the criteria of breach are, and the consequences of breach. Although these documents hardly created a global legislature, there are many mechanisms for creating international law today. There are also international tribunals such as the World Trade Organization, the International Criminal Court, and the International Tribunal for the Law of the Sea.

1.1 Realism

One way to denigrate international law is to challenge its status as law. Another challenge comes from a prominent school of thought in international affairs, known as *realism* (not to be confused with legal realism; see Chapter 2, sec. 2). Realists need not deny that international law is law. They merely deny that it makes much, if any, difference to the conduct of states. Realists understand international actors as motivated by self-interest, understood relatively narrowly, rather than altruism or a desire to do the right thing. States obey international law only when they believe that doing so serves their interests (although farsighted states consider their interests in the long term, not just the short term). Realism proceeds from the premise that states want, above all, to avoid being dominated by other states; that they fear that others will attempt to dominate them; and that they perpetually attempt to dominate one another so as to avoid being dominated, themselves. In this Hobbesian state of affairs, it would be foolish and probably immoral for a leader to allow any moral qualms to stand in the way of advancing his nation's interests (Posner 2003; but see Lefkowitz 2011). Realism has been subjected to extensive critique in the international relations literature. It is opposed by several other schools of thought, but it has not been refuted and remains a viable position.

In the rest of this chapter, I shall assume that positive international law exists. The two major sources of international law are treaty and custom. There are important questions that I must ignore about what makes a norm part of international law.

2. Normative issues

The remainder of this chapter addresses normative issues. Realism is relevant again because it challenges the very project of evaluating international law in moral terms. Realists believe that states never, or almost never, act for moral reasons. This claim entails that even if someone proves, incontrovertibly, that a particular norm of international law is unjust, this proof will have no effect on the behavior of states. Therefore, evaluating international law in moral terms is a waste of time. (Some realists take the stronger position that nation-states simply have no moral obligations to one another, but I shall ignore this position.)

I already noted that realism is a contested position. Even if realism is correct, however, it does not follow that the moral evaluation of international law is pointless. Even if, as realists claim, national leaders never act for moral reasons in the international sphere, most of us are not national leaders. A group of private citizens, for example, might choose to evaluate a proposed international treaty in moral terms. Imagine they conclude that the treaty is just and good international policy. Assume, with the realists, that national leaders generally act in what they believe to be the national interest. Our concerned citizens might then make decisions that lead national leaders to conclude (truly or falsely) that ratification serves the national interest. The concerned citizens might, for example, put political pressure on national leaders to ratify the treaty. Many leaders surely believe that their own political survival is also important to the national interest. Even a leader who believes that ratifying a particular treaty does not serve the national interest may also believe that his own political defeat would be even worse for the nation than ratification. Such a leader may then be motivated to ratify the treaty, even if realism is true.

3. Human rights

In the century prior to the end of the Second World War, the sovereignty of the nation-state was seen as a barrier to international criticism of a state's internal affairs. Each state managed its domestic business without having to answer to international law, except when its actions affected other states in certain ways. All this changed with the adoption of the United Nations Charter in 1945. Today international law regulates not merely the interactions between states, but the treatment by states of their own residents. Above all, international law requires any state within its jurisdiction to respect human rights. States that violate human rights can be sanctioned. In most cases, sanctions involve being denied various rights, privileges, and immunities associated with membership in the community of nations, but international law also licenses military action.

International law embodies several overlapping conceptions of human rights. Conceptions of human rights are relevant to decisions about the use of international military force and humanitarian aid. These conceptions also inform international laws concerning the treatment of prisoners of war and noncombatants in wartime.

Human rights are moral rights that an individual possesses regardless of his membership in a religion, race, ethnicity, nationality, or other group. There are many different proposed lists of human rights, but most lists include rights to life, liberty, freedom of conscience, and subsistence. Human rights can be justified various ways. Utilitarians, for example, argue that protecting human rights maximizes utility. Human rights are necessary to foster fundamental human capabilities. They are entailed by the basic principle that every human being is entitled to equal concern and respect. They are necessary to promote human dignity.

Most human rights are not absolute. Limiting someone's liberty, for example, can be justified under the right conditions. To say that someone has a certain right is just to say that a reason—perhaps a very good reason—is needed to override it.

4. Relativism

Relativists deny the existence of universal human rights. They maintain that whether an individual has a moral right to *x* depends on her community (where *x* could be freedom of expression, basic medical care, etc.). Here is one version of relativism:

> An individual has a moral right to *x* if and only if the members of her community want her to receive *x*.

This view entails that if no one in Nora's community wants her to live, then she has no moral right to life. Critics of relativism (*universalists*) point out that it is often difficult to identify the members of a "community." Each of us belongs to multiple communities: one's nation, town, workplace, religious community, and extended family are all communities. Relativists must explain which of these many communities gets to define one's moral rights. Even within a single community, there can be disagreement. What if half of Nora's community leaps to defend her life, while the other half consciously refuses to do so? Does she have a right to life, or not?

Communities are also not static entities: over time they merge, fracture, and disappear. Human decisions determine the configuration of communities over time. On what basis should we make these decisions?

These questions are especially pressing in the international arena. Even if a nation constitutes a community, it is not the only community to which its residents belong. Moreover, domestic laws may or may not coincide with the beliefs of even a plurality of local residents. The overwhelming majority of South Africans during apartheid were black. They wanted legal rights that apartheid denied to them. Even if relativism is true, this fact would entail that black South Africans had moral rights that apartheid failed to recognize.

Relativism is a problematic position (Harman and Thomson 1996). However, some people who present themselves as relativists are actually expressing other beliefs. One such belief is that we should be careful when judging unfamiliar cultures. Practices and beliefs that seem outrageous to us may, in fact, be justified in their own time and place. Westerners have a sorry history of misjudging other cultures without understanding them.

Even if we conclude, after careful reflection, that human rights are being violated in a foreign land, there is a separate question about the ethics of possible remedies. Using military force in order to prevent human rights violations is sometimes counterproductive. Sanctions always inflict collateral damage on innocent individuals, especially residents of the sanctioned regime. Even public condemnation of a foreign government is a delicate matter. In some cases, no effective remedy may be available. But the fact that good remedies are not always available does not entail relativism about human rights.

5. Group rights and individual rights

The UN Charter protects primarily individual rights. Some argue that group rights should also be protected. A group right is a right that can be asserted only by someone representing a group, not by an individual on his own behalf. Rights asserted on behalf of groups include, among others, rights to land and natural resources, rights to govern themselves, and rights to teach their own languages.

A proponent of group rights could take the position that groups can benefit without benefits accruing to their members. But most proponents of group rights do not take this position. The belief that group rights, in addition to individual rights, should be protected does not entail that groups have a metaphysical existence beyond the existence of individual human beings. Instead, one may believe simply that protecting group rights is an effective means of benefiting individuals.

Normative theories of international law must decide which group rights, if any, the law should protect and what status group rights should have in relation to individual rights. Group rights may be defensible as means to the protection of individual interests. Some group rights can also be justified in terms of corrective justice (see Chapter 5, sec. 3). The descendants of an indigenous people whose land was taken, for example, may acquire a group right to collectively manage land today, or a right to reparations in the form of cash transfers. A postcolonial society might acquire group rights against a previous colonizer for treaty violations a century earlier. Such group rights serve to rectify injustices suffered as a group by the beneficiaries' ancestors.

6. Distributive justice

Some nations have great inequality: millions of citizens live in abject poverty, while a privileged few live comfortable or even luxurious lives. Similar inequalities obtain between wealthy and poorer nations and between the wealthy residents of some nations and poorer residents of others. Both the low absolute level of welfare endured by some and the large gap between the poor and the rich raise questions of distributive justice (see Chapter 3, sec. 2).

Political philosophers have described and defended many competing theories of distributive justice. Some conceptions of justice permit unlimited inequality and unlimited deprivation to prevail, at least if no one else directly causes it. But most conceptions of justice condemn at least the most severe inequalities, and many conceptions require substantial equality. This is not the place to review theories of distributive justice. Let us assume, instead, that we accept a theory of distributive justice that condemns at least some of the inequalities mentioned above. The question for a normative theory of international law concerns the extent to which law can and should attempt to reduce such inequalities.

Let us consider, first, the idea of using international law to reduce inequalities within a single nation. This is a controversial idea for several reasons. First, there are different conceptions of distributive justice. Some doubt that any one of these conceptions is objectively correct. If the leaders of a nation with great internal inequality reject egalitarian conceptions, then what gives foreigners the right to impose egalitarianism via international law? Secondly, even if there is a correct conception of distributive justice, efforts to enforce that conception via law could backfire and cause greater suffering and/or greater inequality.

Let us turn to the idea of using international law to reduce international inequality. As before, there is the concern about choosing the correct theory of justice. We can also ask: under what conditions, if any, do the powerful nations of the world have obligations of justice to reduce international inequality by law? Philosophers offer different answers to these questions. Some philosophers argue that a nation is obligated to reduce inequality between itself and another nation only if it has interacted with the other nation in ways that have brought about the inequality. Others would limit the duty to reduce inequality to cases in which the prospective donor nation has not just brought about the inequality, but has done so in a way that positively harmed the poorer nation. Still others hold that nations with the capacity to reduce inequality have a natural duty to do so even if they did not bring it about. The first two positions, that link the duty to reduce inequality to international interaction, require us to make judgments about the causes of international inequality. In some cases, these judgments are easily made, as when one nation invades another, with which it had no prior dealings, and plunders its natural resources, reducing it from comfort to poverty. In many cases, however, judgments of causal responsibility for inequality are more difficult to make. Some argue that they are usually too difficult to make at the international level, such that we rarely have obligations of justice to reduce international inequality.

7. Secession and self-determination

When a group of citizens share a language, ethnicity, religion, or culture, they sometimes think of themselves as a *people*: Kurds, Palestinians, Quebecois, Tutsi, and so on. Some peoples seek to exercise political self-determination, especially if they constitute a minority within their state. In the most dramatic assertions of self-determination, a people attempts to secede from their current state. The standard secession attempt occurs when a group of citizens try to form a new state on some of their old state's territory (usually territory that the group already occupies) thereby leaving their old state with less territory, fewer resources, and a smaller population. The new state then petitions other nations for full membership in the state system, with its rights and obligations.

Secession has received increasing attention from legal philosophers in the past two decades, inspired by secession attempts (some of them successful) in Serbia, Ethiopia, Canada (Quebec), Sri Lanka, Indonesia, the former Union of Soviet Socialist Republics (USSR), and elsewhere. This section reviews some of the legal-philosophical issues surrounding secession.

Some constitutions actually provide for secession (e.g. Ethiopia; but see Sunstein 1991). Most could be amended to do so. However, few secession attempts actually take place in accordance with constitutional procedures, or even governmental acquiescence. If the government does not acquiesce, then the secession is *unilateral* and often provokes violence. The basic questions are:

(1) Under what conditions, if any, is unilateral secession morally justified?
(2) Under what conditions, if any, should third parties intervene to assist or impede secession attempts?
(3) Under what conditions, if any, should foreign nations or NGOs give formal, legal recognition to a new state that emerges from a secession attempt?

According to Article 1 of the International Covenant of Civil and Political Rights, "[a]ll peoples have the right of self-determination" which allows them to "freely determine their political status." This language does not, however, entail an unconditional right to secede. There are at least two conditions under which international law provides a right to secede. First, colonies are permitted to secede from a colonizing power. Secondly, a people whose sovereign territory has been subjected to aggressive military action is permitted to reclaim that territory as a sovereign state once more.

The more difficult cases involve undemocratic regimes or democracies in which some citizens cannot effectively participate in the democratic process. On some interpretations, international law recognizes a right to secede for groups that are disenfranchised on racial or religious grounds. I shall concentrate on these cases.

First, I should clarify what I mean by a "right to secede," using the Hohfeldian framework (Chapter 3, sec. 2.2). A people has a *liberty-right* to secede if and only if secession is permissible. A liberty-right to secede is a weak kind of right: it does not entail that anyone else, including the state from which secession is attempted, has a duty to refrain from interfering with the attempt. It entails only that the people do not act impermissibly by attempting secession. A *claim-right* is stronger: a people has a claim-right to secede if and only if others have a duty to refrain from interfering with their secession attempt. A state from which a people is attempting to secede must know whether the people has a claim-right to secede, a liberty-right, or neither, before it can formulate a permissible response. So must third parties, such as NGOs and foreign governments, if they consider taking sides in the conflict.

7.1 Who has a right to secede?

Normative theories of secession fall into two categories: *remedial right theories* and *primary right theories*.

7.1.1 Remedial right theories

Remedial right theories understand unilateral secession as a remedy for long-standing, serious injustices—a measure of last resort, akin to revolution. Remedial right theorists disagree about the degree and type of injustice that warrants secession. Some insist that secession is justified only if the state has perpetrated, or at least tolerated, widespread violations of basic human rights, as in cases of genocide, mass dispossession, or systematic rape and torture. Others take a more permissive approach: they would permit secession from states that violate their own agreements with internal peoples regarding political self-determination. Some would also permit secession from states that refuse to recognize a people's morally legitimate claims of self-determination.

Remedial right theorists also disagree about how recent an injustice must be if it is to justify secession. The US government inflicted genocide against Native American tribes in the nineteenth century. Can the tribes invoke that history in support of secession today?

We might understand remedial right theories as making a claim based either on a natural right to defend oneself and others, or on a natural right to receive just compensation for wrongful losses, or both. In either case, the theory does not claim that a state loses its political legitimacy if its government mistreats a minority people. The state does not, for example, lose all of its territorial claims. Rather, the seceding people becomes entitled to a fair portion of the territory, while the state retains the rest. This redrawing of borders inevitably burdens those who remain citizens of the original state, who must now share a smaller territory, but it does not dispossess them entirely. Remedial justice would not allow their total dispossession because not every one of them necessarily supported unjust policies toward the seceding people.

Remedial right theories require and encourage states to treat all peoples justly, and authorize third parties (other nations and NGOs) to offer support to secession movements in states that fail to do so. Critics allege, however, that remedial theories place too many restrictions on secession. Many peoples around the world want and need greater self-determination, even if they cannot point to specific injustices against them. This brings us to ascriptivist theory.

7.1.2 Ascriptivist theory

Whereas remedial right theories differ regarding the injustices that warrant secession, primary right theories do not require any injustice whatsoever as a precursor to secession. The Flemish residents of Belgium, for example, are united by the Dutch language and a shared culture. They have suffered injustices in the past, but these do not rise to the level required by remedial right theories. The Flemish might, nevertheless, be entitled to secede under primary right theories.

On one type of primary right theory, *ascriptivist theory*, the Flemish constitute a people with a right to secede simply because they share language, culture, and ethnicity. In fact, sharing just one of these might suffice for them to constitute a people. The simplest ascriptivist theory holds that every people, so defined, has a moral right to secede from a state shared with other peoples and to form its own state.

Ascriptivists make several arguments in support of their position. One argument is the following:

(1) A group of individuals has a moral right to do whatever is necessary for its members to flourish.
(2) There are many peoples whose members cannot flourish without their own state.
(3) Therefore, every people has a moral right to secede from a state shared with other peoples and to form its own state.

Some ascriptivists support the second premise by observing that throughout history there have been many peoples whose members have been unable to flourish within a state that they do not control. In some cases, majorities have oppressed minorities, outlawing their practices or privately discriminating against them. In other cases, the minority needs resources to sustain its distinctive culture and the state refuses to provide them.

Another defense of the second premise proceeds from the observation that states have difficulty functioning if their citizens belong to more than one people. Democracy, in particular, requires a high level of trust and a willingness to accept political defeat. These attributes may be lacking in a state composed of two peoples, at least if they have a history of animosity. Also, distributive justice often requires that some people accept burdens for the sake of others. The burdened citizens may be prepared to accept a burdensome policy if they identify strongly with the beneficiaries. But if the benefits fall on one people, while the burdens fall on another, then the burdened people may resent the policy and work to overturn it, even if it is required by distributive justice. There may be greater social solidarity in a state comprising a single people.

Critics of ascriptivist theory argue that modern states have developed many effective techniques for protecting the interests of minority peoples within their borders and that social solidarity can exist across peoples, on the basis of shared citizenship itself. The simple claim that every people has a moral right to secede is also widely seen as dangerous and impractical. This is because most modern states contain more than one people and secession is often violent and costly for everyone. A weaker ascriptivist theory accommodates this concern by specifying that although an ascriptive group (e.g. the

Flemish), as such, has a right to secede, their right is overridden if the social costs of secession are too high. The theorist must then explain how high is "too high." If the social costs are too high, then the ascriptivist can insist that the people must be satisfied with less than secession: some legal rights to govern themselves within the larger state, for example, such as Native Americans enjoy with tribal government. This qualified ascriptivist theory is compatible with a remedial theory that is more permissive of secession in response to injustice.

7.1.3 Plebiscitary theories

Plebiscitary theories occupy a kind of middle ground between remedial right theories and ascriptivist theories. They do not require more than the ascriptivist's simple assertion that secession would be good for a people or the state. But they do not require historical injustices, as the remedial theorist does. Instead, they require something akin to a vote. Plebiscitary theory holds that a people has a right to secede if a majority or specified supermajority of its members favor secession. This theory has the advantage of making the choice to secede into a subject for democratic deliberation, rather than pure identity politics. Ascriptivist theories can be seen as assuming, atavistically, that the Flemish ought to secede just because they are Flemish. Yet being Flemish, in this sense, is not a chosen identity. A Flemish individual should have the liberty to choose her own degree of identification with Flanders. Some Flemish individuals see themselves as primarily Flemish, and some of them wish to secede. But other Flemish see themselves as primarily Belgian, European, Jewish, or what have you. Plebiscitary theory gives the Flemish the right to secede if a majority of them (or a supermajority, depending on the theory) endorses secession. Ascriptivist theories, by contrast, could be seen to authorize an outlying minority of Flemish citizens to attempt secession on behalf of all, even if most Flemish citizens oppose the attempt.

Critics also charge that plebiscitary theories foster instability, making the right to secede fluctuate with popular opinion. The boundaries of states are basic structural features of society, even more basic than other features that nations imbed in their basic laws (constitutions or charters), such as the branches of government. A simple national majority has no moral right, for example, to abolish the national legislature, and most constitutions do not allow a simple majority to do so. There is a far stronger case for not allowing a simple majority of a people (themselves typically a national minority) to redraw the boundaries of an entire nation by seceding. Plebiscitary theorists can reply by requiring a supermajority, but even a unanimous vote for secession by the Flemish would comprise a small minority of Belgians. Constitutions exist not just to prevent majorities from tyrannizing minorities, but to prevent minorities from favoring their own interests at everyone else's expense. If the Belgian state threatens the constitutional or human rights of the Flemish, then they may be entitled to secede under remedial right theory. But plebiscitary theories apply precisely in other cases.

Study questions

(1) Is international law less "lawlike" than domestic constitutional law? Why or why not?
(2) Are there any moral restrictions on what national leaders may do on the international stage to advance the interests of their constituents?
(3) Are there any absolute human rights? If so, what makes them absolute?
(4) Is it wrong for developed nations to hold the developing world to standards of "universal" human rights that were drafted by developed nations?
(5) How much are the wealthy nations of the world required to do to reduce poverty, famine, disease, and bloodshed in foreign lands?
(6) Under what conditions should your government recognize a newly formed government that grew out of a successful secession movement? Can we even define "success" for a secession movement without knowing if the international community recognizes the new state as such?

Recommended reading

Altman, Andrew, and Christopher Heath Wellman. 2004. "A Defense of International Criminal Law." *Ethics* 115: 35–67.

Besson, Samantha, and John Tasioulas, eds. 2010. *The Philosophy of International Law*. Oxford: Oxford University Press.

Brilmayer, Lea. 1991. "Secession and Self-Determination: A Territorial Interpretation." *Yale Journal of International Law* 16: 177–202.

Buchanan, Allen. 2004. *Justice, Legitimacy, and Self-Determination*. Oxford: Oxford University Press.

Capps, Patrick, and Julian Rivers. 2010. "Kant's Concept of International Law." *Legal Theory* 16: 229–57.

Cassese, Antonia. 1995. *Self-Determination of Peoples: A Legal Reappraisal*. New York: Cambridge University Press.

Hessler, Kristen. 2005. "Resolving Interpretive Conflicts in International Human Rights Law." *Journal of Political Philosophy* 13: 29–52.

Lefkowitz, David. 2011. "The Principle of Fairness and States' Duty to Obey International Law."
Canadian Journal of Law and Jurisprudence 24: 327–46.

Margalit, Avishai, and Joseph Raz. 1990. National Self-Determination. *Journal of Philosophy* 87:
439–61.

May, Larry. 2005. *Crimes against Humanity: A Normative Account.* Cambridge: Cambridge University
Press.

Meyer, Lukas H. 2009. *Legitimacy, Justice and Public International Law.* Cambridge: Cambridge
University Press.

Miller, David. 1995. *On Nationality.* New York: Clarendon Press.

Moore, Margaret, ed. 1998. *National Self-Determination and Secession.* Oxford: Oxford University
Press.

Murphy, Sean D. 2006. *Principles of International Law.* St. Paul: West Publishing.

Philpott, D. 1995. "A Defense of Self-Determination." *Ethics* 105: 352–85.

Posner, Eric A. 2003. "Do States Have a Moral Obligation to Obey International Law?" *Stanford Law
Review* 55: 1901–19.

Ratner, Steven R. 2005. "Is International Law Impartial?" *Legal Theory* 11: 39–74.

Rawls, John. 2001. *The Law of Peoples.* Cambridge: Harvard University Press.

Sunstein, Cass. 1991. "Constitutionalism and Secession." *University of Chicago Law Review* 58:
633–70.

Waldron, Jeremy. 2008. "Hart and the Principles of Legality." In *The Legacy of H. L. A. Hart*, ed. Matthew
H. Kramer, Claire Grant, Ben Colburn, and Antony Hatzistavrou. Oxford: Oxford University
Press.

Wellman, Christopher Heath. 2005. *A Theory of Secession: The Case for Political Self-Determination.*
Cambridge: Cambridge University Press.

Notes

Preface

1. The latter two terms sometimes refer to domains that are narrower than, broader than, or altogether distinct from legal philosophy in my sense. "Jurisprudence" can refer to (1) legal philosophy in general; (2) a specific branch of legal philosophy, often called "analytical jurisprudence," that studies the nature of law, as opposed to specific bodies of law or evaluations of law; (3) the academic study of law (e.g. the University of Pretoria trains lawyers in the "Department of Jurisprudence"); or (4) a particular body of doctrine applied by courts (e.g. "Australian contract jurisprudence"). "Legal theory" can refer to (1) legal philosophy in general; (2) philosophical inquiry into the nature of law; or (3) all theoretical reflection on law, whether informed by academic philosophy or by another discipline such as linguistics, literary criticism, or social science.

Chapter 1

1. The sovereign could, perhaps, be a group of human beings, although they would need a mechanism for resolving internal conflicts. The important point is that, as a group, they would be above the law.
2. 115 N.Y. 506 (1889).
3. 32 N.J. 358 (1960).
4. Mass. Const. part 1, art. XXX.
5. 5 U.S. (1 Cranch) 137, 163 (1803).

Chapter 2

1. 9 Ex. 341 (Eng. 1854).
2. 3 Murph. & H. 305 (Ex. 1837).

Chapter 3

1. ALM GL ch. 272, § 17 (2012).
2. RI Gen Laws § 11–6-1 (2006).

Chapter 4

1. First published in 1849 as "Resistance to Civil Government."

Chapter 5

1. Named after economists Nicholas Kaldor (1908–86) and Sir John Hicks (1904–89).
2. 159 F.2d 169 (2d Cir. 1947).
3. *Bolton v. Stone* (1951) App. Cas. 850 (H.L.).
4. 248 N.Y. 339 (1928).
5. Restatement 2d of Contracts, § 1.
6. Restatement 2d of Contracts, § 24.
7. Restatement 2d of Contracts, § 71.

Chapter 6

1. MPC § 213.5.
2. MPC § 2.02(a).
3. MPC §§ 210.4, 211.1(b), 220.3.
4. MPC § 3.02(1).
5. 14 Q.B.D. 273 (1884).
6. Re A, [2000] 4 All ER 961.
7. *Regina v. M'Naghten*, 8 Eng. Rep. 718 (1843).
8. Ibid.
9. Not to be confused with libertarians in political philosophy, who believe in minimal government.
10. *Smith v. U.S.*, 36 F.2d 548 (D.C. Cir. 1929).
11. MPC § 401(1), bracketed language appears in original.
12. MPC § 5.02.
13. MPC § 5.03.
14. MPC §§ 5.01(1)(a), (b).
15. MPC § 5.01(2).

Chapter 7

1. Elements adapted from H. L. A. Hart, *Punishment and Responsibility: Essays in the Philosophy of Law* (Oxford: Oxford University Press, 1968).
2. Theft Act 1968, § 1.

3. Execution, of course, also incapacitates. So can various forms of bodily invasion, such as maiming, chemical castration, lobotomy, and so on.

4. Based on Philip K. Dick, "The Minority Report" in *Selected Stories of Philip K. Dick* (New York: Pantheon, 2002), originally published in 1956.

5. *Furman v. Georgia*, 408 U.S. 238 (1972).

6. The case is *Furman v. Georgia*.

7. 481 U.S. 279 (1987).

Chapter 8

1. 143 U.S. 457 (1892).

Chapter 9

1. This hypothetical case is based on *Street v. Queensland Bar Association*, 168 CLR 461 (1989).

2. 5 U.S. 137 (1803).

3. 304 U.S. 144, 152–3 n. 4 (1938) (citations omitted).

4. *Plessy v. Ferguson*, 163 U.S. 537 (1896).

5. A recent survey found that 151 of 198 countries include some form of protection for religion in their constitutions or basic laws (*Global Restrictions on Religion*, Pew Forum on Religion & Public Life, 2009).

6. I shall ignore the fact that the First Amendment only mentions Congress, not state legislatures. The Free Exercise Clause was applied to the states via the Due Process Clause of the Fourteenth Amendment in *Cantwell v. Connecticut*, 310 U.S. 296 (1940), in a move known as "incorporation." It is interesting, however, to ask whether incorporation conflicts with originalism.

7. 374 U.S. 398 (1963).

Glossary

abolitionist regarding capital punishment, one who wishes to abolish the penalty.

acceptance a response to an OFFER that forms a CONTRACT.

actus reus see CONDUCT ELEMENT.

adjudication the process of deciding legal cases and controversies, normally the activity of judges.

analytical jurisprudence a branch of LEGAL PHILOSOPHY concerned with the nature of law (what makes something law and not something else) and the implications of law (what necessarily follows from the fact that something is law).

ascriptivist theory the view that a people have a right to SECEDE simply because they share language, culture, and ethnicity.

attempt a type of INCHOATE OFFENSE in which the defendant tries unsuccessfully to commit a certain complete crime.

authority the condition in virtue of which the state's activities are morally justified; may encompass the right to instruct others, to use coercion, and to impose duties.

autonomy the condition of regulating oneself.

bad samaritan a bystander who fails to assist a stranger in distress.

beneficence doing good.

bias the claim that morally impermissible factors, especially race, influence whether certain convicts are executed.

breach failure to perform on a CONTRACT.

brutalization the alleged tendency of executions to encourage violent crime.

canon of construction an accepted rule or guideline for interpreting certain legal texts.

caprice the claim that convicts who are executed are not selected on a rational basis from others who are equally deserving.

cause-in-fact one of two necessary elements of causation in the law, sometimes understood as an event or condition without which the effect in question would not have occurred.

civil disobedience a form of civil resistance involving deliberate law-breaking under special conditions.

collective property property that is owned by everyone, although not everyone may be entitled to use it.

common property property that everyone is legally entitled to use, such as a public park.

comparative justice similar cases should be treated similarly.

compatibilism the view that at least some people have FREE WILL, although human beings are subject to the same physical laws that govern everything else in the universe; opposes HARD DETERMINISM and LIBERTARIANISM.

comply to conform to the law, for whatever reason; compare to OBEY.

concept a relatively general idea that may exist in different versions, known as CONCEPTIONS (e.g. aesthetic beauty is a single concept of which different artistic schools have different conceptions).

conception a particular version of a certain CONCEPT.

conduct element a voluntary act or failure to act that is necessary to a crime; ACTUS REUS.

consent theory a theory of political obligation according to which such obligations are justified by some form of consent of the governed.

consequentialism a theory holding that an action or rule is morally right if and only if it has consequences at least as good as any other available, regardless of how those consequences come about.

consideration something of value offered in order to persuade another party to enter a CONTRACT.

constructive intent intent that someone did not actually have, but would have had if he had considered the issue.

constructive interpretation interpreting something in a way that takes account of the facts, while casting the object in the best possible light as an object of its kind.

content-independent reason a reason that entails no direct connection between the reason and actions for which it is a reason; for example, reasons generated by the mere fact that someone in authority has given an order.

contract a legally enforceable agreement.

copyright the exclusive right to make copies, license, and otherwise exploit a literary, musical, or artistic work.

corrective justice requiring those who cause wrongful losses to compensate their victims.

countermajoritarian difficulty tension between judicial review and the ideals of democracy, especially pertaining to federal courts in the United States.

criminal law general part of the part of the criminal law concerning all factors that are relevant to deserved punishment other than those that involve causing, attempting, or risking harm to others.

criminal law special part of the part of the criminal law concerning acts that involve causing, attempting, or risking harm to others.

Critical Legal Studies a movement that challenged several basic assumptions about law, including its legitimacy, neutrality, objectivity, and insulation from politics; ascendant in the United States from 1975–2000.

damages money or something of value that a defendant is required to pay to a successful PLAINTIFF as compensation.

dead hand of the past the idea that the drafters of most constitutional provisions have no AUTHORITY over us today; used as an argument against JUDICIAL REVIEW.

deduction a form of reasoning in which a conclusion follows necessarily from the premises, so that the conclusion cannot be false if the premises are true.

default rule in CONTRACT law, a rule that courts apply when a question arises that is not covered by specific contractual language.

defendant a party who is being sued or tried for a crime.

defense an assertion made in order to defeat a civil claim or criminal charge.

deontology a family of moral theories that assign basic significance to concepts such as rights, duties, justice, fairness, equality, autonomy, liberty, and desert; contrasted with CONSEQUENTIALISM, UTILITARIANISM.

deter to discourage someone from committing a crime (e.g. by threat of punishment).

discretion the prerogative of a decision maker to exercise judgment in applying legal NORMS.

distributive justice requiring resources to be justly distributed.

divine law law created by a deity (e.g. the God of the *Bible*).

duress a level of constraint or coercion that constitutes an EXCUSE in criminal law or that suffices to void a CONTRACT executed under its influence.

easy case a case in which the legally correct answer is easy to identify.

efficient there is no better state of affairs, from the perspective of welfare economics.

egalitarianism individuals should be treated equally in certain respects.

elements components of a criminal offense that are jointly necessary and sufficient for its existence.

exclusionary reason a reason to disregard certain other reasons; for example, the fact that an action is illegal may be a reason for me not to treat my desire to perform the action as a reason to do so.

exclusive positivism a version of LEGAL POSITIVISM which holds that there cannot be moral standards of LEGALITY; opposed to INCLUSIVE POSITIVISM.

excuse a circumstance that grants immunity for otherwise criminal conduct; a DEFENDANT who asserts an excuse is claiming that he is less culpable than he would otherwise be for his actions.

external point of view the point of view from which laws are seen as regularities of someone else's behavior; opposed to the INTERNAL POINT OF VIEW.

externality an effect of a transaction on a nonparty; can be positive or negative.

fact finder an individual or group assigned to determine the facts in a trial; a jury in a jury trial or a judge in a bench trial.

fair-play principle if a group of individuals participates in a rule-based cooperative enterprise, and each member restricts his liberty in ways that produce benefits for everyone, then anyone who benefits from the enterprise owes everyone else a duty to submit to all of its rules.

formal legality treating legally similar cases similarly.

formalism treating the form of a case as more important than its substance; MECHANICAL JURISPRUDENCE.

framer's intent what the drafters or ratifiers of a constitutional provision intended for it to mean or accomplish.

free will a certain type of capacity, thought to be possessed by rational agents, to choose a course of action from among various alternatives.

fundamental values interpreting a constitution as the embodiment of some of the basic values of the society.

good samaritan a bystander who assists a stranger in distress.

hard case a case in which the legally correct answer, if there is one, is difficult to identify.

hard determinism the view that no one has FREE WILL because human beings are subject to the same physical laws that govern everything else in the universe and there is no room in the physical world for genuine freedom; opposes LIBERTARIANISM and COMPATIBILISM.

human rights international norms that help to protect everyone, everywhere from political, legal, and social abuses, often understood as a type of NATURAL RIGHT.

hypothetical contract an imaginary agreement between citizens, thought by some to justify the state.

imminent likely to occur at any moment, as in harm.

incapacitate to restrict someone's ability to commit crimes (e.g. by incarceration).

inchoate offense an incomplete part of a complete criminal offense, namely ATTEMPT, solicitation, and conspiracy.

inclusive positivism a version of LEGAL POSITIVISM which holds that there can be moral standards of LEGALITY; opposed to EXCLUSIVE POSITIVISM.

indeterminate possessing more than one possible meaning.

infancy being under a specified age of legal responsibility; constitutes an EXCUSE in criminal law.

insanity a mental defect from which the defendant suffered when he committed the crime and which provides a legal EXCUSE, for example, because he did not understand his action to be unlawful, or was unable to control himself.

intellectual property property resulting from original creative thought, such as patents, COPYRIGHTED materials, and trademarks.

internal point of view the point of view from which laws are seen as giving one reasons for action; opposed to the EXTERNAL POINT OF VIEW.

interpretive question a question concerning the correct interpretation of something.

irrevocability the fact that an executed person cannot be brought back to life if his innocence is later discovered; used as an objection to capital punishment.

judicial review a process whereby the judiciary evaluates acts or rules of other branches of government, especially the review of legislation for constitutionality.

jus ad bellum considerations of justice in the decision to resort to war.

justification a type of DEFENSE asserting that there is a legally sufficient reason for an otherwise criminal act, under the circumstances as they actually are.

Kaldor-Hicks efficient a change is Kaldor-Hicks efficient if a PARETO-OPTIMAL outcome can be reached by arranging sufficient compensation from those who are made better-off to those who are made worse-off, so that all would end up no worse-off than before.

knowledge an actor has knowledge with respect to an element if he believes that it exists or, in the case of result elements, if he believes with "practical certainty" that it exists.

law and economics an intellectual movement originating in the 1960s that uses the tools of economics to analyze law.

legal content the meaning of a legal norm.

legal moralism the view that preventing inherently immoral behavior is always a morally relevant reason for state coercion.

legal nihilism the view that international law is not law.

legal philosophy the philosophical study of law and legal systems; also known as *philosophy of law, jurisprudence*, or *legal theory*.

legal positivism a position within ANALYTICAL JURISPRUDENCE that emphasizes the social nature of law.

legal realism a school of thought emphasizing that judges shape the law, often in accordance with their own policy preferences; originated in the United States in the early twentieth century.

legal reasoning reasoning that aims to reach legal conclusions.

legal system a social system that generates and sustains law.

legality the character of being legal or legally valid; legal validity.

legislative history any of various materials generated in the process of creating legislation, including committee reports, committee hearings, floor debates, and histories of actions taken.

legislator's intent what a legislator intended to express or achieve.

lesser-evils defense an actor who commits an action that would otherwise constitute a crime can assert the lesser-evils defense if the harm he tries to avoid is greater than the harm the act would cause; also *necessity defense*.

lex talionis a wrongdoer should suffer injury similar to what he inflicted; an eye for an eye.

liberalism a political philosophy advocating the freedom of the individual, parliamentary systems of government, nonviolent modification of institutions, and governmental guarantees of individual rights and civil liberties.

libertarianism the view that at least some people have FREE WILL, and that human beings are not subject to the same physical laws that govern everything else in the universe; opposes HARD DETERMINISM and COMPATIBILISM.

living constitutionalism the view that the meaning of a constitution changes over time with the changing needs and values of society.

mechanical jurisprudence see FORMALISM.

mens rea guilty mind or criminal intent in committing the act.

mistake of fact a mistaken belief about facts that are relevant to the legality of an action.

mistake of law a mistaken belief that the law permits, prohibits, or requires an act.

mistake convicting an innocent person, used as an objection to capital punishment.

moral relativism the view that moral facts are relative to something (cultures, individuals, time periods).

natural law theory a school of thought emphasizing necessary connections between law and morality or reason.

natural law law that is knowable to all rational human beings, especially laws of prudence and morality.

natural lawyer a proponent of NATURAL LAW THEORY.

natural right a moral right possessed by each individual just in virtue of being human.

negative liberty an absence of external obstacles or constraints.

negligence failure to exercise the degree of care that the law requires in the circumstances.

nonoriginalism the view that STATUTES or constitutional provisions need not always be understood as they were understood when they were enacted.

norm a standard specifying how someone ought to act or how something ought to be.

obey to deliberately conform to the law because it is the law; compare to COMPLY.

obiter dictum any remarks contained in the opinion of a court that are not necessary to the holding, and hence do not serve as precedent; dictum.

offer a proposal that requires only ACCEPTANCE in order to form a CONTRACT.

open texture the fact that it is sometimes unclear whether or not a certain thing falls within the scope of a certain term.

original position a hypothetical situation, envisioned by John Rawls (1921–2002), in which rational, self-interested parties choose general principles of justice to govern the basic structure of their society, without knowledge of individuating characteristics that could bias their choice.

originalism the view that STATUTES or constitutional provisions should be understood as they were understood when they were enacted.

Pareto-optimal an outcome such that no one can be made better-off without making at least one person worse-off.

personal property property consisting of physical objects or financial instruments.

philosophical anarchism the view that there is no duty to obey the law just because it is the law.

piracy unauthorized reproduction or use of intellectual property.

plaintiff a party who brings suit in a court of law.

plebiscitary theory the view that a people has a right to SECEDE if a majority or specified supermajority of its members favor secession.

policy a NORM or standard setting a goal for improvement in an economic, political, or social feature of the community.

political obligation a moral obligation that one bears simply in virtue of being a citizen or resident, such as a duty to obey the law, to support just institutions, or to serve in the military.

positive law law created by human beings, in contrast to DIVINE LAW or NATURAL LAW.

positive liberty the actual possibility of acting, including whatever internal or external resources are needed.

possession actual holding or occupancy of property, with or without ownership.

power-conferring a law that authorizes someone to act, as opposed to requiring action.

precedent a legal decision or decisions that serve as an authoritative rule or pattern in similar cases arising thereafter.

precedent horizontal precedent created by a court at the same level as, or a lower level than, the present court.

precedent vertical precedent created by a higher court.

prescriptive question a question concerning how things ought to be.

primary rule a rule that requires one to act or to refrain from action.

principle a NORM or standard required by justice, fairness, or another dimension of morality; for example, "innocent until proven guilty."

private law law dealing with the legal relationships of private individuals.

pro tanto reason a reason that has some weight, but that can be overridden by stronger reasons; also known as a *prima facie reason*.

proportional having proper magnitude relative to something else, as in punishment and crime.

proximate cause a CAUSE-IN-FACT with legal relevance, also known as an "adequate," "direct," "effective," "operative," "legal," or "responsible" cause.

public law law concerned with legal relationships between the state and individuals or with the relations among governmental agencies.

purpose an actor has the mental state of purpose with respect to a CONDUCT ELEMENT if and only if he intends to engage in specified conduct while aware of its nature; he has the mental state of PURPOSE with respect to a result element if and only if he has the conscious object of causing that result.

purposivism the view that a legal text should be understood in accordance with the purposes of its drafters or ratifiers.

ratio decidendi the rationale for a decision by a court, that which the decision establishes as PRECEDENT.

realism in international relations theory the view that international actors are motivated by self-interest, understood relatively narrowly, rather than altruism, and hence that international law has little or no effect on their behavior.

reckless action taken without regard for a substantial and unjustifiable risk of which the actor was aware.

regression analysis a statistical procedure for determining a relationship between a dependent variable and an independent variable for a given population.

reliance acting upon another's statement of alleged fact, claim, or promise.

remedial right theory the view that unilateral SECESSION is a remedy for long-standing, serious injustices.

restitution returning to the legal owner property or the monetary value of the owner's loss.

retentionist regarding capital punishment, one who wishes to retain the penalty.

retribution punishing wrongdoers because they deserve it.

retributivism a family of theories holding that the purpose of punishment is RETRIBUTION.

rule of law the idea that all people and institutions are subject to law that is fairly applied and enforced.

rule of recognition a SECONDARY RULE specifying criteria by which to identify a NORM as legally valid within a certain legal system.

rule-skepticism the view that rules cannot dictate a particular result.

sanction an unwelcome consequence inflicted upon someone, as in punishment.

scapegoat someone who is made to bear the blame for others or to suffer in their place.

secede to withdraw formally from a nation, state, or other political union.

secondary rule a rule that concerns PRIMARY RULES, such as RULES OF RECOGNITION, change, and adjudication.

sentencing schedule an assignment of particular sentence ranges to particular crime types.

separability thesis the thesis, originally identified with LEGAL POSITIVISM, that there is no necessary connection between law and morality.

social fact thesis the thesis, important to LEGAL POSITIVISM, that the existence and content of laws are exclusively determined by facts about human mental states and behavior.

stare decisis the principle that courts should recognize a presumption against modifying established PRECEDENT.

statute an enactment made by a legislature and expressed in a formal document.

strict liability liability that is imposed without a finding of fault.

strong paternalism where the state limits someone's liberty for her own sake because it disagrees with her conception of her own welfare.

textualism the view that a legal text should be understood as a reasonable reader would.

tort a wrongful act (other than breach of contract) that results in injury to another's person, property, reputation, or the like, and for which the injured party is entitled to compensation.

tortfeasor one who commits a TORT.

universalism the view that there are moral norms that are correct in every time and place, whether they are socially recognized or not; opposed to MORAL RELATIVISM.

utilitarianism a version of CONSEQUENTIALISM holding that an action or rule is morally right if and only if it maximizes welfare.

weak paternalism where the state limits someone's liberty in order to compensate for his presumed misunderstanding or ignorance of fact.

welfarism the view that human well-being is the only thing with intrinsic value.

Bibliography

The American Heritage Dictionary of the English Language. 4th edn. Boston: Houghton Mifflin, 2000.

Ackerman, Bruce. *We the People: Foundations.* Cambridge, MA: Belknap, 1991.

—. *We the People: Transformations.* Cambridge, MA: Belknap, 2000.

Alexander, Larry. "Constrained by Precedent." *Southern California Law Review* 63 (1989): 1–64.

—. "Deontology at the Threshold." *San Diego Law Review* 37 (2000): 893–912.

—. "Law and Exclusionary Reasons." *Philosophical Topics* 18 (1990): 5–22.

—. "'With Me, It's All Er Nuthin': Formalism in Law and Morality." *University of Chicago Law Review* 66 (1999): 530–65.

Alexander, Larry, and Kimberly Kessler Ferzan. *Crime and Culpability: A Theory of Criminal Law.* Cambridge: Cambridge University Press, 2009.

Alexander, Larry, and Ken Kress. "Against Legal Principles." *Law and Interpretation: Essays in Legal Philosophy.* Ed. Andrei Marmor. Oxford: Clarendon Press, 1995, 279–327.

Alexander, Larry, and Emily Sherwin. *The Rule of Rules.* Durham, NC: Duke University Press, 2001.

Allan, T. R. S. *Law, Liberty, and Justice: The Legal Foundations of British Constitutionalism.* Oxford: Oxford University Press, 1993.

Anderson, Elizabeth. "What Is the Point of Equality?" *Ethics* 109 (1999): 287–337.

Aquinas, Thomas. 1274. *Summa Theologiae.* Ed. Thomas Gilby. Garden City, NY: Image Books, 1969.

Aristotle. 1941. *Nichomachean Ethics.* In *The Basic Works of Aristotle.* Ed. Richard McKeon. New York: Random House .

Atiyah, P. S. *Promises, Morals, and Law.* Oxford: Clarendon Press, 1981.

Austin, John. *The Province of Jurisprudence Determined.* 1832. Ed. Wilfrid E. Rumble. New York: Cambridge University Press, 1995.

Baldus, David C., George Woodworth, and Catherine M. Grosso. "Race and Proportionality since *McCleskey v. Kemp* (1987): Different Actors with Mixed Strategies of Denial and Avoidance." *Columbia Human Rights Law Review* (2007): 143–77.

Baldus, David C., George Woodworth, David Zuckerman, Neil Alan Weiner, and Barbara Broffitt. "An Empirical and Legal Overview, with Recent Findings from Philadelphia." *Cornell Law Review* 83 (1998): 1638–770.

Balkin, J. M. "Ideology as Constraint." *Stanford Law Review* 43 (1991): 1133–69.

Barnett, Randy E. "A Consent Theory of Contract." *Columbia Law Review* 86 (1986): 269–321.

—. "Restitution: A New Paradigm of Criminal Justice." *Ethics* 87 (1977): 279–301.

Barro, Roberto. "Dictatorship and the Rule of Law: Rules and Military Power in Pinochet's Chile." *Democracy and the Rule of Law.* Ed. Jose Maria Maravall and Adam Przeworski. Cambridge: Cambridge University Press, 2003. 188–219.

Bayles, Michael D. "The Justifiability of Civil Disobedience." *Review of Metaphysics* 24 (1970): 3–20.

Bedau, Hugo A. "Civil Disobedience and Personal Responsibility for Injustice." *Monist* 54 (1970): 517–35.

Benson, Peter. "The Basis of Corrective Justice and Its Relation to Distributive Justice." *Iowa Law Review* 77 (1992): 515–624.

Bentham, Jeremy. "Anarchical Fallacies." *The Works of Jeremy Bentham.* 1843. Ed. John Bowring. London: Russell & Russell, 1962.

Berlin, Isaiah. *Four Essays on Liberty.* Oxford: Oxford University Press, 1969.

Bickel, Alexander. *The Least Dangerous Branch.* New Haven: Yale University Press, 1962.

Boonin, David. *The Problem of Punishment.* Cambridge: Cambridge University Press, 2008.

Bork, Robert. "Neutral Principles and Some First Amendment Problems." *Indiana Law Journal* 47 (1971): 1–35.

Brewer, Scott. "Exemplary Reasoning: Semantics, Pragmatics, and the Rational Force of Legal Argument by Analogy." *Harvard Law Review* 109.5 (1996): 923–1028.

Calabresi, Guido. *A Common Law for the Age of Statutes.* Cambridge, MA: Harvard University Press, 1982.

Carothers, Thomas. "The Rule of Law Revival." *Foreign Affairs* 77.2 (1998): 95–106.

Coase, Ronald. "The Problem of Social Cost." *Journal of Law and Economics* 3 (1960): 1–44.

Cohen, Carl. *Civil Disobedience: Conscience, Tactics, and the Law.* New York: Columbia University Press, 1971.

Coleman, Jules. "The Practice of Corrective Justice." *Philosophical Foundations of Tort Law.* Ed. David G. Owen. Oxford: Clarendon Press, 1995.

—. *The Practice of Principle.* Oxford: Oxford University Press, 2001.

—. *Risks and Wrongs.* Cambridge: Cambridge University Press, 1992.

Dalton, Clare. "An Essay in the Deconstruction of Contract Doctrine." *Yale Law Journal* 94 (1985): 997–1114.

Dan-Cohen, Meir. "Decision Rules and Conduct Rules: On Acoustic Separation in Criminal Law." *Harvard Law Review* 97 (1984): 625–77.

Dancy, Jonathan. *Ethics without Principles.* Oxford: Oxford University Press, 2004.

Daniels, Normal. "Equality of What? Welfare, Resources, or Capabilities?" *Philosophy and Phenomenological Research* 50 (supp. vol.) (1990): 273–96.

Darley, John M. "The Ex Ante Function of the Criminal Law." *Law and Society Review* 35 (2001): 165–89.

Davis, Michael. *To Make the Punishment Fit the Crime.* Boulder: Westview Press, 1992.

Devlin, Patrick. *The Enforcement of Morals.* Oxford: Oxford University Press, 1965.

Dezhbakhsh, Hashem, Paul H. Rubin, and Joanna M. Shepherd. "Does Capital Punishment Have a Deterrent Effect? New Evidence from Postmoratorium Panel Data." *American Law and Economics Review* 5.2 (2003): 344–76.

Dicey, A. V. *Introduction to the Law of the Constitution.* 1885. Indianapolis: Liberty Fund, 1982.

Donohue, John J., III, and Justin Wolfers. "Uses and Abuses of Empirical Evidence in the Death Penalty Debate." *Stanford Law Review* 58 (2005): 791–846.

Duff, R. A. *Punishment, Communication, and Community.* Oxford: Oxford University Press, 2001.

Dworkin, Gerald. "Devlin Was Right: Law and the Enforcement of Morality." *William & Mary Law Review* 40 (1999): 927–46.

Dworkin, Ronald. *Freedom's Law: The Moral Reading of the American Constitution*. Cambridge, MA: Harvard University Press, 1996.

—. *Law's Empire*. Cambridge, MA: Harvard University Press, 1986.

—. "Lord Devlin and the Enforcement of Morals." *Taking Rights Seriously*. Cambridge, MA: Harvard University Press, 1977a.

—. "The Model of Rules I." *Taking Rights Seriously*. 1967. Cambridge, MA: Harvard University Press, 1977b. 14–45.

—. "The Original Position." *University of Chicago Law Review* 40 (1973): 500–33.

—. *Taking Rights Seriously*. Cambridge, MA: Harvard University Press, 1977c.

—. "Why Efficiency?" *Hofstra Law Review* 8 (1980): 568–70.

Elster, Jon, and John E. Roemer, eds. *Interpersonal Comparisons of Well-Being*. Cambridge: Cambridge University Press, 1993.

Ely, John Hart. *Democracy and Distrust: A Theory of Judicial Review*. Cambridge, MA: Harvard University Press, 1980.

—. "The Wages of Crying Wolf: A Comment on Roe V. Wade." *Yale Law Journal* 82 (1973): 920–49.

Endicott, Timothy A. O. "The Impossibility of the Rule of Law." *Oxford Journal of Legal Studies* 19 (1999): 1–18.

Enoch, David, and Andrei Marmor. "The Case against Moral Luck." *Law and Philosophy* 26 (2007): 405–36.

Epstein, Richard A. *Simple Rules for a Complex World*. Cambridge, MA: Harvard University Press, 1995.

—. *Takings*. Cambridge, MA: Harvard University Press, 1985.

—. "A Theory of Strict Liability." *Journal of Legal Studies* 2 (1973): 151–204.

Eskridge, William N., Jr. *Dynamic Statutory Interpretation*. Cambridge, MA: Harvard University Press, 1994.

Farber, Daniel, and Suzanna Sherry. *Desperately Seeking Certainty: The Misguided Quest for Constitutional Foundations*. Chicago: University of Chicago Press, 2002.

Farrell, Daniel M. "The Justification of Deterrent Violence." *Ethics* 100 (1990): 301–17.

Feinberg, Joel. "Causing Voluntary Actions." *Metaphysics and Explanation*. Ed. W. H. Capitan and D. D. Merrill. Pittsburgh: University of Pittsburgh Press, 1966. 29–47.

—. "The Expressive Function of Punishment." *Doing and Deserving*. Princeton: Princeton University Press, 1970.

—. *Harm to Others*. Oxford: Oxford University Press, 1984.

—. *Harmless Wrongdoing*. New York: Oxford University Press, 1990.

Finnis, John. *Natural Law and Natural Rights*. Oxford: Clarendon Press, 1980.

—. "On the Incoherence of Legal Positivism." *Notre Dame Law Review* 75 (2000): 1597–611.

Fischer, John Martin, Robert Kane, Derk Pereboom, and Manuel Vargas. *Four Views on Free Will*. Malden, MA: Blackwell, 2007.

Fletcher, George P. "Fairness and Utility in Tort Theory." *Harvard Law Review* 72 (1972): 537–73.

Foot, Philippa. *Natural Goodness*. Oxford: Oxford University Press, 2001.

—. "The Problem of Abortion and the Doctrine of Double Effect." *Oxford Review* 5 (1967): 5–15.

Fortas, Abe. *Concerning Dissent and Civil Disobedience*. New York: New American Library, 1968.

Frank, Jerome. *Law and the Modern Mind*. 1930. Garden City, NJ: Doubleday, 1963.

Freeman, Samuel. "Constitutional Democracy and the Legitimacy of Judicial Review." *Law and Philosophy* 9 (1990/1): 327–70.

Fried, Charles. *Contract as Promise*. Cambridge, MA: Harvard University Press, 1981.

Fuller, Lon L. "The Case of the Speluncean Explorers." *Harvard Law Review* 62 (1949): 616–45.

—. *The Morality of Law*. 2nd rev. edn. New Haven: Yale University Press, 1969.

Fuller, Lon L., and William Perdue, Jr. "The Reliance Interest in Contract Damages." *Yale Law Journal* 46 (1936): 52–96.

Gardner, John. "The Purity and Priority of Private Law." *University of Toronto Law Journal* 46 (1996): 459–93.

Gilbert, Margaret. *A Theory of Political Obligation: Membership, Commitment, and the Bonds of Society*. Oxford: Oxford University Press, 2006.

Goetz, Charles J., and Robert E. Scott. "An Examination of the Basis of Contract." *Yale Law Journal* 89 (1980): 1261–322.

Golash, Deirdre. *The Case against Punishment*. New York: NYU Press, 2005.

Goldman, Alan H. *Practical Rules: When We Need Them and When We Don't*. Cambridge: Cambridge University Press, 2002.

Green, T. H. *Lectures on the Principles of Political Obligation*. London: Longmans, 1907.

Greenawalt, Kent. *Conflicts of Law and Morality*. New York: Oxford University Press, 1987.

—. "The Perplexing Borders of Justification and Excuse." *Columbia Law Review* 84 (1984): 1897–927.

Grotius, Hugo. *The Rights of War and Peace*. 1625. Ed. Richard Tuck. Indianapolis: Liberty Fund, 2005.

Habermas, Jürgen. *Between Facts and Norms*. Trans. William Rehg. Cambridge: MIT Press, 1996.

Hamburger, Philip A. "A Constitutional Right of Religious Exemption: An Historical Perspective." *George Washington Law Review* 60 (1992): 915–48.

Hardin, Garrett. "The Tragedy of the Commons." *Science* 162 (1968): 1243–8.

Harman, Gilbert, and Judith Jarvis Thomson. *Moral Relativism and Moral Objectivity*. Malden, MA: Blackwell, 1996.

Hart, H. L. A. "Are There Any Natural Rights?" *Philosophical Review* 64 (1955): 175–91.

—. "Commands and Authoritative Legal Reasons." *Essays on Bentham*. Oxford: Oxford University Press, 1982. 243–68.

—. *The Concept of Law*. 1961. 2nd ed. Oxford: Oxford University Press, 1994.

—. *Law, Liberty, and Morality*. Stanford, CA: Stanford University Press, 1963.

Hart, H. L. A., and Tony Honoré. *Causation in the Law*. Oxford: Clarendon Press, 1959.

Hart, Henry M., and Albert M. Sacks. 1958. *The Legal Process: Basic Problems in the Making and Application of Law*. Westbury, NY: Foundation Press, 1994.

Haskar, Vinit. *Rights, Communities and Disobedience: Liberalism and Gandhi*. New Delhi: Oxford University Press, 2001.

Hayek, Friedrich A. *Law, Legislation and Liberty*. Vol. 1. 1821. Chicago: University of Chicago Press, 1978.

Hegel, G. W. F. *Elements of the Philosophy of Right*. Ed. Allen Wood. Cambridge: Cambridge University Press, 1991.

Himma, Kenneth. "H. L. A. Hart and the Practical Difference Thesis." *Legal Theory* 6 (2000): 1–43.

Hobbes, Thomas. *Leviathan*. 1651.

Hohfeld, Wesley Newcomb. *Fundamental Legal Conceptions*. New Haven: Yale University Press, 1919.

Hooker, Brad. *Ideal Code, Real World: A Rule-Consequentialist Theory of Morality*. Oxford: Oxford University Press, 2000.

Horwitz, Morton J. "The Rule of Law: An Unqualified Human Good?" *Yale Law Journal* 86.3 (1977): 561–6.

Hume, David. "Of the Original Contract." *Hume's Ethical Writings*. 1777. Ed. Alasdair MacIntyre. London: University of Notre Dame Press, 1965.

Hutchinson, Allan C., and Derek Morgan. "Calabresian Sunset: Statutes in the Shade." *Columbia Law Review* 82 (1982): 1752–78.

International Commission of Jurists. *The Rule of Law in a Free Society: A Report of the International Congress of Jurists*. Geneva, 1959.

Kagan, Shelly. *The Limits of Morality*. Oxford: Clarendon Press, 1989.

Kant, Immanuel. *Critique of Pure Reason*. 1787. Cambridge: Cambridge University Press, 1998.

Kaplow, Louis. "Rules versus Standards: An Economic Analysis." *Duke Law Journal* 42 (1992): 557–629.

Keating, Gregory. "A Social Contract Conception of the Tort Law of Accidents." *Philosophy and the Law of Torts*. Ed. Gerald J. Postema. New York: Cambridge University Press, 2001.

Keeton, Robert E. *Legal Cause in the Law of Torts*. Columbus: Ohio State University Press, 1963.

Kelsen, Hans. *The Pure Theory of Law*. 1960. Trans. M. Knight. Berkeley: University of California Press, 1967.

Kennedy, Duncan. *A Critique of Adjudication (fin de siècle)*. Cambridge, MA: Harvard University Press, 1997.

Kennedy, Randall L. "*McCleskey v. Kemp*: Race, Capital Punishment, and the Supreme Court." *Harvard Law Review* 101.7 (1988): 1388–443.

Kershnar, Stephen. *For Torture: A Rights-Based Defense*. Lanham, MD: Lexington Books, 2011.

King, Martin Luther, Jr. "Letter from Birmingham City Jail." *Civil Disobedience: Theory and Practice*. 1963. Ed. Hugo Adam Bedau. Indianapolis: Bobbs-Merrill, 1969.

Klosko, George. "Political Obligation and Gratitude." *Philosophy and Public Affairs* 17 (1989): 191–211.

—. *The Principle of Fairness and Political Obligation*. Lanham, MD: Rowman & Littlefield, 1992.

Kramer, Matthew. "How Moral Principles Can Enter into the Law." *Legal Theory* 6 (2000): 83–108.

Kretzmann, Norman. "Lex Iniusta Non Est Lex: Laws on Trial in Aquinas' Court of Conscience." *American Journal of Jurisprudence* 33 (1988): 99–122.

Kymlicka, William. *Contemporary Political Philosophy: An Introduction*. 2nd edn. Oxford: Oxford University Press, 2001.

Laudan, Larry. "The Rules of Trial, Political Morality and the Costs of Error: Or, Is Proof Beyond a Reasonable Doubt Doing More Harm Than Good?" *Oxford Studies in Philosophy of Law*. Ed. Leslie Green and Brian Leiter. Vol. 1. Oxford: Oxford University Press, 2011.

Lawson, Gary, and Guy Seidman. "Originalism as a Legal Enterprise." *Constitutional Commentary* 23 (2006): 47–80.

Lefkowitz, David. "The Principle of Fairness and States' Duty to Obey International Law." *Canadian Journal of Law and Jurisprudence* 24 (2011): 327–46.

Leiter, Brian. "Legal Realism." *A Companion to Philosophy of Law and Legal Theory*. Ed. Dennis Patterson. Malden, MA: Blackwell, 1996. 261–79.

—. "Legal Realism and Legal Positivism Reconsidered." *Ethics* 111 (2001): 278–301.

Levi, Edward. *An Introduction to Legal Reasoning*. Chicago: University of Chicago Press, 1949.

Lewellyn, Karl. "Remarks on the Theory of Appellate Decision and the Rules or Canons About How Statutes Are to Be Construed." *Vanderbilt Law Review* 3 (1950): 395–406.

Lewis, David. *Convention*. Cambridge, MA: Harvard University Press, 1969.

Lippke, Richard L. "To Waive or Not to Waive: The Right to Trial and Plea Bargaining." *Criminal Law and Philosophy* 2 (2008): 181–99.

Locke, John. *Two Treatises of Government*. 1688. Ed. Peter Laslett. Cambridge: Cambridge University Press, 1988.

MacCormick, Neil. *Legal Reasoning and Legal Theory*. Oxford: Clarendon Press, 1978.

—. *Rhetoric and the Rule of Law: A Theory of Legal Reasoning*. Oxford: Oxford University Press, 2005.

Mackie, J. L. *The Cement of the Universe: A Study of Causation*. Oxford: Clarendon Press, 1974.

—. *Ethics: Inventing Right and Wrong*. Harmondsworth: Penguin Books, 1977.

MacKinnon, Catharine A. "'Freedom from Unreal Loyalties': On Fidelity in Constitutional Interpretation." *Fordham Law Review* 65 (1997): 1773–80.

Marmor, Andrei. "The Rule of Law and Its Limits." *Law and Philosophy* 23 (2004): 1–43.

—. *Social Conventions: From Language to Law*. Princeton: Princeton University Press, 2009.

McConnell, Michael W. "The Origins and Historical Understanding of Free Exercise of Religion." *Harvard Law Review* 103 (1990): 1409–517.

—. "Textualism and the Dead Hand of the Past." *George Washington Law Review* 66 (1998): 1127–40.

McMahan, Jeff. "Self-Defense and the Problem of the Innocent Attacker." *Ethics* 104 (1994): 252–90.

Mill, J. S. *Utilitarianism*. 1861.

Montague, Philip. *Punishment as Societal-Defense*. Lanham, MD: Rowman & Littlefield, 1995.

Moore, Michael S. *Causation and Responsibility*. New York: Oxford University Press, 2009.

—. "The Independent Moral Significance of Wrongdoing." *Placing Blame*. Oxford: Oxford University Press, 1997.

—. "The Moral Worth of Retribution." *Responsibility, Character, and the Emotions: New Essays in Moral Psychology*. Ed. Ferdinand Schoeman. Cambridge: Cambridge University Press, 1987. 179–219.

Morreall, John. "The Justifiability of Violent Civil Disobedience." *Canadian Journal of Philosophy* 6 (1976): 35–47.

Morris, Herbert. *On Guilt and Innocence: Essays in Legal Philosophy and Moral Psychology*. Berkeley: University of California Press, 1976.

Murphy, Mark C. "Natural Law Jurisprudence." *Legal Theory* 9 (2003): 241–67.

Murphy, Sean D. *Principles of International Law*. St. Paul: West Publishing, 2006.

Nagel, Thomas. "Equality." *Mortal Questions*. Cambridge: Cambridge University Press, 1979.

Nathanson, Stephen. *An Eye for an Eye: The Immorality of Punishing by Death*. 2nd edn. Lanham, MD: Rowman & Littlefield, 2001.

Nozick, Robert. *Anarchy, State, and Utopia*. New York: Basic Books, 1974.

Nussbaum, Martha C. "The Costs of Tragedy: Some Moral Limits of Cost-Benefit Analysis." *Journal of Legal Studies* 29 (2000): 1005–36.

O'Connor, Gary E. "Restatement (First) of Statutory Interpretation." *N.Y.U. Journal of Legislation & Public Policy* 7 (2003/4): 333–64.

Perry, Ronen. "Correlativity." *Law and Philosophy* 28 (2009): 537–84.

Perry, Stephen. "The Distributive Turn: Mischief, Misfortune, and Tort Law." *Quinnipiac Law Review* 16 (1996): 315–38.

—. "The Moral Foundations of Tort Law." *Iowa Law Review* 77 (1992): 449–514.

—. "Second-Order Reasons, Uncertainty, and Legal Theory." *Southern California Law Review* 62 (1989): 913–94.

Pettit, Philip. "The Consequentialist Can Recognise Rights." *Philosophical Quarterly* 38 (1988): 42–55.

Plato. *Crito*. In *Plato: Complete Works*. Eds. John M. Cooper and D. S. Hutchinson. Indianapolis: Hackett, 1997.

Polinsky, A. Mitchell. *An Introduction to Law and Economics*. 2nd edn. Boston: Little, Brown, and Co., 1989.

Posner, Eric A. "Do States Have a Moral Obligation to Obey International Law?" *Stanford Law Review* 55 (2003): 1901–19.

Posner, Richard A. *Economic Analysis of Law*. 8th edn. New York: Aspen, 2010.

Postema, Gerald J. "Introduction: Search for an Explanatory Theory of Torts." *Philosophy and the Law of Torts*. Ed. Gerald J. Postema. Cambridge: Cambridge University Press, 2001. 1–21.

Pound, Roscoe. "Mechanical Jurisprudence." *Columbia Law Review* 8.8 (1908): 605–23.

Quine, W. V. *Word and Object*. Cambridge, MA: MIT Press, 1964.

Quinn, Warren. "The Right to Threaten and the Right to Punish." *Philosophy and Public Affairs* 14 (1985): 327–73.

Radin, Max. "The Theory of Judicial Decision: Or How Judges Think." *American Bar Association Journal* 11 (1925): 357–62.

Rawls, John. "Legal Obligation and the Duty of Fair Play." *Law and Philosophy*. Ed. Sidney Hook. New York: NYU Press, 1964.

—. *A Theory of Justice*. Cambridge, MA: Harvard University Press, 1971.

Raz, Joseph. *The Authority of Law*. Oxford: Clarendon Press, 1979a.

—. *The Concept of a Legal System*. 1970. 2nd edn. Oxford: Oxford University Press, 1980.

—. "Legal Positivism and the Sources of Law." *The Authority of Law*. Oxford: Clarendon Press, 1979b. 37–52.

—. *The Morality of Freedom*. Oxford: Clarendon Press, 1986.

—. "The Rule of Law and Its Virtue." *The Authority of Law*. Oxford: Clarendon Press, 1979c. 210–29.

Regan, Donald H. "Authority and Value: Reflections on Raz's *Morality of Freedom*." *Southern California Law Review* 62 (1989): 995–1095.

Reiman, Jeffrey H. "Justice, Civilization, and the Death Penalty: Answering Van Den Haag." *Philosophy & Public Affairs* 14.2 (1985): 115–48.

Ridge, Michael, and Sean McKeever. *Principled Ethics: Generalism as a Regulative Ideal*. Oxford: Oxford University Press, 2006.

Rosenberg, Gerald N. *The Hollow Hope: Can Courts Bring About Social Change?* 2nd edn. Chicago: University of Chicago Press, 1993.

Ross, W. D. *The Right and the Good*. Oxford: Clarendon Press, 1930.

Rothbard, Murray. *For a New Liberty*. New York: Libertarian Review Foundation, 1978.

Sarat, Austin D. *When the State Kills: Capital Punishment and the American Condition*. Princeton: Princeton University Press, 2001.

Sarat, Austin D., and Charles Ogletree, eds. *When Law Fails: Making Sense of Miscarriages of Justice*. New York: New York University Press, 2009.

Satz, Debra. *Why Some Things Should Not Be for Sale*. New York: Oxford University Press, 2010.

Scalia, Antonin. *A Matter of Interpretation: Federal Courts and the Law*. Princeton: Princeton University Press, 1997.

—. "The Rule of Law as a Law of Rules." *University of Chicago Law Review* 56 (1989): 1175–88.

Schauer, Frederick. "Is the Common Law Law?" *California Law Review* 77 (1989): 455–71.

—. *Playing by the Rules: A Philosophical Examination of Rule-Based Decision-Making in Law and in Life*. Oxford: Oxford University Press, 1991.

—. "Precedent." *Stanford Law Review* 29 (1987): 571–605.

Scheffler, Samuel. *The Rejection of Consequentialism*. 1982. Rev. edn. Oxford: Oxford University Press, 1994.

Schmidtz, David. "Islands in a Sea of Obligation: Limits of the Duty to Rescue." *Law and Philosophy* 19 (2000): 683–705.

Seavey, Warren A. "Mr. Justice Cardozo and the Law of Torts." *Harvard Law Review* 52 (1939): 371–407.

Sen, Amartya. "The Discipline of Cost-Benefit Analysis." *Journal of Legal Studies* 29 (2000): 931–52.

Shapiro, Scott. *Legality*. Cambridge, MA: Belknap, 2011.

Shepherd, Joanna M. "Deterrence versus Brutalization: Capital Punishment's Differing Impacts among States." *Michigan Law Review* 104 (2005): 203–55.

Simmons, A. John. *Moral Principles and Political Obligations*. Princeton: Princeton University Press, 1979.

Singer, Peter. *Democracy and Disobedience*. Oxford: Clarendon Press, 1973.

Smart, J. J. C. "Utilitarianism and Squeamishness." *Utilitarianism and Its Critics*. Ed. Jonathan Glover. New York: Macmillan, 1990.

Solum, Lawrence B. "Equity and the Rule of Law." *The Rule of Law*. Ed. Ian Shapiro. New York: NYU Press, 1994. 120–47.

Soper, Philip. *The Ethics of Deference: Learning from Law's Morals*. Cambridge: Cambridge University Press, 2002.

Stapleton, Jane. "Choosing What We Mean by 'Causation' In the Law." *Missouri Law Review* 73 (2008): 433–80.

Steiker, Carol S. "No, Capital Punishment Is Not Morally Required: Deterrence, Deontology, and the Death Penalty." *Stanford Law Review* 58 (2005): 751–89.

Stein, Michael Ashley. "*Priestley v. Fowler* (1837) and the Emerging Tort of Negligence." *Boston College Law Review* 44 (2003): 689–731.

Stone, Martin. "The Significance of Doing and Suffering." *Philosophy and the Law of Torts*. Ed. Gerald J. Postema. New York: Cambridge University Press, 2001.

Sunstein, Cass R., ed. *Behavioral Law and Economics*. Cambridge: Cambridge University Press, 2000.

—. "Constitutionalism and Secession." *University of Chicago Law Review* 58 (1991): 633–70.

—. "Justice Scalia's Democratic Formalism." *Yale Law Journal* 107 (1997): 529–67.

—. "On Academic Fads and Fashions." *Michigan Law Review* 99 (2001): 1251–64.

—. "On Analogical Reasoning." *Harvard Law Review* 106.3 (1993): 741–91.

Sunstein, Cass R., and Adrian Vermeule. "Deterring Murder: A Reply." *Stanford Law Review* 58 (2006): 847–57.

—. "Is Capital Punishment Morally Required?" *Stanford Law Review* 58 (2005): 703–50.

Sypnowich, Christine. *The Concept of Socialist Law*. Oxford: Clarendon Press, 1990.

Tamanaha, Brian Z. *Law as a Means to an End: Threat to the Rule of Law*. Law in Context. New York: Cambridge University Press, 2006.

—. *On the Rule of Law: History, Politics, Theory*. Cambridge: Cambridge University Press, 2004.

Thompson, E. P. *Whigs and Hunters*. New York: Pantheon, 1975.

Thomson, Judith Jarvis. *The Realm of Rights*. Cambridge, MA: Harvard University Press, 1990.

Tinkler, Justine E. "'People Are Too Quick to Take Offense': The Effects of Legal Information and Beliefs on Definitions of Sexual Harassment." *Law and Social Inquiry* 33 (2008): 417–45.

Unger, Roberto Mangabeira. *What Should Legal Analysis Become?* London: Verso, 1996.

Waldron, Jeremy. "Hart and the Principles of Legality." *The Legacy of H. L. A. Hart*. Ed. Matthew H. Kramer, Claire Grant, Ben Colburn, and Antony Hatzistavrou. Oxford: Oxford University Press, 2008.

—. *Law and Disagreement*. Oxford: Oxford University Press, 1999.

—. "Moments of Carelessness and Massive Loss." *Philosophical Foundations of Tort Law*. Ed. David G. Owen. Oxford: Clarendon Press, 1995. 387–408.

—. "The Rule of Law in Contemporary Liberal Theory." *Ratio Juris* 2 (1989): 79–96.

Walker, A. D. M. "Political Obligation and the Argument from Gratitude." *Philosophy and Public Affairs* 17 (1988): 191–211.

Waluchow, W. J. *Inclusive Legal Positivism*. Oxford: Clarendon Press, 1994.

Wasserstrom, Richard A. "Strict Liability in the Criminal Law." *Stanford Law Review* 12.4 (1960): 731–45.

Weber, Max. *Max Weber on Law in Economy and Society*. 1925. Ed. Max Rheinstein. New York: Simon & Schuster, 1967.

Weinrib, Ernest J. *The Idea of Private Law*. Cambridge, MA: Harvard University Press, 1995.

—. "Understanding Tort Law." *Valparaiso Law Review* 23 (1989): 485–526.

Wellman, Carl. *An Approach to Rights*. Dordrecht: Kluwer, 1997.

White, Lawrence H. "Can Economics Rank Slavery against Free Labor in Terms of Efficiency?" *Politics, Philosophy and Economics* 7 (2008): 327–40.

Williams, Glanville. "The Risk Principle." *Law Quarterly Review* 77 (1961): 179–212.

Wittgenstein, Ludwig. *Philosophical Investigations*. 1953. Trans. G. E. M. Anscombe. Oxford: Basil Blackwell, 1967.

The Wolfenden Report. New York: Stein and Day, 1963.

Wolff, Robert Paul. *In Defense of Anarchism*. New York: Harper and Row, 1970.

Wright, Richard W. "Causation in Tort Law." *California Law Review* 73 (1985): 1735–828.

—. "Right, Justice and Tort Law." *Philosophical Foundations of Tort Law*. Ed. David G. Owen. Oxford: Clarendon Press, 1995. 159–82.

Zapf, Christian, and Eben Moglen. "Linguistic Indeterminacy and the Rule of Law: On the Perils of Misunderstanding Wittgenstein." *Georgetown Law Journal* 84 (1996): 485–520.

Index

acceptance (contract) 140

Ackerman, Bruce A. 238–9

actus reus *see* criminal law, conduct

Adams, John 24

adjudication, theories of 39

Alexander, Larry,

    on criminal law 156, 175

    on exclusionary reasons 21

    on legal principles 44

    on precedent 46

    on rule of law 28

    on threshold nonconsequentiaism 64

analogy *see* reasoning, analogical

anarchism,

    philosophical 91

    political 50

Aquinas, St Thomas 3, 16, 96, 99

Aristotle 17, 65, 128–9

Atiyah, P. S. 144

attempt (criminal) 76, 173–7, 192

    complete versus incomplete 174–7

Augustine, St 16

Austin, John 3, 12, 16, 245–6

authority 19, 47

    legitimate 20, 91

    practical 20

    theoretical 19

autonomy 22, 26, 67–9, 76

    versus heteronomy 68

Bad Samaritan Laws 80–8

Balkin, Jack 38

Barnett, Randy E. 146

Bedau, Hugo 101

beneficence 51

Bentham, Jeremy 3, 51, 55, 184

    on rights 60

Berlin, Isaiah 67

Bickel, Alexander 229

blackmail 167

Blackstone, Sir William 16

breach (contract) 141

Brennan, William 222

Brown v. Board of Education 238–9

Bush v. Gore 28

but-for cause *see* causation, cause-in-fact

Calabresi, Guido 121, 217

canons of construction (statutory) 222–3

capital punishment 197–205

    arguments for abolition of 200–5

        bias/racism 204–5

        caprice/arbitrariness 202–3

        civilization/humanity 201–2

        inconsistency 201

        mistake/irrevocability 202–3

    brutalization effect of 199

    consequentialist arguments for retention

        of 198–200

    retention versus abolition 197

    retributivist arguments for retention of 197–8

Cardozo, Benjamin 138

Carolene Products Co., United States v. 237–8

Carroll Towing, U.S. v. 126

case law *see* precedent

case of first impression 44–5

causation 87, 128, 132–9

    cause-in-fact 133–4

    legal 133

    proximate 133, 135–9